J. B. C Munro

Commercial Law

A Text-Book for Commercial Classes

J. B. C Munro

Commercial Law
A Text-Book for Commercial Classes

ISBN/EAN: 9783337178574

Printed in Europe, USA, Canada, Australia, Japan

Cover: Foto ©Suzi / pixelio.de

More available books at **www.hansebooks.com**

COMMERCIAL LAW

AN ELEMENTARY TEXT-BOOK FOR
COMMERCIAL CLASSES

BY

J. E. C. MUNRO, LL.M.

OF THE MIDDLE TEMPLE, BARRISTER-AT-LAW
FORMERLY PROFESSOR OF LAW IN THE OWENS COLLEGE, MANCHESTER

London

MACMILLAN AND CO.

AND NEW YORK

1893

PREFACE

THE object of this little book is to provide an elementary text-book on Commercial Law for schools and colleges. Lectures on Commercial Law are now given every winter in many of our large towns. These lectures attract bankers, accountants, and young business men. The want of a text-book has long been felt, as the existing works are too advanced for practical use. In writing this work I have aimed at brevity and simplicity of statement. As a rule cases are not quoted, but many of the illustrations embodied in the text are taken from decided cases. At the end of each chapter or part, reference is made to the leading text-books, to which the reader is referred for further information.

As the book is written mainly for those who are unfamiliar with legal terms, I have added a "glossary" of some terms used in the text that seemed on reading the proofs to require explanation. I have to express my grateful thanks to Dr. James Gow, the editor of the series, Mr. William Baker of Lincoln's Inn, and Mr. J.

C. Graham of the Inner Temple for kind assistance and valuable suggestions during the progress of the work.

I have also to thank Mr. John Macdonell, one of the editors of Smith's *Mercantile Law*, and Mr. T. E. Scrutton, the author of *Charter-parties and Bills of Lading*, for permission to use the forms of a charter-party and a bill of lading printed in the text.

J. E. C. MUNRO.

2 NEW SQUARE,
  LINCOLN'S INN.

CONTENTS

PART I

PART II

CONTRACTS

PART III

THE LEADING COMMERCIAL CONTRACTS

PART I

MERCANTILE PERSONS AND MERCANTILE PROPERTY

§ 1. Mercantile Persons. — Commercial transactions are carried on by individuals or sole traders, partnerships, companies, and by their agents.

§ 2. Sole Traders. — No distinction is now drawn between subjects and aliens as regards capacity to trade, except that an alien cannot own a British ship. If an alien purchase a British ship, the ship thereupon ceases to possess a British character. During war a subject cannot trade with the enemy except by license of the Crown.

Married women were formerly under trading disabilities, inasmuch as they could not bind themselves personally by contract except in the city of London. But now a married woman may carry on a trade as if she were single, when she has obtained a protection order or is living apart under a judicial separation. She can also bind herself so as to affect her separate estate by contract. In respect of her contracts she is in a more favourable position than a man. A man is liable to be imprisoned for disobeying an order of a court to pay a debt, but when a married woman with separate estate contracts a debt, she cannot be imprisoned, the property alone being liable (§§ 44-46).

S   B

Persons under twenty-one can, as a rule, bind themselves absolutely for necessaries only (§§ 39-43).

The executors and administrators of a deceased trader are liable to see to the payment of his debts out of his assets, and may be concerned in carrying on the business. An executor is a person appointed as such by a will. An administrator is a person appointed by the Court of Probate where a man has died without making a will, or where he has made a will and has appointed no one as executor.

§ 3. **Partnerships.**—Partnership is the relation which exists between persons carrying on a business in common with a view to profit. Persons who enter into partnership with one another are called a firm. In Scotland the "firm" is legally a distinct person from the members, but this rule does not prevail in England, though English law recognises the firm for certain purposes. The relations of partners to one another will be considered in a subsequent chapter, but it may be here pointed out that each member of a partnership is an agent of the firm and of the other partners for the purposes of the business of the partnership. Third parties therefore in dealing with a member of a firm are dealing at the same time with the other members.

§ 4. **Companies.**—A company may be defined as a number of persons incorporated by law, so that the company has a distinct personality apart from the persons who compose it. An unincorporated company is merely a partnership, and has no legal existence apart from its members ; contracts are entered into with the partners as individuals, and every member is liable for the debts of the partnership. In the case of an incorporated company, contracts are entered into with the company itself and therefore creditors can only proceed against the property of the company.

§ 5. **How Incorporation takes place.** — A company may be incorporated (*a*) by royal charter; (*b*) by special Act of Parliament ; (*c*) by a certificate issued under an Act of Parliament.

(*a*) The Crown in virtue of its prerogative may incorporate a number of persons as a company. In some cases charters are issued under and by authority of Acts of Parliament, as, for example, the charter incorporating the Bank of England.

(*b*) Sometimes an Act of Parliament is specially passed for the purpose of incorporating a company. For example, railway companies are often formed by special Acts.

(*c*) Under the Joint Stock Companies Acts, seven persons can obtain a certificate of incorporation as a company, provided certain conditions are fulfilled. The seven persons usually subscribe their names to two documents, called the memorandum and the articles of association respectively. The memorandum is a concise statement of the objects of the company; the articles are the rules to be followed in carrying out such objects. A memorandum is essential, but the articles are not absolutely necessary, the Acts containing articles that apply where special articles have not been framed. The registrar of joint stock companies issues a certificate that has the effect of incorporating into a company the persons who sign the memorandum, together with such other persons as may from time to time become members of the company.

§ 6. Limited and Unlimited Liability.—The memorandum of a limited company must state that the liability is "limited," and to what extent. In a limited company the liability of members for the debts of the company is limited to the amount stated, and it is usual to limit the liability to the amount of the shares held. In an unlimited company the liability of members is unlimited. In no case, however, can a creditor of a company sue a member of the company for a debt contracted by the company. Creditors have to be content with taking proceedings against the company itself, and if the company cannot pay, proceedings, as we shall see later on, may be taken to wind up the company, and the law will compel every member to contribute that which is due from him in respect of his shares. If the liability, for example, is limited to

£10 a share, and this has not been paid, no more than £10 can be demanded; if £5 has been paid, £5 can be demanded. On the other hand, if the liability be un-limited, each member can be compelled to contribute until all the debts of the company are discharged.

§ 7. Seven Members required.—If a company carries on business for six months after the number of its members is less than seven, every member who is aware that the number of members has been reduced below the number prescribed by law, becomes personally liable for the payment of all the debts of the company contracted subsequent to such six months. Care therefore should be taken so that the number of members is never less than seven.

§ 8. The Memorandum.—The law requires the memorandum to contain the following particulars in the case of an "unlimited" company:—

1. The name of the company.
2. The place where the registered office is situated.
3. The objects for which the company is established.

If the company be "limited," the memorandum must also contain—

4. The word "limited" in addition to the name of the company.
5. A declaration that the liability of the members is limited.
6. The amount of capital divided into shares of a certain amount.

The memorandum is the charter of the company, and defines and limits the powers of the company. It cannot be altered without the consent of a court.

§ 9. The Articles of Association.—The articles of association prescribe the rules to be observed in the administration of the company's affairs. They usually relate to calls upon shares, the transfer and forfeiture of shares, the increase or reduction of capital, the borrowing of money, proceedings at meetings, the election, retirement and powers of directors, the auditing of accounts, the declaration of dividends, winding up, and the distribution of assets. As a rule the articles of association can be altered by the company.

§ 10. Directors.—The articles usually declare that the management of the business shall be vested in the directors. The shareholders are thus excluded from the management, though they necessarily exercise great control through their power of censuring or removing a director. The directors cannot validly do any act not within the powers of the company.

As a rule their powers are prescribed by the articles. The usual powers given are to acquire property, to enter into contracts, to appoint officials and trustees, to bring or defend actions, to give receipts, to refer disputes to arbitration, to invest moneys, to form a reserve fund, and to recommend the amount of the dividend.

§ 11. Shares.—The capital of a company is always, as we have seen, divided into shares. The persons who sign the memorandum and articles have to state opposite their names how many shares they take. Other shareholders obtain shares by applying for them. An application is accepted by the directors allotting the shares, and the posting of the notice of allotment to the applicant makes him liable to take and pay for the shares. The applicant is usually required to remit a portion of the amount of each share when he makes his application, and another portion when the shares are allotted to him. Subsequent payments are termed "calls," and the articles usually authorise the directors to make calls from time to time until the whole amount is paid. Certificates may be issued by the directors certifying the number of shares held by a shareholder, and such certificate is *prima facie* evidence that the holder owns the shares.

§ 12. Winding up.—A company may be wound up or dissolved (1) compulsorily, (2) voluntarily, or (3) subject to supervision.

1. The Chancery Division of the High Court of Justice will order a company to be wound up—

    (*a*) When the company has passed a resolution requiring the company to be wound up by the court.

    (*b*) When the company does not commence business within a year from its incorporation, or suspends business for a year.

(c) Whenever the number of members is less than seven.

(d) When the company is unable to pay its debts.

(e) When the court thinks that it is just and equitable that it should be wound up.

The company itself, any shareholder, or a creditor may ask the court to make the order. If the order be made, a liquidator is usually appointed to assist the court; his chief duties are to realise the property of the company and to pay its debts so far as the property will permit.

2. A company may, without going to the court, wind up its affairs voluntarily, but this will not prevent a creditor from asking the court for a compulsory order. Voluntary winding up is often resorted to where it is desired to re-construct the company on a new basis. The company authorise the winding up by resolution, and appoint a liqui-dator for the purpose.

3. In some case where a voluntary winding up has been resolved upon, the court may order the winding up to proceed under its supervision. This course has the ad-vantage that the assistance of the court can be readily obtained when necessary.

By an Act of Parliament passed in 1890, the winding up of companies is subject to the control of the Board of Trade. The procedure is similar to that followed in bankruptcy.

§ 13. **Mercantile Property.**—Mercantile transactions relate usually to moveable property. Such property takes the form of a material thing or a right of action. A bale of cotton is a material thing, but a share in a company is really a right of action. Land or immoveable property is often required for trading purposes, and attention may therefore be directed to some of the more important forms of mercantile property and their chief characteristics.

§ 14. **Land.**—Land, where it is owned for partnership purposes, is regarded as partnership property. The law will not interfere with its descent, but it will compel the person who takes it to hold it for the benefit of the partner-ship (§ 116). Land is now liable for the payment of debts.

§ 15. **Moveable Property.**—Moveable property is the subject of absolute ownership, and hence parties buying goods are not obliged to trace the title of the vendor, as they have to do in the case of land.   Sales in open market as a rule confer a good title (§ 158).   Moveables, with certain exceptions, such as heirlooms, fixtures, and growing crops, descend to the executor or administrator for the benefit of the next of kin, subject to the payment of debts.

Special rules are applied to British ships.   In order to be entitled to the name and privileges of a British ship she must be owned and registered as one, except in the case of ships not exceeding 15 tons, employed on the rivers and coasts of the United Kingdom or of a British possession. The property in a British ship is regarded as divided into 64 equal parts, and it would apparently follow that 64 is the maximum number of owners.   But the law allows any number of persons not exceeding five to be registered as joint owners, such joint owners being regarded as one person for the purpose of registration.   A company, too, may be registered in its corporate name.   Shares in a ship are transferred by a prescribed form of bill of sale under seal.

The word "chattel" is often used in England to denote moveable property, but the leading classification of property in English law is not "immoveables" and "moveables," but "real" and "personal" property.   Personal property includes not only moveables, but certain interests in land, such as leaseholds—if the owner of such property dies intestate, the property descends to the next of kin after all debts have been paid.   Real property includes all estates that amount to an interest not less than an estate for life.

§ 16. Rights of Action.—Moveable property is usually divided into material things and rights of action.   The former class includes everything that is tangible or possesses a material form; the latter class includes all claims or rights, especially claims to the payment of sums of money. If A. possesses ten sovereigns, the sovereigns are material things; if B. owes A. ten sovereigns, A. has a right to bring an action against B. for the money.

The chief forms of right of action that need be considered are shares, stock, debentures, debenture stock, copyright, designs, patents, trademarks, and goodwill.

§ 17. Shares.—The proportion of capital subscribed by a member of a company is divided into shares. The allotment of shares in reply to an application constitutes a contract between the company and the member that the latter will contribute the amount of the shares when called upon so to do in accordance with the agreed conditions. A shareholder can never call upon the company to pay him out the amount he contributed. He remains a shareholder until he procures some one else to take his place. A share can always be transferred subject to the company's regulations. The shareholders' names are registered, and usually each shareholder is entitled to a certificate stating the number of shares he holds (§ 11).

§ 18. Stock.—The term "stock" is applied to denote either the amount of capital contributed to a company or the amount advanced to a government. Stock differs from shares in that (1) it is always fully paid, and (2) it can be transferred in fractional parts. Sometimes a company, when its shares are fully paid up, converts them into stock for convenience of transfer.

A portion of the national debt is called the funded debt, and the holder of stock in the funds has a right to a perpetual annuity, subject to the right of the State to redeem such annuity by the payment of a stipulated sum. For instance, £100 3 per cent stock is the right to receive a perpetual annuity of £3 per annum, subject to the right of the Government to redeem such annuity by the payment of £100.

The public funds consist of several kinds of stock, the nature and legal incidents of each kind being fixed by the Act of Parliament creating it. The most important stock is known as consols.

Stock in the public funds is transferred by signature of the books at the Bank of England. The owner may attend personally to authorise the transfer, or he may appoint an agent for the purpose, by writing under his hand and seal attested by two witnesses. In some cases stock may be represented by certificates payable to bearer, and then the stock can be transferred by delivery of the certificate.

§ 19. Debenture.—The word "debenture" is used in various senses, but as a rule it signifies a document under seal of a company given to secure the repayment of money advanced to the company, such repayment being usually secured by a charge on the whole or part of the property of the company. A debenture may, however, be issued without any such charge. The debenture holder looks to the property charged as the security for his money, and generally stipulates that he will be entitled to certain remedies in case the money is not repaid when due.

§ 20. Debenture Stock. — A company is sometimes authorised to issue debenture stock. Such stock is a charge on the undertaking of the company prior to all shares or stock, and the interest has priority over all dividends. Holders of this stock cannot require payment of the principal money paid up upon it. The stock gives, in fact, a perpetual annuity. The holder is a creditor and not a member of the company.

§ 21. Copyright.—Copyright is the exclusive right of multiplying copies of an original work or composition. Under the Copyright Acts, copyright in books, pamphlets, sheet music, maps, charts, and plans lasts for forty-two years, *or* during the lifetime of the author, and seven years after his death, whichever period is the longer. The copyright of an article in a review belongs to the author, unless the owner of the review has bought the copyright. An action cannot be maintained for the infringement of copyright unless the copyright has been registered.

§ 22. Designs.—Any new or original design applicable to any article of manufacture or to any substance, whether it relate to the pattern, the shape, or the ornament thereof, may be registered at the proper office. By such registration copyright is acquired in the design for five years from the date of registration. A design will not be registered where it has been previously published in the United Kingdom. The design has to be registered for a particular class of goods.

§ 23. Patents.—A patent is the exclusive right of making, using, or vending a new invention for a period of fourteen years. The right is conferred by letters patent, granted under seal by the Crown, but during the period between the acceptance of an application at the patent office and the formal grant, the applicant is protected to the extent that he may use and publish the patent. The applicant has to lodge a general description of the patent when he sends in his application; subsequently he has to lodge a detailed description called the complete specification. The Crown in making the grant does not take upon itself to say whether the invention is new or not. A patentee is therefore liable to find his patent invalid, because some one has previously patented or published the subject matter. A record of all patents is kept at the patent office, and this record can always be searched. The time for which a patent is granted may be extended by the Judicial Committee of the Privy Council where the patentee has not received adequate remuneration.

§ 24. Trademarks and Goodwill.—A trademark is a mark applied to goods in order to denote their make or quality, or to indicate the firm who exported or manufactured them. By registering a trademark the right to its exclusive user is acquired. A trademark may consist of a name printed in a distinctive manner, the signature of the applicant, or any distinctive device, mark, brand, heading, label, ticket, or fancy word or words not in common use.

A trademark can only be assigned along with the goodwill of a business.

A goodwill is nothing more than the expectation that the old customers of a firm will continue their dealings after the business has been transferred to a new firm. The purchaser of a goodwill usually stipulates for his protection that the vendor will not carry on the same business in the neighbourhood. The extent to which such stipulations are valid will be considered in a subsequent chapter (§ 80).

§ 25. Authorities.—The treatises on Personal Property by Mr. Williams and by Mr. Goodeve contain a concise account of the various forms of moveable property, as well as chapters on companies. Reference may be also made to Mr. J. W. Smith's *Compendium of Mercantile Law* on the subject matter of this and the following chapters.

PART II

CONTRACTS

CHAPTER I

THE FORMATION OF CONTRACTS

§ 26. Definition of a Contract.—A contract is an agreement enforceable by law.

This definition of a contract does not profess to enumerate all the elements that are required to constitute a contract. It merely embodies two of the more important characteristics of every contract, viz. (1) that a contract is an agreement, and (2) that it is an agreement that the law will enforce. It is therefore necessary to examine the nature of an agreement, and to enumerate the various elements an agreement must possess, in order to be regarded as a contract.

§ 27. What is an Agreement.—An agreement is an offer or proposal by one person made to and accepted by another person relating to some act to be done or not to be done by one of such persons towards the other.

An agreement therefore implies (*a*) two persons at least, (*b*) an offer, and (*c*) an acceptance.

Two parties at least are required to every agreement, since it is the result of a common intention expressed by two or more minds. Either party may be a natural person, *e.g.* a man or a woman, or an artificial person, *e.g.* a corporation.   The limitations that the law has imposed on the capacity of natural or artificial persons of entering into contracts will be considered later on.

§ 28. **Offer and Acceptance.** — Every agreement, no matter of how complicated a nature, may be resolved into (1) an offer on one side, and (2) an acceptance on the other.   The simplest type of case is where A. says to B., " Will you buy 1000 yards of cloth at 6d. per yard ? " and B. replies, " Yes."   A more complicated case is where a long correspondence takes place between buyer and seller, eventually resulting in goods being sold.   But all the stipulations and conditions contained in the letters can be thrown into the form of an offer and an acceptance. An offer may also be made by advertisement, as, for example, where a reward is offered to any person who will restore lost property ; the restoration of the property amounts to an acceptance.   The time-tables of a railway company form an offer to carry any person, subject to the terms and conditions stated ; the purchase of a ticket amounts to an acceptance.   A bid at an auction is an offer; the fall of the hammer an acceptance of the highest bid. Many other simple forms of offer and acceptance have been introduced by the custom of trade.

§ 29. **Intention to invite Offers.** — In some cases it is difficult to say whether there is an offer or merely an intimation that offers are or will be invited.   For instance :—

A. advertises that he has goods to sell at a certain price. B. goes to his shop and says I will take the goods at the advertised price.   Is B.'s statement to be regarded as an acceptance of an offer made by A., or is it to be taken merely as an offer by B. which A. is entitled to refuse ?   The answer depends in this as in other cases entirely on what was the real intention of the party in advertising, such intention to be collected from the nature of the transaction.

It has been held that the advertisement of a sale by auction does not amount to such a definite offer to sell the goods that there is a contract with those who attend the sale to the effect that the goods will be sold.   The courts regard such an advertisement, if made in good faith, as an intimation of an intention to sell, and not as a binding undertaking to sell.   On this principle an advertisement of a sale by tender is merely an invitation of offers, and does not imply that the highest offer will be accepted.

§ 30. **Communication of Offer and Acceptance.**—The parties must communicate to one another their common intention.   Unless the offer be communicated, there is no opportunity for acceptance, and a mere intention to accept has no legal effect.   If A. offers to sell goods to B., and B. resolves to buy them at the price mentioned, but never communicates his intention to A., there is no agreement for the sale of the goods.   The communication of the acceptance may, as we have seen, take the form of the doing of an act.   For example, when an order is sent for goods, the offer to purchase implied in the order may be accepted formally, or by the actual sending of the goods.

§ 31. **When is the Communication complete ?**—The communication of an acceptance is complete when it is put in course of transmission to the proposer, so as to be out of the power of the acceptor.   As a proposer may revoke his proposal before acceptance, it is of great importance to determine the point of time from which an acceptance dates. Where the acceptance is oral no difficulty occurs, but where the acceptance is made by letter or telegram, the question arises, does the acceptance date from the moment of posting the letter or sending the telegram, or from the moment when the letter or telegram is received by the proposer ?   It has at length been decided that where an offer is made by letter or by telegram, the acceptance is complete the moment the letter of acceptance or the telegram is despatched.   Some say that the rule is based on the principle that where A. makes an offer to B. by letter, A. is understood to authorise B. to send an acceptance by post.

The acceptance being complete the moment the letter is posted, it follows that there is a binding contract, though the letter containing the acceptance is never received.   The letter may be lost during transmission, but both persons are bound by the contract.

If it is desired to exclude the operation of the rule, the offer should state expressly that the acceptance is not to be binding until the acceptance has been received.

An acceptance may be implied from the conduct of the acceptor. An omnibus company by running its buses offers to carry safely any person who pays the fare. The getting into an omnibus is an acceptance. In the case of an order for goods, the offer as we have seen may be accepted by the sending of the goods.

§ 32. **Nature of the Acceptance.**—The acceptance must be absolute and identical with the terms of the offer.

If there is any variation between the offer and the acceptance, there is no agreement, and the acceptance with its variation is regarded as a new proposal.

A. offered to sell B. a quantity of " good " barley, and B. replied by accepting the offer of the " fine " barley. As it appeared that the words " good " and " fine " were used in the trade to denote different qualities, it was decided that there was no acceptance.

When a broker is employed to sell goods, he is regarded as an agent to act for both buyer and seller. He sends to the seller a " sold note," and to the buyer a " bought note." Both these notes ought to be identical, since if they vary in their terms, *e.g.* as to description of goods, or as to mode of payment, it may be held that there is no contract.

The acceptance of the offer must be by the person to whom the offer is made. A. sent an order for goods to B., who, unknown to A., had sold his business to C. The order was opened by C. and executed by him, but it was held that C. could not recover the price of the goods from A., inasmuch as the original offer had been made to B. and not to C.

§ 33. **Revocation of Offer.**—An offer may be revoked up to the moment of acceptance, but not afterwards.

Until the offer is accepted there is no legal relation between the parties, and therefore the proposer may at any moment revoke his offer. Hence a bidder at an auction may withdraw his bid before the hammer falls. A merchant who has ordered goods by post may withdraw the order provided an acceptance has not been posted.

An offer may be revoked though it expressly allows a certain time for acceptance.

Very frequently a proposal contains a statement that the offer will be kept open until a certain day or a certain hour. For instance, A. writes to B. making him an offer of certain goods, and stating that he will keep the offer open for a certain time.   A. is not bound to keep the offer open for such time, since he is under no legal duty to do so.   His words are regarded merely as an intimation that after the expiration of the time mentioned the offer will not continue. Hence where three days were given by a merchant to an intending buyer of goods to make up his mind, and within the three days the buyer went to the seller for the purpose of accepting the offer, but before he accepted the offer the seller declined to sell, saying he had offered the goods elsewhere, it was held that this amounted to a revocation, and that there was no contract.

A tender to supply goods during a stated time to a company or institution made in reply to an advertisement, is an offer that may be revoked during the period the time is running.   By giving orders from time to time on the terms of the tender, the company or institution convert the tender into a binding contract for all goods actually ordered, but this does not prevent the party tendering from withdrawing as regards any future supply.

§ 34. Express and Implied Revocations. — The revocation may be either express or implied.

Express notice may be given by letter or telegram, or orally, and in order to prevent all misunderstanding, it is desirable always to give notice expressly.   The form of the notice is immaterial, but it must be given by the proposer or his agent duly authorised.

Implied revocation is a revocation implied from the conduct of the parties.   For instance, if A. offers goods to B., but before B. accepts A. sells them to C.   If B. has notice or knowledge of such sale he cannot proceed to accept A.'s offer.   The sale to C. is regarded as an implied revocation of the offer made to B.   But suppose B. has no knowledge of the sale to C., is he at liberty to accept A.'s offer ?   The

point has not yet been decided, but Mr. Pollock answers
in the affirmative. The result would be that A. would have
sold the goods twice over, and would have to pay damages
to one of the parties if he is unable to fulfil both contracts.
It is therefore very desirable that a merchant who has made
an offer of goods to one person should not sell them to
another until he has withdrawn his first offer.

§ 35. Communication of Revocation.—An express revocation, to be effective, must be communicated to the
person to whom the offer is made ; but in the case of an
implied revocation, knowledge of the revocation is sufficient.

A revocation not communicated is altogether inoperative.
An intention or determination to revoke an offer is not
sufficient. " The law," says Sir W. Anson, " regards the
offerer as making his offer during every instant of time
that his letter is travelling, and during the period which
may be considered as a reasonable time for acceptance."
The party to whom the offer is made is therefore entitled
to consider that it is still being made, unless he hears to the
contrary, and that his acceptance concludes a binding contract. An implied revocation, *i.e.* where the goods offered
for sale to A. are sold to B., appears to be only effective if
A. has notice of such sale.

§ 36. From what time Revocation dates.—The communication of a revocation is not complete until it is
received.

We have seen (§ 31) that the communication of an
acceptance by post is complete the moment the letter is
posted, but in the case of a revocation the communication
is not complete until it has actually reached the proposer.
A Cardiff firm wrote on the 1st October to a New York
firm offering 1000 boxes of tin plates at a certain price, and
asked for a reply by cable. On the 8th October the Cardiff
firm wrote a letter withdrawing the offer. The first letter
containing the offer reached New York on the 11th October, and the New York firm at once cabled accepting the
offer. On the 20th October the letter withdrawing the
offer was received. The Cardiff firm refused to forward
the goods, alleging that they revoked their offer by their

letter of the 11th October; but the court held that the revocation could only date from the 20th October, the date the second letter was received, and inasmuch as the offer had been duly accepted on the 11th, there was a binding contract.

§ 37. **What Agreements are Contracts?**—Assuming the offer not to be revoked, but accepted, there arises an agreement. But an agreement of itself is not enforceable at law. It is therefore necessary to ascertain what agreements the law will enforce. Briefly stated, an agreement to be enforceable must possess three characteristics :—

1. The parties to it must possess legal capacity to enter into the agreement.
2. The agreement must be made in a certain form or be supported by a consideration.
3. The subject matter must be lawful.

These three conditions will now be considered.

CHAPTER II

CAPACITY OF PARTIES TO CONTRACT

§ 38. General Rule.—Every natural person is competent to enter into a contract who is of full age and of sound mind, and is not specially disqualified by law.

No distinction is now drawn between subjects and aliens as regards capacity to contract, but alien enemies are subject to certain disabilities during war.

The capacity of an artificial person, such as a corporation, to contract depends mainly upon the purpose of its existence, except where it is expressly defined in the instrument or statute creating it.

INFANTS

§ 39.—A person under the age of twenty-one is an "infant." The position of infants in regard to contracts may be summed up in the following propositions :—

- (*a*) Contracts made with infants relating to (1) loans of money, (2) sales of goods other than necessaries, and (3) accounts stated, are absolutely void.
- (*b*) Contracts made with infants relating to necessaries or for their benefit are valid.
- (*c*) By custom in certain places and by Act of Parliament, infants may enter into special kinds of contracts.
- (*d*) All other contracts made with infants may be avoided by them either before or within a reasonable time of their coming of age.

§ 40. (*a*) **Void Contracts of Infants.**—It follows from the principles above laid down that if a merchant or shopkeeper supplies goods to an infant which are not necessaries, or if a money-lender lends him money, or if an account be stated of dealings with the infant, the merchant, the shopkeeper, the money-lender, or the person stating the account, has no remedy against the infant. The infant may pay what is due if he likes, but he is not bound to do so. Even if he represent himself to be of full age, the contract is void. The courts will not, however, allow any person, even an infant, to take advantage of a fraud. And though they must bow to the rule that says the contract is void, they will, on the ground of the fraudulent misrepresentation, compel the infant to restore any benefit he may have derived under the contract.

§ 41. (*b*) **Contracts of Infants for Necessaries.**—It is an old rule that an infant may enter into a binding contract for the supply of " necessaries " for his own use. " The word ' necessaries,' " said Baron Parke, " is not confined in its strict sense to such articles as were necessary to the support of life, but extended to articles fit to maintain the particular person in the state, degree, and condition of life in which he is." Food and clothing are examples of necessaries, but it would be impossible to give any list, inasmuch as what would be regarded as necessaries at one time or to one person, would be held not to be necessaries at another time, or to another person. Luxuries and ornaments, such as cigars and jewellery, are not regarded as necessaries except under very special circumstances. It is for the judge before whom the case is tried to say whether the articles can reasonably be considered as necessaries at all, but if he thinks the question an open one, the jury will be asked to say whether the particular things supplied were, under all the circumstances, to be regarded as necessaries. A few examples taken from decided cases will illustrate the above principles.

Livery for a servant, a horse, and a regimental uniform were regarded as necessaries where they were specially suitable to the position in life of the infant. On the other hand, a pair of jewelled solitaires that cost £25 were held not to be necessaries for a young man of large fortune. A watch may be regarded as a necessary, but its price must bear some relation to the circumstances of the purchaser.

§ 42. (*c*) **Special Contracts of Infants.**—By custom and by statute infants are authorised to enter into special contracts. These contracts relate rather to real property than to mercantile law, but it may be pointed out that, according to the custom of London, an infant unmarried and above the age of fourteen, though under twenty-one, may bind himself apprentice to a freeman of London by indenture with proper covenants.

§ 43. (*d*) **Voidable Contracts of Infants.**—We have seen that contracts of infants for goods sold, for money lent, and contracts in the form of accounts stated, are void, whilst contracts of infants for necessaries and contracts specially authorised by custom or statute are good. It remains to point out that all other contracts can be enforced by an infant if he chooses, but such contracts cannot be enforced against him. Formerly an infant was allowed, on coming of age, to ratify any contract that he had entered into during infancy, but in 1874 this power was taken away by the Infants Relief Act, which enacted that no action can be brought against a person upon any promise made after he attains his majority, to pay any debt contracted during infancy, or upon any ratification made after full age of any promise or contract made during infancy.

MARRIED WOMEN

§ 44. **Old Rule.**—The old common law regarded a husband and wife as one person, and disqualified the wife from entering into contracts binding on her personally. The custom of the city of London, however, permitted a married woman to trade, and for that purpose to make valid contracts, and by personal service a woman might acquire certain rights, but even in these cases the husband had to be a party to any action brought by or against her.

A married woman divorced or judicially separated from

her husband has the capacity to contract as if she were unmarried. A protecting order from a magistrate confers on her a similar capacity.

§ 45. Separate Estate.—At common law the moveable property of a wife belonged to the husband, and he acquired by marriage important interests in her immoveable property such as land. In short, subject to certain limitations, the property of the wife belonged to the husband. In course of time the doctrine came to be established that a married woman might by means of a trustee hold property for her own use independent of the husband. To such property the term "separate estate" was applied. Not only was she allowed to hold such property, but she was allowed to enter into contracts regarding it. Such contracts were regarded as not binding her personally, but as only binding the separate estate. In other words, if she were sued on a contract and judgment was recovered, she could not be committed to prison for refusing to pay. The doctrine of separate estate has been greatly extended by Acts of Parliament, but the principle still remains that the contracts of a married woman bind her separate estate only. The Married Women's Property Act 1882 says: "A married woman shall be capable of entering into and rendering herself liable in respect of and to the extent of her separate property on any contract," and of suing and being sued, as if she were a single woman.

There is a method by which a married woman may be prevented from binding her separate estate, viz. by using in the instrument granting her the property words restricting her from alienation. In such a case she has no power to bind her estate by contract. This disability lasts during marriage, and if she becomes a widow the power to contract revives.

§ 46. Contracts binding Separate Estate.—It is essential to the validity of the contract that at the time it is made the married woman should have some separate property, otherwise the contract is void. The value of such property may be very much less than the amount she contracts to pay; that is immaterial as far as the validity of the contract is concerned.   If the contract be valid, it will bind not only the separate estate she possessed at the time the contract was made, but also after acquired separate estate.

On the other hand, if she has no separate estate at the moment of time the contract is made, the contract is void, even though she should acquire such estate afterwards.

§ 47. As Agent for Husband.—A married woman residing with her husband has an implied authority to contract on behalf of the husband for a reasonable supply of goods and service for the household.   The authority may be revoked at any time, and it is desirable that notice of revocation should be given to those with whom she has been accustomed to deal.   The duty of proving that the wife has authority rests with the party seeking to enforce the wife's contract against the husband.   The husband being bound in law to maintain his wife, she can, if he fails to support her in a manner suitable to his station, bind him as his agent for what she requires.   The husband cannot deprive the wife of this authority.   If, however, the wife voluntarily leaves the husband's house and lives apart, she loses all right to pledge his credit, and those supplying her with goods do so at their own risk.

§ 48. Contracts with Husband.—A married woman may contract with her husband in respect of her separate estate.   She may, for example, lend him money out of such estate.   She may also enter into a contract with him relating to any litigation between them, or for a judicial separation.   But as regards other kinds of contracts, she cannot as a rule contract with him directly.

CORPORATIONS AND COMPANIES

§ 49. Definition.—A corporation is an artificial person created by law having a perpetual succession, a distinctive name, and a common seal.   Not being a natural person, it can only contract through an agent, and such agent must have the requisite authority to enter into the contract.

§ 50. Powers of Contracting.—The powers of a corporation to enter into contracts may be defined or limited in the instrument of incorporation. Where this is not the case regard must be had to its constitution and purposes. In the case of limited companies, the powers of contracting are defined in the "memorandum of association." A contract which is beyond the powers of a corporation is said to be *ultra vires* and is void.

§ 51. Form of Contracting.—As a general rule, a corporation can bind itself by contract only by a deed, *i.e.* by a writing under the common seal. To this there are many exceptions. Where the matter is of slight importance or of frequent occurrence the seal is not necessary. Hence the agent of a corporation may engage clerks, and the guardians of a poor law union may order ordinary provisions for a workhouse, by word of mouth. Trading corporations may enter into contracts in the usual course of business without the corporate seal (§ 65).

LUNATICS

§ 52. Contracts for Necessaries.—Every person is presumed to be of sound mind until the contrary appear. It may, however, occur that one of the parties to a contract is of unsound mind, and the question arises what effect has this on the contract or on the capacity to contract. By unsound mind is meant incapable of understanding the effects of the contract.

A contract for the supply of necessaries to a lunatic or his wife is good. The debt is chargeable against the lunatic's estate. By necessaries is meant articles necessary to the estate and condition of the lunatic.

§ 53. Contracts during Lucid Intervals.—A lunatic differs from an idiot in that he may at times have lucid intervals, *i.e.* be perfectly sane. During such intervals he can enter into a contract. But so long as the insanity lasts the lunatic is regarded as incapable of understanding the nature and consequences of any legal act. Some authorities have thought that if a lunatic enters into a contract, the fact of the lunacy being known to the other party, the contract is absolutely void, *i.e.* it has no legal effect whatever. But the better opinion seems to be that the lunatic on attaining a lucid interval may either adopt or confirm the contract.

§ 54. Contracts without Notice of Insanity.—Where a person contracts with another without any notice of insanity, the contract is valid. Hence where a person of unsound mind bought annuities from an insurance company, and the company had no knowledge of the insanity, it was held after the death of the lunatic that the purchase ought not to be set aside.

§ 55. Contracts with Notice of Insanity.—A contract made with a person of unsound mind by a person knowing of such unsoundness of mind is voidable. By "voidable" is meant that if an action be brought against the lunatic to enforce the contract, proof of lunacy will be a good defence.

§ 56. Effect of Insanity subsequent to a Contract.—The fact that one of the parties to a contract becomes insane subsequent to the making of the contract, does not as a rule affect its validity. But the insanity of a principal revokes the authority of the agent, and the insanity of a person engaged to be married releases the other from the contract to marry.

§ 57. Drunkenness. — A person who by reason of drunkenness has placed himself in a condition analogous to insanity, is regarded, as far as the capacity to contract is concerned, as of unsound mind. The same rules apply as in the case of lunacy. If therefore a person enters into a contract with another, knowing him to be so drunk as not to understand what he is doing, such contract is voidable by the party of whom advantage has been taken.

CHAPTER III

THE FORM OF AND CONSIDERATION FOR CONTRACTS

§ 58. Classes of Contracts.—An agreement, in order to be enforceable as a contract, must be entered into before a Court of Record, or be under seal, or be supported by a consideration. Hence there are three classes of contracts in English law : (1) contracts of record, (2) contracts under seal, and (3) simple contracts. Certain contracts belonging to the last mentioned class require, in addition to a consideration, that they should be embodied in a certain form, *e.g.* in writing. Simple contracts may therefore be divided into two sub-classes : (1) those requiring, (2) those not requiring a special form.

CONTRACTS OF RECORD

§ 59. What is a Record ?—A record is a memorandum of a Court of Record entered on the rolls of the court. Certain entries on the rolls are regarded as amounting to a contract. The record proves itself, and no evidence to the contrary is admitted.

§ 60. Judgment Debts.—The only contract of record that requires notice here is a judgment recovered in an action. If one man brings an action for the price of goods and obtains judgment, such judgment is entered on the rolls of the court, and is said to give rise to a debt or contract of record between the plaintiff and defendant. A judgment debt has now no priority over an ordinary debt in the administration of the assets of a deceased person.

CONTRACTS UNDER SEAL

§ 61. How entered into.—A contract under seal is entered into by the delivery of a written or printed document bearing the seal of the person making delivery. If both parties are to be bound, the document should bear both their seals. It follows that a contract under seal requires three requisites : (1) writing or printing, (2) sealing, and (3) delivery. Signing may be added as a fourth requisite, though there is good reason for saying that, except in certain special contracts, it is not absolutely essential. The document is usually called a deed.

A deed ought to be written or printed on paper or parchment, and not upon wood or cloth, but it is immaterial whether the contents be written or printed, or whether a pen or pencil be used.

§ 62. Sealing.—The deed must bear the seal or seals of the party or parties to be bound. The use of sealing wax and of a seal to make an impression on the wax is unnecessary ; a wafer or an impression made by an instrument is sufficient.

§ 63. Signing.—The signatures of the parties ought always to be added to a deed, but by law they are only absolutely essential in certain cases.

§ 64. Delivery.—The "delivery" of the deed makes the deed take effect as regards the party making the delivery. The actual handing over of the deed is the simplest form of delivery, but the use of any words indicating that the person wishes the deed to become operative will amount to delivery.

Usually the seals are affixed beforehand, and the party executes the deed by placing his finger on the seal, saying, "I deliver this as my act and deed." This amounts to both sealing and delivery. The importance of delivery lies in the fact that the moment it takes place the deed takes effect.

The delivery may be made conditionally, and then the deed does not take effect until the condition is performed. Until such performance the deed is called an escrow.

If any of the material parts of a deed are omitted and delivery is made, the deed is void and the omissions cannot be subsequently supplied. The document when completed should be re-executed. The omission of an immaterial part, such as the date, will not invalidate a deed.

Shares in limited companies are usually transferable by deed. Sometimes the deed of transfer is executed without the name of the purchaser being inserted. Such a transfer does not pass a legal title to the shares, though it may give a right to have the shares duly transferred. The practice of the Stock Exchange in allowing the purchasing broker to fill in the name of the buyer, is not recognised by the courts.

§ 65. **Contracts that required to be made under Seal.**—In ordinary commercial transactions, such as the selling and buying of goods, it is not necessary to use a deed. But in the following cases the contract must be made under seal :—

1. Contracts transferring shares in companies.

By the Companies Act of 1862, section 22, shares in companies subject to the Act are to be transferred in the manner provided by the regulations of the Company. As a general rule such regulations require a deed for every transfer.

2. A contract transferring a British ship. Merchant Shipping Act, 1854, s. 55.

3. A contract for the sale of a piece of sculpture with copyright. 54 Geo. 3, c. 56.

4. Contracts entered into with corporations. A corporation such as a municipal corporation or a joint stock company is regarded as an "artificial person." In other words, the corporation itself has to be distinguished from the persons composing it. Every corporation has its own special seal, and the presence on a document of an impres-

sion made by such seal is evidence [1] that the corporation was a party to the document. The affixing of the seal makes the document perfect, and delivery is not required, as in the case of deeds made between individuals.

In the case of a trading corporation such as a company it would be very inconvenient to carry out the rule in every case, and it has been established that a *trading* corporation may by its agents and servants enter into simple contracts relating to the objects and purposes for which the corporation was founded. Hence where a gas company orders gas meters, or an iron company iron rails, or a shipping company ship provisions, the contract is good though not made under seal. To require a seal would tend to prevent the company from carrying out the objects for which it was founded. For similar reasons a trading company may draw and accept bills of exchange.

It must, however, be remembered that if the contract does not relate to the purposes for which the company was incorporated, it will not be binding on the company unless the company's seal is attached. For instance, where a company of copper miners gave an order for iron, it was held that this order was so far away from the business of the company that it ought to have been under seal.

In the case of non-trading corporations, such as municipal corporations, the rule requiring all contracts to be under seal is relaxed as regards contracts relating to matters of trifling or of daily occurrence, such as the hiring of a servant, or the ordering of necessaries for a workhouse, as well as regards contracts of urgent necessity such as those relating to repairs, necessitated by the severity of the weather or other emergency.

But it is desirable in all contracts of any importance to obtain the seal of the corporation, unless the legislature has expressly exempted such contracts from the necessity of sealing.

---

[1] Whether a person has sealed a deed or not, is a question of evidence or proof.

§ 66. A Consideration necessary.—It is a principle of English law that an agreement, if it does not amount to a contract of record or a contract under seal, must, in order to be enforced, be supported by some consideration. As mercantile contracts are seldom made under seal, it may be laid down as a general rule that all mercantile agreements, in order to be binding, must be supported by a consideration. Special statutes require in addition certain contracts to be in writing, so that a distinction may be drawn between (1) contracts that require both writing and consideration, and (2) contracts that require a consideration only.

§ 67. Contracts required to be in Writing. — The following are the chief examples of contracts relating to mercantile transactions that are required to be in writing :—

1. The acceptance of a bill of exchange.

2. The acknowledgment of a debt otherwise barred by the statute of limitation. A creditor cannot recover a simple debt after six years have elapsed, unless the debtor before the expiration of such six years makes a payment on account or gives an acknowledgment that he owes the money. Such acknowledgment must be in writing and be signed by the debtor or his agent.

3. Any promise made by one person (A.) to another person (B.) to answer for the debt, default, or miscarriage of a third person (C.) For instance, where A. promises B. that if he (B.) will supply goods to C., he (A.) will be answerable for the price of the goods if C. does not pay, B. should not supply the goods unless the promise is reduced to writing. It will be observed that it is assumed that the third person (C.) obtains the goods on credit, he is therefore primarily liable to pay. A. undertakes to be liable in case C. does not fulfil his promise. In all such cases the rule applies, and the promise should be given in writing, and be signed by the promiser or his agent

authorised for that purpose. If no writing be given, and C. fails to pay for the goods, no action can be brought against A.

4. Any agreement not to be performed within the space of one year from the making thereof.

This rule is applied only to agreements that clearly show by their tenor that the parties contemplated performance after the expiration of one year. For instance, a contract of partnership for ten years, a sale of goods where the goods are not to be delivered or paid for until after the expiration of twelve months, a contract of service for three years — such contracts indicate the intention of the parties to postpone performance for one year.

But if the contract is so framed that no such intention is indicated, and it is one that may be performed within the year, or if it may be performed within the year by one of the parties, then it is not within the rule: for instance, a contract to deliver goods within six months, and to receive payment within eighteen months, or a contract for the sale of goods, the price to be paid by yearly instalments.

5. Contracts for the sale of goods of £10 in value or over, where there is no acceptance of the whole or part of the goods, and no payment or part payment of the price.

Inasmuch as wholesale transactions are usually for goods of a greater value than £10, and are entered into without an immediate tender of the goods or the price, this class of contracts will embrace the greater number of wholesale purchases and sales. The above rule is based on the 17th section of the Statute of Frauds and on Lord Tenterden's Act (9 Geo. 4, c. 14, § 7), which enact that in order that a sale of goods of the value of £10 and upwards shall be binding, one of three things must occur, viz. (1) acceptance of the whole or part of the goods, or (2) receipt of part of the price, or (3) writing signed by the party liable.

The rule will be fully discussed in the chapter dealing with the contract of sale.

§ 68. **Oral Contracts.**—We now pass to those contracts

that need not be expressed in any particular form, that is to say, contracts that may be entered into by word of mouth. The class is a very important one. It includes all sales where the value of the article sold does not amount to £10, and as most single retail transactions relate to goods under £10 value, it will be understood that an enormous number of these contracts are entered into during the course of the year.

As a matter of fact, oral contracts for the sale and purchase of goods of a greater value than £10 are daily entered into. In strict law such contracts are not binding, but the force of commercial opinion ensures their due observance. If it became known on any exchange that a particular merchant was in the habit, when convenient, of disregarding his contracts on the ground that they ought to have been put in writing, no one would enter into business relations with him.

Reference has already been made to the fact that a contract in writing (as distinguished from a contract under seal) requires what in law is called a consideration. The same principle applies to oral contracts.. We may therefore lay down the following rule: Every contract, whether written or oral, not being made under seal, requires a consideration.

§ 69. **What is a Consideration ?**—The simplest example of a consideration is money. A. buys goods from B. at a price of £20. The £20 is the consideration promised by A. to B. for the goods. But the goods themselves may be regarded as the "consideration" given to A. by B. in exchange for the money. The consideration then is the equivalent or return given for a promise.

But a consideration need not necessarily be money or goods ; it may be some service or task. For instance, if a carrier undertakes to carry your luggage for a certain sum, the carrying of the luggage is a sufficient consideration to give rise to a valid contract.

The consideration may also be an omission to do that which a person is entitled to do. For instance, A. may be entitled to sue B. for a debt, A. may agree not to sue for a time provided an extra £5 be paid down ; here the consideration given by B. is £5, the consideration given by A. the giving of time for payment.

Marriage is a valid consideration between the parties to a marriage, and will support a promise made to either or both of such parties by a third party. On the other hand, blood relationship or love or affection is not sufficient to support an ordinary contract.

A consideration then is a *quid pro quo;* and it is the legal term used to denote the "something" that every person must give in order to obtain "something" in return.

§ 70. Executed, Executory, and Past Considerations.
—When a consideration is an act to be done, such as the payment of money, and the money is paid at the time the contract is entered into, the consideration is said to be "executed"; but if the money be not so paid, the consideration is said to be "executory." A "past" consideration is one executed and past before the contract is made. We shall see later on that an "executed" or an "executory" consideration is, but a "past" consideration is not, sufficient to support a simple contract.

§ 71. Rules relating to Consideration. — (*a*) The
amount of the consideration given is immaterial so long as it is of some value.

The law leaves the parties to make their own bargain. It insists that there shall be some price, but leaves the price to be fixed by agreement. If therefore a merchant in want of money sells his goods at a very low price, he can-not afterwards upset the sale on account of the small price he received. It is only when the inadequacy of the consideration is so gross as to amount to fraud that a court will interfere to set aside the contract (§ 90).

(*b*) A promise to do that which a man is bound to do will not amount to a consideration.

A promise by A. to B. to do that which he (A.) is already legally bound to do is of no advantage to B., because B. knows that the act must be performed in any case. It will not therefore be a good consideration for something promised on the part of B. The asking of time for pay-ment of a debt is a good example of this type of case. A creditor is pressing a debtor for payment, and is threaten-ing legal proceedings. The debtor asks for a fortnight's delay, and the creditor grants it, but before the fortnight expires he issues a writ. The debtor cannot legally complain. If he sets up as a defence the promise by the creditor to give further time, the answer will be that as the debtor was legally bound to pay at once, he gave nothing in return for the promise to wait, and therefore the promise of the creditor was not binding. On the other hand, if the debtor had given something for the extra time, then there would have been a valid contract.

(c) The consideration must not be so vague that it would be impossible for a court to enforce it.

(d) The consideration must be lawful.

The promise to do an unlawful act will not be a good consideration. And if any part of the consideration is illegal, it generally renders the whole transaction illegal (§ 75).

(e) The consideration must not be a past benefit.

This rule may be best explained by an illustration. A. purchased a horse from B. At a subsequent time A. inquired if the horse was sound, and B. thereupon gave A. a warranty of soundness. In other words, B. entered into a contract with A. to the effect that he warranted the soundness of the horse. Such a warranty was not binding, inasmuch as A. gave B. nothing—no consideration for it. Had the warranty been given at the time of the sale it would have been binding as part of the transaction.

§ 72. **Waiver of Exemption from Liability.**—A debtor, as we have seen, is not bound to pay a debt after six years have expired. The debtor may, however, waive his right, and if he promises to pay the debt after the six years have expired, he will be bound by his promise. Some writers think this promise is to be regarded as based on a consideration already received.

§ 73. **Proof of Consideration.**—The plaintiff who is trying to enforce a simple contract must show that he gave some consideration to the defendant in respect of the defendant's promise. The holder of a bill of exchange is not bound by this rule. If he is suing another party on the bill, the burden of showing that no consideration was given lies on the defendant.

CHAPTER IV

THE LEGALITY OF THE AGREEMENT

§ 74. Introductory.—We have seen that an agreement, to be enforced as a contract, must not be unlawful. The question then arises, What agreements are unlawful? In answering this question no attempt will be made to enumerate all the various kinds of unlawful agreements, as it will be sufficient for the purposes of this work if attention be directed to the leading unlawful agreements relating to trade.

§ 75. Where the Object is Unlawful.—An agreement for an unlawful purpose is void. An unlawful purpose is one that is prohibited by law. It is unlawful, for instance, to sell goods to be shipped in a prohibited trade, or to sell beer to be retailed without a license. In all such cases the seller, if not voluntarily paid for the goods, cannot recover the price. Upon the same principle money lent for an illegal purpose cannot be recovered.

§ 76. Where an Insurer has no Interest in the Policy.—An insurance of a ship where the insurer has no interest in the ship is void. The object of this rule is to prevent insurances being entered into by way of wager.

The same principle is applied to life and fire insurance. A man may insure his own life, but he cannot insure the life of another unless he has an "interest" in such life at the time of effecting the insurance; and only a person who has an interest in property can insure it against loss by fire (§ 164).

§ 77. Where Goods are sold on Sunday.—By a statute

passed in the reign of King Charles II., tradesmen are prohibited under a penalty from exercising any business on Sunday. An action cannot be brought upon an agreement made in violation of the statute, and hence where a horse-dealer bought a horse with a warranty on Sunday, he could not sue for breach of warranty (§ 147). In order that the statute may apply, the agreement must be one made in the course of the ordinary business of the tradesman. If, how-ever, goods be sold on Sunday, and both parties carry out the agreement, the property in the goods will pass to the buyer.

§ 78. **Where Goods are sold by Improper Weights or Measures.**—By the Weights and Measures Act of 1878 all agreements for work or goods agreed for by weight or measure are, in the absence of any agreement to the contrary, to be regarded as made with reference to the imperial weights and measures, and if not so made, they are to be void. But the weights and measures of the metric system may be used in agreements.

§ 79. **Where certain Goods are not sold in accord-ance with Law.**—Dead game killed in this country can be sold only during a certain time of the year by licensed dealers.

Intoxicating liquors can be sold only in licensed premises. The retailer of spirituous liquors is prohibited from taking any pledge for the payment of the price, and as a rule the retailer of all kinds of intoxicants is unable to sue for the price.

Coal must be sold by the weight, and a weight ticket be delivered to the buyer with any quantity over two hundredweight; otherwise a penalty is incurred, and the seller cannot recover the price. Bread, except fancy bread, must also be sold by weight if the purchaser so desire.

§ 80. **Where the Agreement is in restraint of Trade.**—As a general principle a trader is entitled to carry on a lawful business at his own discretion and in his own way, and any agreement to the contrary is void. Hence where a number of manufacturers agreed to regulate the wages and hours of work of their employees, and to manage their establishments in accordance with the views of the majority, it was held that this agreement, being in restraint of trade in so far as it deprived each one from controlling his own business, was not enforceable.

It is, however, not unlawful for a number of trades to agree to share the trade between them in such a way as to prevent competition, at least so long as there are no unreasonable restraints placed upon the parties.

The law permits agreements to be entered into that appear to be in a partial restraint of trade, on the ground that ultimately trade will be benefited. The chief agreements of this kind relate to the sale of a business.

After the sale of the goodwill of a business the seller, in the absence of any contract to the contrary, is free to carry on a similar trade, and to solicit his former customers in the usual way of business. In order to prevent the seller taking this course, it is usual to insert in the document by which the sale is effected a stipulation or contract restraining the seller from trading within such limits as regards place and time as are reasonably necessary for the protection of the business the buyer has acquired.

A restraint unlimited as regards space is generally held to be unreasonable. For example, a covenant by a brewer not to carry on the business of a brewer elsewhere was held unreasonable. On the other hand, covenants by a milkman not to set up in business within five miles for two years, and of a butcher not to carry on the same trade within five miles, were held reasonable. The custom of the trade is an important element in determining what is reasonable.

A restraint reasonably limited as to space may, in some cases, be unlimited as to time, inasmuch as this may be necessary to secure him the full enjoyment of that which he has bought. Hence the seller may agree not to carry on a similar business during his life.

The agreement must be founded on a valuable consideration, but the amount of the consideration is immaterial.

Similar principles are applied to agreements by which a retiring partner binds himself not to compete with the firm, or by which a servant or agent undertakes not to compete with his employer after the period of employment has ended.

§ 81. **Where the Agreement is a Fraud on Creditors.** —All agreements made for the purpose of defrauding third parties are void. If therefore a debtor who is insolvent enters into an arrangement with his creditors that they will accept part payment of all debts due in full discharge of such debts, he is not allowed to favour one creditor at the expense of the others. A creditor who stipulates with the debtor for a preference in favour of himself cannot enforce such agreement.

§ 82. **When the Agreement is in Fraud of the Bankrupt Laws.**—Any agreement on the part of the creditors of a bankrupt, or of the bankrupt himself, tending to interfere with the just application of the bankrupt law is illegal and void. An agreement by a creditor not to oppose the bankrupt's discharge, or an agreement interfering with the equal distribution of the assets, is void. So too is an agreement buying the vote of a creditor in the interests of the bankrupt.

CHAPTER V

§ 83. Possibility at Time of Contracting.—An agreement, in order to be enforceable at law, must be possible of performance. As we are at present concerned with the formation of contracts, the possibility of performance to be considered is that which exists at the time the agreement is made. If such possibility exist then there is *primâ facie* a good contract.

At a subsequent time events may occur that render it impossible for one or other of the parties to fulfil the obligation undertaken, and the effect of such events on the legal position of the parties requires to be examined.

§ 84. Kinds of Impossibility.—Three kinds of impossibility may be specified :—

1. Absolute impossibility : that is to say, impossibility inherent in the nature of the act promised, as, for instance, where a man agrees with another to make water run up a hill, or undertakes to fly across the ocean.

2. Legal impossibility : that is to say, where the act promised is prohibited by law.

3. Actual impossibility : that is to say, where the act promised becomes impossible owing to circumstances.

§ 85. Absolute Impossibility. — If an agreement is impossible in itself, it is void, as the parties to it cannot be supposed to have entered into an absurd agreement. The question of what is or is not impossible in itself depends largely on the progress of knowledge. What is apparently impossible at one time, becomes possible at a later stage of the earth's history.

§ 86. Legal Impossibility.—Where the performance of an agreement is legally impossible there is no valid contract. Every person is supposed to know the law, and the parties to the agreement are taken to have been aware that in law it could not be carried out. For instance, if A. professes to discharge B. from a debt due to C. without having any authority from C. to do so, the discharge is void, as a valid discharge for a debt can be given only by the debtor or his agent.

§ 87. Actual Impossibility.—Where the act to be done is not impossible in itself, and is not prohibited by law, it may become impossible in fact, owing to particular circumstances occurring subsequently. As a general rule the agreement is valid and the party who has undertaken the performance is liable. A few examples will illustrate the principle. Where a ship was to be loaded with usual despatch, and the loading was delayed by the occurrence of a frost, the party loading was held liable for the delay. Where a builder undertook to erect a building within a certain time in accordance with plans to be furnished, and it turned out that the plans were such that the buildings could not be erected within the time prescribed, the builder was held liable. In both these cases the parties might have protected themselves by the insertion of proper stipulations in the agreement. Unexpected difficulties therefore do not serve as an excuse for non-performance of the terms of an agreement.

There are certain exceptions to the principle, but they will be referred to under the head of Performance and Discharge of Agreements (§ 102).

CHAPTER VI

EFFECTS OF MISTAKE, MISREPRESENTATION, OR FRAUD

§ 88. **Reality of Consent.**—A contract which on the face of it is for a legal and possible object, possesses the proper form or consideration, and is made between parties capable of contracting, may, however, have no legal effect or a limited legal effect if it appear that there was no real agreement. This may happen in three ways : (1) where there was a " mistake," the parties meaning different things ; (2) where there was " misrepresentation," by one of the parties that induced the other to contract ; and (3) where there was " fraud," *i.e.* an intentional misrepresentation.

§ 89. **Mistake.**—As a general rule one party to a contract is not allowed to avoid it by alleging that he made a " mistake." The word " mistake " may, however, be used in various senses. It may mean a mistake as to expectations. A. buys goods thinking the market is going to rise, when in fact it falls. It may mean a mistake as to the utility of the article for a particular purpose, as, for instance, where a person buys a stove which he finds too small for heating purposes. Or it may mean mistake in wording the offer or the acceptance, *e.g.* where A. orders 100 tons when he only meant 10 tons. Other uses of the word might easily be given. We are, however, concerned with a technical use of the term to denote certain circumstances that are recognised by the courts as indicating a want of that real consent that is essential to every contract. These circumstances may be divided into five classes :—

1. Where the contract relates to a thing believed by both parties to exist when it has ceased to exist.
2. Where one party contracts with another person believing him to be a third party.
3. Where one party, not being negligent, is mistaken as to the real nature of the contract.
4. Where there is a mutual mistake as to the identity of the thing sold.
5. Where one party is mistaken as to the nature of the promise given, and such mistake is known to the other party.

§ 90. (1) **Mistake as to the Existence of the Subject Matter.**—When a cargo at sea is sold, the parties not knowing whether it is afloat or not, are regarded as contracting on the supposition that the cargo is afloat.   If it eventually turns out that the vessel and cargo had been wrecked and lost at the moment the contract was made, the contract is not binding, and the loss will fall on the seller and not upon the buyer.   So too where a cargo of corn supposed to be on a voyage to England was sold, when in fact it had become so heated that it had already been sold at Tunis, the court held the contract void on the ground that it implied that the corn was in existence as such, and that it was capable of delivery.

It would probably be more correct to classify all these cases under failure of an implied condition that the thing sold is in existence, and belongs to the vendor.

It is important to remember that such an implied condition is only imported into contracts of a certain type, *i.e.* when the parties are to be taken as contemplating an existing thing belonging to the vendor.   There is no rule of law to prohibit A. from selling to B. that which does not belong to A.   Stock Exchange dealings take place daily in stocks and shares that do not belong to the vendor, and such dealings are valid.   Non-existing property may be bought and sold if there is a possibility of its existence, and the parties are aware of its non-existence.   For example, A. may sell B. a crop to be raised on a certain field.

§ 91. (2) **Mistake as to Party.**—The usual type of case

in which one party contracts with another believing him to be a third party, is due as a rule to the fraud or dishonesty of the other party. A. was accustomed to buy goods from B.: an order for goods from A. directed to B. came into C.'s hands, who had bought B.'s business. C. executed the order without informing A. of the change in the proprietorship of the business. It was held that A. was not obliged to pay for the goods, as there was no contract between A. and C.

If A. by imitating the signature of B. obtains goods from C., the property in the goods will not pass to A., as there is no real contract of sale between A. and C. In this case C. thinks he is contracting with B.

§ 92. (3) **Mistake as to the Nature of the Contract.**— Where a blind man or a man who cannot read has a written contract falsely read out to him, so that the contract as read is entirely different from the contract as written, and afterwards signs the contract, it will not be binding on him. Under such circumstances "the mind of the signer did not accompany the signature." Hence where a very old man signed a bill of exchange (§ 238), being told that it was a guarantee (§ 188), and the bill was endorsed over to a party who sued him upon it, it was held that the amount could not be recovered against him. And where an illiterate man executed a deed releasing "all claims," which was represented to him as a deed releasing "arrear of rent" only, it was held that the deed was void.

In order that the contract may be avoided in these cases, it is necessary that there should be an absence of negligence. He who signs a written document without informing himself of the contents when he is able so to do, is negligent, and will be bound by his document.

§ 93. (4) **Mistake as to the Identity of the Thing sold.**—If A. intends to sell one thing, and B. to buy another, there is an absence of that common intention that is the essence of every agreement. Cases occur where different things are described by the same name, and it is quite possible for the parties to agree upon a contract thinking they mean the same subject matter when in fact they do not. A. purchased from B. a cargo of cotton "to arrive *ex* 'Peerless' from Bombay " : it so happened that there were two ships sailing from Bombay named 'Peerless,' and A. meant one vessel and B. the other. It was held that there was no contract.

§ 94. (5) **Mistake of One Party known to the Other.**— In all contracts of sale the law as a rule leaves the buyer to use his own judgment, and if he makes any mistake as to the quality of the thing sold, the loss falls upon himself (§ 146). To this rule there are, as we shall see (§ 147), certain exceptions; for example, where the vendor is regarded as warranting the quality of the thing sold. If therefore A. buys from B. a length of cloth believing it to be of better quality than it really is, B. making no representations on the subject, and A. not communicating his views to B., the contract is good. But if A. buys the cloth thinking it is made entirely of silk, when it is made of a mixture of silk and cotton, and B. knows that A. thinks that he (B.) is selling the cloth as pure silk, the sale is void. Of course A. might protect himself by asking B. to warrant the cloth to be pure silk, but we are assuming that there is no warranty asked for or given. It is also assumed that B. makes no representation of any kind; he is merely supposed to know that A. thinks that he (B.) is selling pure silk. The following example may also be given : A. bought some oats from B. ; the oats were new, but A. thought they were old, and B. knew that A. thought that he (B.) was selling old oats; it was held that the sale was void.

§ 95. **Misrepresentation.**—Previous to or at the time of entering into a contract representations may be made by either party to the other with the object of inducing him to agree to the terms proposed. A vendor of goods, for instance, may represent them as being the manufacture of a particular firm, or as possessing certain qualities. Another type of representation may be seen in the statements contained in the prospectus of a company inviting the public to take shares. Closely connected with misrepresentations is the non-disclosure of facts known to one party and not to the other. In certain contracts, such as insurance (§ 163), the fullest disclosure of all material facts is required, but apart from these contracts one party is not bound to disclose to the other facts that he knows, and which might affect the other party's judgment. For instance, a seller of goods is not obliged to point out defects to the purchaser. Actual misrepresentation is forbidden, and a contract is liable to be set aside where a misrepresentation is made, even though the person making it believes he is speaking the truth. In order that a misrepresentation may avoid the contract, it must be (1) of fact and not of law, (2) made by a party to the contract, and (3) the misrepresentation must have induced the contract acted on the misrepresentation.

1. The misrepresentation must be of fact.

Every one is supposed to know the law, and therefore the courts will not avoid a contract where one party entered into it on the faith of a representation of its legal effects which was untrue. There are exceptions to this rule, as, for example, where such an advantage has been taken by one party of the other as to amount to a fraud.

The representation must not be a mere opinion — an opinion is not a fact. Hence statements of "belief" are not representations of fact.

2. The misrepresentation must be made by a party to the contract.

If A. contracts with B. on the faith of representations made by C., he cannot avoid the contract. But if B. is the agent of C., the question arises, Are principals responsible for the misrepresentations of their agents? As a rule a principal is only liable for the act of his agent if it is within the scope of his authority (§ 128), and hence if the misrepresentation was within the agent's authority, the contract of the principal is void. Directors are agents of the company, and if they induce persons to contract with the company by misrepresentations, such contracts are liable to be avoided.

3. The misrepresentation must have induced the contract.

A party to a contract cannot avoid a contract on the ground of misrepresentation, if such misrepresentation did not induce him to make the contract. The misrepresentation, in other words, must relate to a material fact; and a fact is said to be material when it would affect the judgment of a reasonable man, acting on the principles which men follow in the kind of business to which the contract relates.   It is no reply to an alleged misrepresentation to say that the other party might have ascertained the truth— the making of the representation tends to put the other party off his guard.   Nor is it any reply to prove that the party making it believed in its truth.   There is no duty, in the cases of which we are speaking, of making any representations whatever, and he who makes them and thereby induces a party to enter into a contract with him cannot enforce such contract.

§ 96. Fraud. — A misrepresentation will amount to fraud where the party making it (1) knows that it is untrue, or (2) makes it recklessly, not caring whether it be true or false.

That knowledge of the falsehood of the thing asserted is necessary to fraud, has always been recognised.   But the circumstances under which false statements made without such knowledge amount to fraud, have been the subject of much discussion.   It is not sufficient that the false statement be made carelessly, it must be made recklessly.   An honest belief in the truth of the statement excludes the idea of fraud.

For example, where the directors of a company stated in a prospectus that the company had the right to use steam power, honestly believing this to be true, when in fact the company had no such power, it was held that there was no fraud.

Whether a false statement is made recklessly or whether there are reasonable grounds for believing it to be true is a matter of evidence.   Careful inquiry is made into the circumstances under which the statement was made, or upon which the belief was founded.   A man may deliberately represent himself as having a belief which he does not possess.   This will amount to fraud; the person is wilfully misrepresenting his state of mind, which is a matter of fact.

The distinction between misrepresentation and fraud lies in this, that in fraud there is a wilful misrepresentation. Fraud involves misrepresentation, but requires in addition either a knowledge that the statement is untrue, or a reckless state of mind as to its truth or falsehood.

§ 97. Remedies in case of Misrepresentation or Fraud.

1. Contracts induced by misrepresentation or fraud are not void but voidable, *i.e.* the party injured may elect to uphold the contract or to avoid it.

If he upholds the contract, he may claim damages for such loss as he has sustained. If he desires to avoid the contract, he must give notice of such intention to the other side. He cannot, however, take this course if he has taken any benefit under the contract, or if circumstances have so altered that the parties cannot be placed in their original position, or if third parties have acquired rights under it.

2. In the case of fraud an action may be brought for deceit.

Fraud is a wrong giving rise to an action for damages, apart from any damages that can be claimed for any loss arising under the contract.

CHAPTER VII

THE ASSIGNMENT OF CONTRACTS

§ **98. Introductory.**—An unperformed contract gives rise to certain rights and duties. The rights belong to, and the duties are binding on the parties to the contract. A person who is not a party to the contract cannot enforce the rights or be compelled to undertake the duties. It may, however, happen that one of the parties may desire to transfer his rights or his liabilities to another person, and we have to examine how far the law will recognise such transfer. A distinction must be drawn between rights and duties or liabilities.

§ **99. Liabilities cannot be assigned.**—The law does not permit a person who has promised to do anything under a contract to transfer such duty to another person. If A. contracts with B. that he, B., shall manufacture and supply certain goods, B. is not allowed to transfer the duty of fulfilling the contract to C. A. may have been induced to make the contract by his reliance on the credit and character of B.: in any case the law assumes that A. contracted with B., and with B. alone.

A liability, however, may be assigned with the consent of the party entitled to call for performance. This practically amounts to a rescission of the contract with one person and the making of a new contract with another.

§ **100. Assignment of Rights.**—Formerly it was a rule that rights under a contract were not assignable, but partly by the decisions of the courts and partly through the operation of statutes, such rights can now be assigned. Special provision has been made for assigning rights under certain contracts, *e.g.* in the case of policies of insurance and shares in companies. In all these cases the provisions of the statute must be observed.

The right to receive money under a bill of exchange or a promissory note may be transferred by delivery of the bill or note if it is payable to bearer, and by endorsement and delivery if it is payable to order (§ 246). No notice is required to be given to the party liable to pay ; it is not necessary for the assignee to show that he gave any consideration ; and he is not affected by any defect in the title of prior holders. These characteristics are summed up in the word "negotiable." A bank-note is an example of a negotiable instrument. It can be transferred by delivery, the transferee has not to give notice to the bank that it has come into his hands, and he is entitled to receive gold in exchange for it from the bank named, though some previous holder may have stolen it.

All debts, *i.e.* rights to receive money, may be assigned in writing signed by the assignor, provided the assignment be absolute. The assignee must give notice of the assignment to the person liable to pay, whose consent, however, is not necessary. The assignee takes subject to any "equities," *i.e.* claims to which the debt was subject previous to assignment.

§ 101. **Assignment of Rights and Liabilities by Operation of Law.** — We have seen that a liability under a contract cannot be assigned to another by the party upon whom the liability is cast by the contract. What an individual cannot do, the law may do, and in some cases does it. For instance, the purchaser of a lease is by law bound to pay the rent and to discharge other liabilities imposed by the lease on the original lessee. If a husband receives property through his wife, he is liable to the debts contracted by her before marriage to the extent of such property. Death often operates as a transfer of both rights and liabilities. For instance, the legal representatives of a deceased man take all his personal property ; all liabilities attached to such property pass to them as well as the benefit of all rights of action.   On bankruptcy all rights of action belonging to the bankrupt pass to the trustee, though as far as liabilities are concerned the trustee can in some cases disclaim them.

CHAPTER VIII

PERFORMANCE, BREACH, AND DISCHARGE OF CONTRACTS

§ 102. Duty of Performance.—The parties to a contract are bound to carry out their respective promises. If the contract be silent as to the mode of performance, it must be performed in accordance with the usage of the place where it was made. In all cases the performance must be a *bona-fide* performance, and not a compliance with the mere letter of the agreement. Where no time is fixed, performance must be within a reasonable time. In some cases the performance by one party is made to depend on something to be done previously by the other; where this happens, performance is not due until the act agreed upon has been performed.

§ 103. Payment.—When a sum of money has to be paid, the payment, unless the parties otherwise agree, should be made in legal-tender money (§ 154). A bill or note is often taken in payment of a debt, but as a rule this is to be regarded as merely extending the time for payment, so that if the money be not paid when the bill or note is due, the creditor may still sue on the original contract. But if the creditor has taken the bill or note in discharge of the debt, then he has to rely on the rights of action given by the bill, and the original contract is at end.

§ 104. Tender.—In the case of a sale of goods, a tender of the price or of the goods amounts to performance on the part of the person tendering. In the case of a tender of goods, the tender should be unconditional, and be made at the proper time and place, and the person to whom the tender is made should have a reasonable opportunity of examining the goods.

In the case of money, such a sum should be offered as will enable the creditor to take exactly what is due without giving change (§ 154).

BREACH OF CONTRACT

§ 105. **Effect of Breach.**—A breach of contract by one party gives the other party a right of action for damages, and, in the following cases, discharges such other party from the necessity of performing his share of the agreement: (1) when the party renounces his liabilities; (2) when he makes it impossible that he can fulfil the contract; and (3) when he totally fails to perform what he has promised.

§ 106. (1) **Renunciation.**—Where one party gives the other notice that he will not carry out a contract, the latter may treat the contract as at an end, and bring an action for damages. For instance, if A. engage B. as a servant from the 1st June, and before the 1st of June A. writes to B. that he will not require his services, B. may bring an action for damages at once against A. In order that a renunciation should amount to a discharge of a contract, it is necessary (1) that the renunciation should be of the whole contract, and (2) that the renunciation should be treated as a discharge. If subsequent to renunciation performance is insisted on, the contract remains.

§ 107. (2) **Impossibility.**—If one of the parties to a contract by his own act renders it impossible for him to perform it, the other party is excused performance, and may at once bring an action for damages. For example, if A. gives B. an option (which B. accepts) to purchase an article within a certain time, but before the option is exercised sells it to some one else, the contract is at an end (§ 87).

§ 108. (3) **Failure to Perform.**—Where the performance of a promise forms the consideration for the performance of another promise, failure to perform the one excuses the performance of the other. As for example, where A. buys goods and promises to pay for them on delivery, here delivery must be made before payment can be demanded. But if the promise and not the performance of it was the real consideration on either side, the contract must be performed on one side though it be broken on the other, the injured party having his remedy in an action for damages. As for example, where A. bought land from B. and covenanted to pay for it on the 1st April, and B. covenanted to convey the land to A., no time being fixed for the conveyance: as soon as the 1st April arrived, B. was entitled to sue for the purchase money though he had not conveyed nor offered to convey the land to A.

§ 109. Remedies for Breach.—We have seen that in many cases of breach of contract the party injured is discharged from performance of his promise. Apart from this, he is entitled to bring an action for damages. The amount of damages recovered is supposed to represent the loss sustained so far as it was in contemplation of the parties. Where the parties cannot agree on the amount, it has to be fixed by a judge or a jury.

Instead of awarding damages, the courts might order the defaulting party to perform the contract. This course is usually adopted in regard to sales of land, but in the case of the sale of goods the courts consider that damages are a more appropriate remedy: and specific performance is only decreed when the articles sold cannot on account of their intrinsic qualities be represented adequately by damages.

DISCHARGE

§ 110. Discharge of Contracts.—A contract may be discharged or rescinded in the following ways :—

1. By consent. The parties may agree before performance that the contract shall be no longer binding. If the contract has been under seal, the discharge must also be under seal. The discharge may take

the form of the substitution of a new contract for the old one.

2. By fulfilment of a proviso for discharge. The original agreement may contain a clause to the effect that under certain circumstances it is to be at an end.

3. By operation of law. The alteration of a written contract will under certain circumstances operate as a discharge ; and when a bankrupt obtains his order of discharge, he is discharged from all debts provable under the bankruptcy.

4. Performance, as we have seen, puts an end to the contract.

5. Breach of contract, as we have also seen, often operates as a discharge.

§ 111. Authorities on Contracts.—The work of Sir William Anson on the Law of Contract will be found very useful by the student. Sir F. Pollock's treatise on Contracts is more advanced. A Digest of the Law of Contract is published by Mr. Leake ; whilst works such as Addison on Contract discuss all forms of contracts.

PART III

THE LEADING COMMERCIAL CONTRACTS

CHAPTER I

PARTNERSHIP

§ 112. **Its Nature.**—Partnership has already been defined as the relation that subsists between persons carrying on a business with a view to profit. The partners may make any agreement they please as to the amount of capital, labour, or skill that each one is to contribute to the business, but the sharing of the profits is absolutely essential to a partnership. If an agreement, for instance, be made that one of the partners is to have no share in the profits, he is not a partner. The mere receipt of a share of the profits will not of itself be conclusive as to the existence of a partnership. The executors of a partner may, after his death, be entitled to a share of the profits, but the receipt of such share will not necessarily make the executors partners. Sharing profits is, however, evidence of partnership, but it is not conclusive—all the facts of the case must be examined and the real intention of the parties ascertained. A widow or child of a deceased partner may receive by way of annuity a portion of the profits without becoming thereby a partner. Interest to a creditor may vary with the profits, or take the form of a share of the profits without the lender becoming thereby a partner.

But parties are not permitted to exercise the powers of a partner and at the same time under the cover of some arrangement escape the liabilities of a partner. A creditor who lends money in consideration of a share in the profits is obliged, in case the borrower becomes bankrupt, to postpone his claims until all the other creditors are paid. But if his debt is secured by any charge or mortgage, his rights under such charge or mortgage remain unaffected.

§ 113. Power of a Partner to bind the Firm.—Every partner is an agent of the firm and of his other partners for the purposes of the partnership. As between the partners and third parties, each partner is taken to have full authority without any express agreement to enter into contracts binding on himself and his co-partners, so long as such contracts relate to the usual and ordinary business of the partnership. He may therefore sell any goods belonging to the firm, buy any goods required for the business, engage clerks, and receive all debts due. The exact limits of a partner's authority naturally depend on the character of the business of the firm. Where the firm is carrying on some trade, a partner, as a rule, has in addition to the above powers full authority to make and accept bills of exchange in the name of the firm. He may also borrow money on the firm's credit, and for that purpose pledge any goods belonging to the firm.

On the other hand, a partner is not an agent to bind the firm in matters not connected with the firm's business, unless he is specially authorised.

A partner, for instance, is not regarded as having authority to bind the firm by a document under seal. An express authority from the firm for such a purpose is required, and such authority must be under seal. Nor can a partner give a guarantee in the firm's name without special authority, unless it is the usage in the firm, or in other firms engaged in the like business, so to do. Nor can a partner bind his firm by a submission to arbitration.

The general authority of a partner to bind the firm may be restricted by agreement between the partners, but such agreement will not affect third parties unless they have

notice of it.   If a third party, having notice of such agreement, enters into a contract with the partner outside his
restricted authority, the firm is not bound by it.   In order
to prevent any controversy arising as to the scope of the
notice, care should be taken to warn third parties that the
firm will not be answerable for the acts of the partner outside of his limited authority.

A partner who enters into an unauthorised contract
may, however, be personally liable upon it.

§ 114. **Liability of Partners.**—A partner during his
lifetime is liable jointly with the other partners for all the
debts and obligations of the firm incurred while he is a
partner.   A partner's liability begins when he enters the
partnership; he is not liable for debts previously incurred.
By retiring from the firm, and giving notice to that effect,
he ceases to be liable for subsequent debts.   But so long
as he is a member of the firm, liability attaches to him
jointly with his co-partners.

On the death of a partner the partnership is dissolved,
and his private property then becomes liable to the payment of partnership debts in so far as they are unpaid, but
subject to the prior payment of his own private debts.   It
follows from this rule that the creditors of a partnership
have, on the death of a partner, a claim upon his private or
separate property that they do not possess during his lifetime.

The practical effect of the rule is that the firm's assets
are liable for the payment of the firm's debts ; the separate
property of the deceased partner is liable for his separate
debts ; but if the firm's assets are insufficient to pay
creditors, they can recover what is unpaid from the assets
of the deceased that remain, after paying his private debts.

In Scotland the law as to liability is different to that
in England.   There a partner during his lifetime is individually as well as jointly liable for the debts of the firm.

§ 115. **Liability of Persons "holding out."**—If a
man, by words or conduct, represents himself as a partner,
or allows others to do so, he is liable as a partner to any one
who, on the faith of such representation, gives credit to the
firm.   The mere use of a man's name without his know-

ledge will not make him liable as a partner, the use of the name must be with his assent. A retiring partner, in order to avoid liability, ought always to give public notice of his retirement.

The principle of "holding out" does not apply to the executors of a deceased partner who permit the old name to be continued in use.

§ 116. Partnership Property.—All property originally brought into the partnership-stock, or subsequently acquired for the purposes of the firm, is regarded as partnership property. Hence if one partner buys land or shares with the money, and on account of, the firm, they will be regarded as the property of the firm, though the partner takes an assignment to himself.

When land becomes partnership property, it is as between the partners regarded as moveable and personal estate, and hence the legal representatives of a deceased partner, and not his heir, are entitled to such property.

§ 117. Rights and Duties of Partners.—The chief rights and duties of partners, in default of any agreement to the contrary, as between themselves are as follows :—

1. All the partners are entitled to share equally in the capital and profits of the business, and must contribute equally towards all losses.

In the absence of any agreement to the contrary, a partner is not entitled to any remuneration for his services beyond his share of the profits, if any. Until the profits are actually ascertained, a partner is not entitled to any interest on capital subscribed by him. But where he makes an advance to the firm beyond the amount of capital he agreed to subscribe, he is entitled to interest at the rate of five per cent per annum from the date of such advance.

2. A partner in the course of the partnership business must not make any undisclosed profit for himself.

Hence he must account for any benefit derived by him without the consent of the other partners from any transaction concerning the partnership, or from any use by him of the partnership property, name, or business connection.

A partner too, if he carries on a business of the same nature as the partnership, and competing with it, must hand over to the firm all the profit he makes, unless he has the consent of his co-partners to the carrying on of such competing business.

3. Every partner is entitled to be indemnified by the firm in respect of payments made and personal liabilities incurred in the ordinary business of the firm, or for the preservation of the property of the firm.

4. Every partner is entitled to take part in the management of the partnership business.

Where any difference occurs, it is to be decided by a majority of the partners. But in three cases, the will of the majority is not recognised : (1) where a change is to be made in the nature of the partnership business, the consent of all the existing partners is required ; (2) a majority cannot expel a partner unless there is a clause to that effect in the partnership agreement; and (3) a new partner cannot be introduced without the consent of all the existing partners.

5. Partners are bound to render true accounts and full information of all things affecting the partnership to any partner or his legal representatives.

6. Every partner is entitled to have access to and to inspect and copy the partnership-books, which are to be kept at the place where the business is carried on.

§ 118. Dissolution of Partnership.—Subject to any agreement between the partners, a partnership is dissolved—

1. If entered into for a single undertaking, by the termination of the undertaking.

2. If entered into for a fixed term, by the expiration of that term.

3. If no fixed term has been agreed upon, by any partner giving notice to the other partners of his intention to dissolve the partnership. It is desirable that this notice be in writing.

4. By the death of a partner.

5. By the bankruptcy of a partner.

A partnership may, notwithstanding any agreement of the parties, be dissolved—

1. By the happening of any event that renders the business of the firm illegal.

2. By a decree of the court.

The court will, as a rule, order a dissolution of partnership where circumstances have arisen that render it just and equitable that the partnership should be dissolved; where one partner is found a lunatic after inquiry ; where a partner becomes permanently incapable of carrying out his partnership agreement ; where a partner has been guilty of conduct prejudicially affecting the carrying on of the business, or where the business can only be carried on at a loss.

§ 119. **Effects of Dissolution.**—After a dissolution, the authority of each partner to bind the firm continues as far as may be necessary to wind up the affairs of the partnership, but not otherwise. The property of the firm must be realised and applied in the following order : in paying (1) the debts and liabilities of the firm ; (2) any advances made by a partner; (3) what is due to the partners in respect of capital. Any surplus left is to be divided equally amongst the partners.

These rules are to be taken as subject to the terms of the partnership agreement.

§ 120. **Authorities.**—The greater portion of the law of partnership has been codified in the Partnership Act of 1890. Sir F. Pollock's Digest of the Law of Partnership includes this Act. A larger treatise is the standard work of Lord Justice Lindley.

CHAPTER II

PRINCIPAL AND AGENT

§ 121. Introductory.—An agent is a person employed to do an act on behalf of another. The person for whom such act is done is called the principal. The division of labour has been carried to such an extent in connection with the distribution of goods, that sellers as well as buyers often find it to their advantage to effect sales and purchases through the agency of third parties.

Any person who has capacity to enter into a contract may appoint an agent : any person may, as regards third parties, be appointed agent, even though he be a minor. An agent is usually remunerated by commission or salary, but no consideration or payment is necessary to create agency.

§ 122. Kinds of Agents.—The chief classes of mercantile agents are factors, brokers, commission agents, and *del credere* agents.

A factor is an agent for sale to whom possession of the goods is given.

A broker is an agent employed by two parties to negotiate a contract between them. There are several kinds of brokers. A broker for sale is an agent to sell or purchase commodities—he is not entrusted with the possession of the goods. A stock and share broker is an agent employed to sell or buy stocks or shares. An insurance broker is an agent employed to effect a policy of insurance.

A commission agent is an agent employed not by two parties, but by one party to either sell or buy goods.

A *del credere* agent is an agent for sale who gives an undertaking to his principal that the parties with whom he contracts will fulfil their engagements.

A distinction is sometimes drawn between "special" and "general" agents. A special agent is one who has authority to act in a special case only. A general agent is one who is employed in many cases. The authority of the former is derived from his special authority; the authority of the latter is inferred from the previous cases in which he has acted.

§ 123. Appointment of Agents.—An agent may be appointed expressly by any form of words, except in special cases, where a special form is required.[1] It is generally desirable to have the terms of the appointment reduced to writing, so as to avoid any subsequent dispute as to the extent of the agent's authority.

The relation of principal and agent may be inferred from the conduct of the parties. A servant who is habitually sent by his employer to order goods from a shopkeeper is regarded as the employer's agent, and a wife who is permitted by her husband to order necessaries for the household becomes his agent.

§ 124. Ratification.—Ratification of the acts done by one person on behalf of another is discussed by some writers under the head of appointment of agent. By ratification is meant the adoption of a contract by one person made by another on his behalf, but without his authority. It is not every act of another person that can be ratified, so as to make the person ratifying a party to the act and responsible for it. But where a contract is made by B. on behalf of A., without A.'s authority, in respect of something that A. can lawfully do, A. may adopt the contract and become liable on it, whether it be to his detriment or his advantage. The ratification may be by either words or conduct.

§ 125. The Authority of Agents.—The authority of an agent may be express or implied.

An authority is said to be express when it is given by

---

[1] *E.g.* An agent to execute a deed must be appointed by deed.

words spoken or written. The advantage of a written authority is that the written document furnishes excellent evidence as to the extent of authority conferred.

An authority is said to be implied when it is inferred from the circumstances of the case. For example, if A. is in the habit of sending his servant B. to buy goods from C. on credit, C. is justified in supposing that the servant has authority to buy on credit. If, however, the servant was in the habit of buying for cash, and he asks for goods on credit, the shopkeeper ought at once to inquire if the servant has authority to buy on credit. If he has no such authority, the employer will not be liable to pay for the goods.

An agent authorised to do any act has authority to do every lawful act necessary in order to do such act. Hence an agent employed to carry on a business may purchase all articles necessary to such business. An agent employed to sell, may do everything requisite to effect a sale, *e.g.* he can sell on credit when this is the usage of the business; an insurance agent can adjust and settle a loss; a debt-collecting agent can give receipts.

§ 126. **Duties of Agents.**—*Obedience.*—An agent ought to observe the directions of the principal. This is the primary duty of an agent, and any losses resulting from a failure to obey instructions must be borne by him. All orders as to time, price, and quality should be observed. In many cases a discretion is given to him; in such a case he may take what course seems best.

In the absence of any instructions, he ought to follow the usual course of business at the place where the business is to be transacted.

Skill.—The agent must conduct the business with as much skill as is generally possessed by persons engaged in a similar business. An agent ought to possess the skill requisite to enable him to discharge what he undertakes. If he is incompetent, and fails to disclose this incompetence to his employer, he must make good any resulting loss. Perfect skill is not required, only that which is possessed by those engaged in the particular business in question.

Diligence.—The agent must not only possess sufficient

skill and use it, but he must also act with reasonable diligence, *i.e.* with the diligence that would be shown by a competent man.   Hence if an insurance broker fails to have the usual insurance clauses inserted in a policy, he must make good any loss, or if an agent for sale sells on credit without making proper inquiries as to the solvency of the purchaser, he also must make good any loss.

Emergencies.—In all cases of emergency the agent should communicate with the principal.   This rule specially applies to the non-acceptance or dishonouring of bills of exchange.

Fidelity.—An agent is not allowed to use his position in order to benefit himself beyond his agreed remuneration. An agent for sale is not allowed to purchase for himself, unless he discloses every material fact to the principal.   If the agent deals in the business of the agency on his own account, he must hand over all profit made.   Fidelity to the principal is absolutely necessary.

Accounts.—An agent must keep proper accounts, and render them when required to his principal.   A failure to keep accounts may deprive the agent of any right to his commission, and a failure to furnish accounts to the principal renders him liable to an action.

Moneys.—All sums received on the principal's account should be paid over, but the agent may retain out of such sums any moneys due to himself in respect of advances made or expenses incurred in conducting the business, as well as his own remuneration.   Payment of remuneration is not, as a rule, due until the act authorised is done.

Commission.—An agent is entitled to retain any property, papers, or books of the principal until the amount due for commission and expenses has been paid.

§ 127. Duties of Principal to Agent.—*Reimbursing Expenses.*—The principal must reimburse the agent all the expenses he has necessarily incurred in carrying out the agency.   The agent cannot recover needless expenses.

Payment of Remuneration.—The principal must also pay the agent the agreed salary or commission.   The agent can, as we have seen, retain his remuneration out of moneys that come into his hands for his principal. The agent may, however, forfeit his right to remuneration through misconduct.

The principal must indemnify the agent against the consequences of all lawful acts done by the agent under the authority conferred upon him. Hence if the agent by authority of the principal brings or defends an action, the principal must reimburse him all costs incurred in such action.

Wrongful Acts.—Where a principal directs an agent to do a wrongful act to a third party, and the agent, acting *bona fide*, and having no knowledge that the act is wrongful, obeys the direction, the principal must make good to the agent any loss he sustains. Hence if the agent innocently makes a false representation as to the quality of goods by the direction of the principal, the latter is liable.

§ 128. Position of Third Parties.—As a general rule, all contracts entered into by an agent as agent, are regarded as entered into by the principal, so long as the contract was within the scope of the agent's authority. It is immaterial whether the *name* of the principal be disclosed or not, provided the third party knew he was entering into a contract with *an agent* as such, and the parties intended that the principal should be bound. In order to protect himself from any liability, the agent should always take care that the contract is so drawn as to make the principal liable.

It follows that, as a rule, an agent cannot enforce a contract entered into by him as agent on behalf of a principal, and that he incurs no liability on such contract. But to this rule there are certain exceptions.

1. Where the agent does not disclose the name of his principal, the presumption arises that credit was given to the agent. The question to be decided in each case is, to whom was credit really given?
2. Where the contract relates to the sale or purchase of goods for a merchant resident abroad, it has been held that, without express authority, an agent cannot pledge the foreign merchant's credit, and is himself personally liable.

3. Where the agent contracts to be personally liable, he is liable.

4. An agent may be personally liable by the custom of a particular trade.

The agent may not disclose the fact that he is agent, and the third party may be entirely ignorant that he is dealing with an agent. In such a case the agent is liable to the third party ; but if the third party discover that there is a principal, he may elect whether to proceed against the agent or the principal. B., for example, acting as agent for A., but not disclosing the fact of agency, sells goods to C., C. is entitled to look to B. for completion of the contract ; but if C. finds out that A. was B.'s principal, he may (if necessary) sue either A. or B. The principal, if he desires to enforce the contract, can only do so by submitting to all rights and obligations existing between the agent and the third party. In other words, if performance is sought by the principal from the third party, the third party is to have the same rights as if he were sued by the agent.

§ 129. **Falsely representing Oneself to be Agent.**— If a man who has no authority to act as agent professes to enter into a contract on behalf of another, and there is a principal named who might adopt the contract, but does not do so, the agent can neither sue nor be sued on the contract. The agent is, however, liable to the third party for pretending to be an agent.

But if there be no principal who could adopt the contract, e.g. where the alleged principal is fictitious, the agent is held to have contracted in person, and may be sued as principal by the third party.

§ 130. **Position of Special Classes of Agents.** — Special rules, derived partly from the usage of trade and partly from statute, apply to certain classes of agents.

Factors.—A factor has, as we have seen, possession of the goods. He is entitled to sell them in his own name, he may sell on the usual terms as to credit, and receive and give a receipt for the price. Under the Factors' Act of 1889, he has an implied authority to pledge the goods. His right to remuneration is protected by the lien given him by law for the balance of his account. So long as the goods are in his possession, a third party who has no notice of the revocation of the factor's authority is protected as regards any lawful dealings with the factor relating to the goods (§ 127).

Brokers.—A broker for sale is supposed to be employed for the purpose of negotiating a sale. As soon as the contract is arranged, his duties are, in the absence of any agreement to the contrary, at an end. He has no authority as broker to receive the price.

Usually, however, a broker who is engaged in an established trade is assumed to have authority to buy or sell in accordance with the well-established usages of the trade, provided such usages do not change the essential character of the broker's employment. A usage for a broker for sale to purchase for himself is not one that would be recognised by the courts.

A broker may by the terms of his employment be given a wide discretion, and then in buying and selling he may exercise such discretion.

An *Auctioneer* is an agent for the public sale of property. Until the fall of the hammer he is the agent of the seller alone; but when the hammer falls he is agent of both parties, to do what is necessary to make the bargain binding, under the Statute of Frauds (§ 137).

He has possession of the goods and can receive payment for them in cash, but not by bill. He may receive payment by cheque, provided the cheque be duly honoured.

§ 131. Sub-agents.—An agent cannot, as a rule, employ another person to perform what he has undertaken to do, as the principal is supposed to have employed the agent to do the thing himself.

By the custom of trade in certain trades, or by consent of the principal, sub-agents may be employed. In choosing a sub-agent as much diligence will be required of the agent as in the execution of the undertaking.

Where a sub-agent is properly employed, he represents the principal, as regards third parties, just as if he had originally been appointed by him; but the sub-agent is responsible, as a rule, for his acts to the agent, and the agent is responsible for the acts of the sub-agent to the principal.

An agent should be careful not to appoint a sub-agent until he has satisfied himself that he has authority so to do. If it should turn out that no such authority existed, the agent and not the principal will be bound by the acts of the sub-agent towards both the principal and third parties.

§ 132. **Termination of Agency.** — The relation of principal and agent may be terminated in the following ways :—

1. By mutual consent, as, for example, where the principal and the agent agree to bring the relationship to an end.
2. By revocation on the part of the principal.

As a rule, the principal can at any time revoke the agent's authority without the agent's consent, provided the agent has no interest in its continuance ; but he should give notice of such revocation, not only to the agent, but to the public, or at least to those with whom he is accustomed to deal. A person dealing with an agent is entitled, as a rule, to assume that the agent's authority continues until notice is given him that it is revoked. Where the agent has an interest in the execution of the authority, the principal cannot revoke the authority without the agent's consent, unless the original contract stated that it was to be revocable without such consent. Hence if a person is appointed agent for a definite time at a fixed salary, he cannot be dismissed before the time expires, unless he receives compensation.

3. By the agent renouncing the business.

An agent may withdraw from the agency, but if the agency was undertaken for a consideration, the agent must make good to the principal any loss arising from the renunciation.

4. By the expiration of time or the completion of the business.
5. By the death of either principal or agent.

All contracts entered into by the agent after the death of the principal are not binding on the estate of the deceased principal, even though the third party dealing with the agent has no notice of the death.

6. By the principal or agent becoming of unsound mind.

7. By the bankruptcy of the principal.

§ 133. **Authorities.**—Sir William Anson's work on the Law of Contracts contains the leading principles relating to agency. *Principal and Agent*, by Mr. W. Evans, discusses the subject in detail.

CHAPTER III

§ 134. Definition.—A contract of sale is a contract whereby the seller transfers or agrees to transfer the property in goods to the buyer for a money consideration called price, which the latter pays or agrees to pay. The object of the contract is to transfer the ownership or property in the goods from the seller to the buyer. By "property" is meant the general property in the goods, as distinguished from a special right such as possession. The owner of an article may, for instance, have given it in pledge, but that does not prevent him selling his "property" in the article, *i.e.* the right to redeem the pledge, and such sale will not affect the special right of the pawnbroker. Again, a merchant may have borrowed money from his bankers on the security of goods : this will not prevent him from selling the goods, though the buyer will, as a rule, acquire the goods subject to the rights of the bank.

§ 135. A Sale and an Agreement for Sale.—It is important to note the distinction drawn in the above definition between a "transfer" and an "agreement to transfer." The former is often called a "sale," and the latter an "agreement to sell." A contract, as a rule, leaves one or both of the parties to it under an obligation or a number of obligations to do or perform something. For instance, in the wholesale market where transactions are carried out on a large scale by means of credit, a purchase usually leaves the seller under the obligation to deliver the goods, and the buyer under the obligation to pay the price at the time and place agreed upon. Here at the moment of time the contract is made performance is on both sides postponed to a future date, and the distinction between the making of the contract and its performance is very marked. The contract is an "agreement to sell"; but in the retail market, where articles are often sold for cash and delivery is at once made, the formation of the contract and its performance take place practically at the same moment. For instance, a person enters a shop, purchases a pound of tea, pays for it and takes it away: here the contract is performed at the same time as it is entered into. The contract is a "sale." The importance of the distinction between a "sale" and an "agreement to sell" lies in the fact that the former does, and the latter does not, transfer the property from the vendor to the buyer. In a "sale" the property passes at once, in an "agreement for sale" the goods remain the property of the vendor until the time for delivery has arrived, or the conditions subject to which the property is to pass to the purchaser are fulfilled.

§ 136. **The Price.**—The consideration given by the buyer to the seller is called "price," and price always implies money. If goods be given without any consideration, there is a "gift"; if goods be given in exchange for goods, there is a "barter." As a rule, the price is fixed by the contract, but the parties may leave it to subsequent arrangement,—a course not often adopted, as it is likely to lead to litigation.

It is not unusual in certain cases for the parties where they cannot fix the price to leave it to be fixed in an agreed manner. Such an arrangement is legal. The usual manner adopted is to refer the price to valuers, and the price so fixed is as much a part of the contract as if it had been inserted in it.

Where none of the above methods are adopted for fixing the price, the buyer must pay a reasonable price. A reasonable price means "such a price as the jury upon the trial of the cause shall under all the circumstances decide to be reasonable. This price may or may not agree with the current price of the commodity." An example

may be given of a contract of sale where no price was fixed.
A. ordered B. to build a new carriage with certain appoint-
ments, the whole to be ready by a certain date. The
carriage was built, but on B. sending in his bill for £480,
A. refused to take the carriage or to pay for it, alleging
amongst other things that the omission of the price from
the order invalidated the contract. The court held the
contract was good, inasmuch as where the price was left
uncertain, the law implied that a reasonable price would be
paid.

§ 137. **The Form of the Contract of Sale.**—Up to the
reign of Charles II. no special formalities were required as
regards a sale of goods. The contract might have been
oral or written, or partly oral and partly written. But in
the twenty-ninth year of the reign of that sovereign, the
celebrated statute called the Statute of Frauds was passed,
and by the seventeenth section an important change was
introduced as regards the sale of goods of the value of £10
and upwards. We have therefore to consider the form of
the contract where the value of the goods is (1) below £10,
(2) £10 and upwards.

    (1) *Goods below £10 in value.*—A contract for the sale
      of goods below £10 in value may be
        1. Oral.
        2. Written.
        3. Partly oral and partly written.
        4. By deed.
        5. Implied from the conduct of the parties.

A deed is rarely used to effect a contract for the sale of
moveable property, at least where it is tangible. In the
case of rights of action, such as shares in companies, a deed
is usually necessary. Orders for goods are often given and
accepted by letters; here the contract is to be gathered
from the whole correspondence. Oral contracts, especially
in small retail transactions, are the most usual. The
moment the seller and the buyer agree as to what is to be
sold and the price, there is contract of sale. The question
as to when the ownership of the thing sold will pass to the
purchaser will be treated subsequently (§ 155).

§ 138. (2) **Goods of the Value of £10 and upwards.**— Speaking generally, the effect of the Statute of Frauds upon contracts for the sale of goods of the value of £10 and upwards, is to require over and above the ordinary requisites of a contract the fulfilment of one of the three following provisions : [1]—

(*a*) The acceptance by the buyer of part of the goods sold, and actual receipt of the same.

(*b*) The giving of something in earnest to bind the bargain or in part payment.

(*c*) The making of a note or memorandum in writing of the contract signed by the party to be charged, or his duly authorised agent.

§ 139. (*a*) **Acceptance and Receipt.**—The buyer must not merely *accept* part of the goods, but must also *receive* them, and the contract will not be good unless he does both. " The *acceptance* of part of the goods," said Lord Blackburn,[2] " is an assent by the buyer meant to be final that this part of the goods is to be taken by him as his property under the contract, and as so far satisfying the contract. So long as the buyer can, without self-contradiction, declare that the goods are not to be taken in fulfilment of the contract, he has not accepted them. And it is immaterial whether his refusal to take the goods be reasonable or not. If he refuses the goods, assigning grounds false or frivolous, or assigning no reasons at all, it is still clear that he does not accept the goods, and the question is not whether he *ought* to accept, but whether he *has* accepted them. The question of acceptance or not is a question as to what was the intention of the buyer as signified by his outward acts.

---

[1] The words of the section are : " And be it enacted that from and after the four-and-twentieth day of June [1677], no contract for the sale of any goods, wares, or merchandises for the value of £10 sterling or upwards shall be allowed to be good, except the buyer shall accept part of the goods so sold, and actually receive the same or give something in earnest to bind the bargain or in part payment, or that some note or memorandum in writing of the said bargain be made and signed by the parties to be charged by such contract, or their agents thereunto lawfully authorised."

[2] Blackburn on Sale, 2nd ed. p. 16.

"The receipt of the goods is the taking possession of them. When the seller gives to the buyer the actual control of the goods, and the buyer accepts such control, he has actually received them. Such a receipt is often evidence of an acceptance, but it is not the same thing : indeed the receipt by the buyer may be and often is for the express purpose of seeing whether he will accept or not. If goods of a particular description are ordered to be sent by a carrier, the buyer must in every case receive the package, to see whether it answers his orders or not : it may even be reasonable to try part of the goods by using them ; but though this is a very actual receipt, it is no acceptance so long as the buyer can consistently object to the goods as not answering his order. It follows from this that a receipt of goods by a carrier, or on board ship, though a sufficient delivery to the purchaser, is not an acceptance by him so as to bind the contract, for the carrier, if he be an agent to receive, is clearly not one to accept the goods."

The exercise of the right of ownership over the goods amounts to receipt and acceptance, *e.g.* where the purchaser of a stack of hay resold it. The taking of a sample, which by the terms of the contract was to be part of the goods sold, may amount to acceptance. Mere examination of goods is not acceptance.

The question as to whether there has been an acceptance or a receipt of part of the goods is a question of fact, and not one of law. Where the matter is tried before a judge and jury, the latter have to decide "whether under all the circumstances the acts which the buyer does or forbears to do amount to an acceptance" (§ 153).

§ 140. (*b*) **Earnest or Part Payment.**—"Earnest" means money or other article given by the buyer to the seller, and accepted by the latter as indicative of his assent to the sale. The giving of earnest is unusual in commercial transactions, but in some country fairs a shilling or other coin is given as earnest in the sale of cattle or the hiring of servants. In one reported case, the owner of a horse sent his servant to a fair to sell it ; an offer of £45 was made, and the vendor's servant taking a shilling in his hand, drew the edge of it across the hand of the purchaser, and then replaced the shilling in his own pocket, a proceeding called by the witnesses "striking the bargain" : it was held there was no "giving of earnest" within the meaning of the Statute of Frauds.

"Part payment" means payment of part of the price, either in money or in anything that is accepted in part satisfaction of the price.   An agreement to set off a debt due to the buyer, the transfer of a bill or note, or the payment of interest due, will each amount to part payment.

§ 141. (c) **Memorandum or Note in Writing.**—The third method of making a valid contract for the sale of goods of the value of £10 and upwards, is by some note or memorandum in writing of the bargain, signed by the parties to be charged, or their agents.

Two points require consideration—

1. The form of the memorandum in writing.
2. How and by whom it should be signed.

§ 142. **The Form of the Memorandum.**—The memorandum need not be on one piece of paper; it may be contained on several pieces written at different times, provided the one that is signed makes such reference to the other papers as will enable the court to construe them all as one document.   A series of letters between the vendor and the purchaser is an excellent example of a memorandum contained on several pieces of paper.

It is, however, essential that the evidence of the connection of the different writings should appear from the documents themselves, as oral evidence is not admissible to connect a signed paper with others unsigned.   " In order to embody in the letter any other document or memorandum or instrument in writing, so as to make it part of a special contract contained in that letter, the letter must either set out the writing referred to, or so clearly and definitely refer to the writing, that by force of the reference, the writing itself becomes part of the instrument " which refers to it.

§ 143. **What the Memorandum ought to contain.**— First, the name or a description of the party with whom the bargain is made.

Without such name or description it is impossible to say who are the parties to the bargain, and the writing is therefore incomplete, as it contains only part of the contract. When, therefore, the agent of the purchaser wrote down in a memorandum book the terms of a sale as follows: "Bought of A. 20 puncheons of treacle, £37 : 10s., to be delivered by the 10th December," and A. signed the memorandum, it was held that this was insufficient, as it did not show who was the purchaser.

The memorandum ought always, as a matter of precaution, to contain the names of both the vendor and the purchaser as such. But if instead of the name a description of either party sufficient to identify him be given, that will be sufficient. For instance, the name of a partnership is regarded as sufficiently describing the members of the firm who compose it. It has also been held that where an agent signs a contract without disclosing his principal, such contract is good as against the principal, who may sue or be sued in his own name, on the ground that the act of the agent in signing the agreement in pursuance of his authority, is the act of the principal.

Secondly, the terms of the bargain.

The memorandum should state what is sold and the quantity sold ; the price, if a price has been fixed ; the mode of payment, if this has been arranged ; as well as the other terms and conditions agreed upon. In short, the memorandum should show the whole bargain. As a rule, when the terms of a sale are reduced to writing, and signed by one party, there is a presumption that all the terms have been embodied in the memorandum, and as Lord Blackburn points out, "It is a difficult thing for a party to prove that a written admission signed by himself does not contain the whole truth. The jury would properly be very unwilling to find that the writing did not contain the whole agreement, unless there was some good reason given to explain the inaccuracy." [1]

Thirdly, the signature of the party to be charged.

It has long been settled that the only signature required is that of the party against whom the contract is to be

[1] Blackburn on Sale, 2nd ed. p. 58.

enforced.   If the vendor has to bring an action for the
price, he must produce a memorandum in writing of the
terms of the contract signed by the purchaser: if the
purchaser has to sue for the articles sold, he must produce
a similar memorandum, signed by the vendor.

It follows from this, that if A. offer B. in writing (*e.g.* by
letter) to sell him a certain quantity of goods at a given
price, and B. accepts the offer *orally*, B. can, if necessary,
sue A., inasmuch as there is a memorandum signed by A.;
but A., if necessary, could not successfully sue B., as there is
no memorandum signed by B.   A vendor should therefore
always secure the signature of the purchaser, and the
purchaser that of the vendor.

The signature need not be the actual subscription of the
name : a mark intended as a signature is sufficient.   A mere
description is not enough, and it is doubtful if the use of
initials amounts to signature.

The signature may be in print ; and as the statute does
not specifically require the signature to be at the end of the
memorandum, it may be at the beginning or in the middle.
If, however, the alleged signature is not at the end of the
document, the question arises, with what intention was the
name inserted ?   If it is introduced merely incidentally, that
is not sufficient.   The name "must be so placed as to show
that it was intended to relate and refer to, and that in fact
it does relate and refer to every part of the instrument."

§ 144. Signature by an Agent.—The signature of a
party to the contract may be made by an agent " thereunto
lawfully authorised."

The agent must be a third party, inasmuch as it has
been held that one of the parties cannot act as agent for the
other in order to sign the contract.

The authority given to the agent to sign need not be in
writing, and the fact of agency may be established in the
same way as in other cases of agency (§ 123).

An auctioneer is an agent with a power of sale from the
vendor, and therefore has an implied authority to sign the
contract of sale embodied in the condition of sale on his
behalf.   The auctioneer has, however, no authority from

the highest bidder to make a contract for him, but the moment the lot is knocked down, the highest bidder becomes the purchaser, and in law (provided the sale is a public one) he is held to authorise the auctioneer to sign the contract on his behalf. The auctioneer, by entering the purchasers' names and the price opposite each lot in the catalogue, makes the contracts binding on the purchasers.

An auctioneer's clerk is not the agent of both parties ; he is the agent of the auctioneer, and he can only sign on behalf of the parties where he is specially authorised so to do.

A broker for sale is a person whose trade is to "find purchasers for those who wish to sell, and vendors for those who wish to buy, and to negotiate and superintend the making of the bargain between them." [1] As the agent for both parties, he has authority to sign a memorandum, so as to make the contract binding.

When a broker succeeds in effecting a sale, he usually enters the terms in his broker's book and adds his signature. This signed entry constitutes the contract between the parties, and is binding on both. The broker, as such, having authority to make a memorandum of the contract between buyer and seller, a signed entry in his book is sufficient evidence of a memorandum by a duly authorised agent within the meaning of the Statute of Frauds.

As a rule, a broker prepares two copies of the entry, and signs them. One is called the "sold note," and is sent to the vendor. In substance it takes this form : " Sold for A. B. to C. D." The following is an example :—

" To Messrs. A. B.—Sold for your account to Messrs. C. and D. the following parcels of Spanish wool (a few bags more or less) of each mark, viz. (*specifying them and the rates of price*) customary tare and allowance. To be paid for by acceptances at two, four, six, and eight months. —Signed, M., *Broker.*"

The other note is called the "bought note." In substance it takes this form, "Bought for C. D. of A." The following is an example :—

[1] Blackburn on Sale, 2nd ed. p. 78.

"Bought for Messrs. C. D. of Messrs. A. B. from 80 to
100 tons of palm oil, of merchantable quality, free from dirt
and water, at £26 per ton, payable per cash, etc. The
above oil warranted to arrive on or before the 30th June
(current), *ex* 'Premier,' Fullerton, Cape Coast. Customary
allowances.—Signed, T. W., *Broker*."

The party receiving and keeping either a bought or a sold
note is held to know that the person signing it is acting as
his broker, and to authorise him to do so. It is the better
opinion that the bought and sold notes do not constitute
the contract that is contained in the signed entry in the
broker's books, but the value of the bought and sold notes
consists in this, that in the absence of any entry in the
broker's books, or in the case of the entry being unsigned,
the bought and sold notes, if they agree, and if they contain
the names of the parties, and all the other terms of the
bargain, are sufficient to satisfy the Statute of Frauds.
Indeed, either note alone will satisfy the statute if there be
no variance between it and the other note.

Difficult questions arise where the two notes differ from
each other, or from the signed entry. The rules applicable
in such cases will be found in the works of Lord Blackburn
and Mr. Benjamin on the sale of goods.[1]

§ 145. **Variations of a Written Contract.**—Where a
contract of sale has been reduced to writing, any variation
of its terms ought also to be put in writing. It is a well-
established rule that a contract required to be in writing by
the Statute of Frauds cannot be enlarged or varied by an
oral agreement. Any verbal alteration will have the effect
of preventing any action being brought on the contract as
altered.

In some cases a verbal alteration has been held to
amount to a rescission of the original contract and the substitution of a new one for it, inasmuch as there is nothing
in the 17th section to prevent a written contract being
rescinded by a verbal agreement.

§ 146. **Caveat Emptor.**—As a general rule, on a sale
of goods, the buyer takes all risk as to quality, fitness, or

[1] See Benjamin on Sale, p. 268, where the leading rules are summarised.

condition of the goods. The buyer is supposed to examine the goods before the purchase, and he cannot afterwards complain that defects were not pointed out. " The buyer is always anxious to buy as cheaply as he can, and is sufficiently prone to find imaginary faults in order to get a good bargain, and the vendor is equally at liberty to praise his merchandise in order to enhance its value, if he abstain from a fraudulent representation of facts, provided the buyer have a full and fair opportunity of inspection, and no means are used for hiding the defects. If the buyer is unwilling to bargain on these terms, he can protect himself against his own want of care or skill by requiring a warranty from the vendor of any matters the risk of which he is unwilling to take upon himself." [1]

§ 147. Conditions and Warranties.—A contract of sale may be subject to any conditions agreed to by the parties, and may be accompanied by one or more warranties, expressed or implied, given by the seller to the buyer.

A warranty is an express or implied statement of something which the party undertakes shall be part of the contract, as, for example, where the seller warrants that a horse is sound, that a cargo of corn is of a certain quality, that the goods were manufactured by a particular firm, or that the commodity sold contains a definite percentage of some chemical ingredient.

No particular form of words is required : in every case it is a question for a jury whether the words used were intended to amount to a warranty or not. Any affirmation at the time of sale is a warranty, provided it appear in evidence to have been so intended. " In determining whether it was so intended," says Mr. Benjamin, " a decisive test is whether the vendor assumes to assert a *fact* of which the buyer is ignorant, or merely states an *opinion* or judgment upon a matter of which the vendor has no special knowledge, and on which the buyer may be expected also to have an opinion and to exercise his judgment. In the former case there is a warranty, in the latter not."

A representation to amount to a warranty requires to be

[1] Benjamin on Sale, p. 405.   [2] *Ibid.* p. 609.

made at the time the contract is entered into.   Representations anterior to the contract, though they may give rise to actions, are not warranties, *e.g.* where the vendor, the day before the sale of a horse at Tattersall's, said to the purchaser, "He is perfectly sound in every respect," this remark was held not to be part of the contract.

A warranty may, however, be given after a sale, provided some consideration be given for it—the warranty in this case really forms an additional and separate contract.

§ 148. Implied Warranties.—In certain cases the law implies a condition or a warranty.

1. Where goods are sold by description, there is an implied condition that the goods shall correspond with the description.   "If you contract to sell peas, you cannot oblige a party to take beans" (Lord Blackburn in Bowes *v.* Shand, 2 App. Cas. p. 480). A contract to sell rice shipped at Madras in March and April is not fulfilled by shipping rice in February.

2. Where goods are ordered by description from a seller who deals in goods of that description, and the buyer has no opportunity of examining the goods, there is an implied warranty that the goods shall be of merchantable quality and condition.

A firm of Liverpool merchants purchased certain bales of "Manilla hemp" to be shipped from Singapore.   The hemp was delivered in such a damaged condition that it was not merchantable.   It was held that the purchaser was entitled to damages, since the buyer bought for the purpose of sale, and the seller could not on any other supposition than that the article was merchantable have found a customer for his goods, and the buyer must be taken to have trusted to the judgment, knowledge, and information of the seller, as it is clear that he could exercise no judgment of his own.

No warranty, however, is implied where the buyer has an opportunity of inspecting the goods, inasmuch as he can exercise his own judgment in the matter.

3. Four warranties or conditions are implied in a sale by sample.

(*a*) That the bulk of the goods shall correspond with the *description*.

(*b*) That the bulk shall correspond with the sample in *quality* and *condition*.

The first of these rules is not exactly a warranty, since warranty rather relates to quality: it is a part of the general rule already referred to that where goods are sold by description it is implied that they shall correspond with the description. Hence where the purchase was of "foreign refined rape oil, warranted only equal to samples," and the oil tendered was equal to sample, but was not "foreign refined rape oil," it was held that the purchaser was not bound to accept it.

The second rule embodies the leading principle relating to sale by sample—the seller is held to undertake that the bulk shall agree with the sample.

(*c*) That the buyer shall have a reasonable opportunity of comparing the bulk with the sample.

If the buyer desires to inspect the bulk, he should make his request at a proper and convenient time.

(*d*) That the goods shall be free from any defect rendering them unmerchantable, which would not be apparent on a reasonable examination of the sample.

At one time it was maintained that, upon a sale of goods by sample, no warranty that they were merchantable could be implied, but this view has not been adopted by the courts.

A firm of Manchester merchants agreed to manufacture and supply 2500 pieces of gray shirtings according to sample at 18s. 6d. per piece, each piece to weigh 7 lbs. The goods were manufactured and delivered in England, but on their arrival at Calcutta, it was found that 15 per cent of the weight of the goods consisted of China clay, introduced into the texture for the purpose of making them weigh the 7 lbs. per piece. At the time the goods were delivered to the purchaser's agent in England, the agent could not by inspection have ascertained that any foreign ingredient had been added. The court held that the shirtings delivered ought to have been *merchantable*, notwithstanding that they were purchased by sample, and not

G

being merchantable, owing to the presence of the China clay, the purchaser was entitled to damages.

A firm of cloth merchants ordered from a firm of cloth manufacturers at Bradford a quantity of cloth, described as "mixt worsted coatings," which were to be, in "quality and weight," equal to certain numbered samples. The coatings were, as the manufacturers knew, intended for sale to tailors and others. The coatings delivered were made in the same form as the samples, but on account of the want of cohesion between the warp and the weft, they gave way under the strain of ordinary wear, and a large quantity was returned to the cloth merchants. The merchants refused to pay for the goods, and when an action was brought against them they claimed damages for breach of contract. At the trial it was found that though the cloth was not merchantable, it corresponded with the sample; but it was also found that the defect was not apparent or discoverable upon such an inspection as was ordinary and usual upon worsted cloths of the class. The House of Lords unanimously held that upon such a contract there was an implied warranty that the goods should be fit for use in the manner in which goods of the same quality and general character ordinarily would be used. "When a purchaser," said Lord Herschell, "states generally the nature of the article he requires, and asks the manufacturer to supply specimens of the mode in which he proposes to carry out the order, he trusts to the skill of the manufacturer just as much as if he asked for no such specimens; and I think he has a right to rely on the samples supplied representing a manufactured article which will be fit for the purposes for which such an article is ordinarily used, just as much as he has a right to rely on manufactured goods supplied on an order without samples complying with such a warranty."

4. Where there is a contract for a sale of goods by a manufacturer, as such, there is, in the absence of any trade usage to the contrary, an implied warranty that the goods are of the seller's own manufacture.

A firm of shipbuilders entered into a contract to buy

from a firm of iron manufacturers 2000 tons iron ship-plates, to be of the quality known as "Crown." Before the plates were all delivered, the manufacturers closed their works and offered to complete the contract by delivering iron plates of "Crown" quality, but made by another firm. It was held by the court that the manufacturers were bound to supply plates of their own manufacture, and not plates made by other firms.

5. Where the buyer, relying on the seller's skill or judgment, orders goods for a particular purpose known to the seller, and the goods are of a description which it is in the course of the seller's business to supply (whether he be a manufacturer or not), there is an implied warranty that the goods shall be reasonably fit for such purpose.

An examination of this rule shows that three conditions are necessary to imply the warranty.

(1) The buyer must rely on the seller's skill.

(2) The goods must be ordered for a special purpose known to the seller.

(3) The goods must be of a description which the seller supplies in the course of his business.

A few examples will illustrate these points.

A carriage-pole was ordered from a carriage-builder for a carriage: the pole supplied broke, on account of its not being fit and proper for the carriage, and the horses were injured. The carriage-builder was held liable; all the above conditions being fulfilled.

A butcher bought from a meat-salesman a carcase which he inspected before purchase; no warranty was implied here, as the first condition, viz. relying on the seller's skill, was not fulfilled.

A farmer, who had bought from a butcher the carcase of a pig, sold it to another farmer. The meat turned out to be diseased, but it was held that there was no warranty that the meat was fit for food, inasmuch as the vendor farmer was not a dealer in meat; here the third condition was wanting.

6. An implied warranty of quality, fitness, or condition

may be annexed to a contract of sale by the usage of trade.

In the sale of certain drugs, it is usual to state in the catalogue whether they are sea-damaged or not, and in the absence of a statement that they were sea-damaged, it was always assumed that they were free from such a defect. This custom was held to be equivalent to an implied warranty of freedom from sea-damage.

§ 149. **Duty of the Seller to deliver.**—The primary duty of a seller of goods is to *deliver* them in accordance with the terms of the contract. By *delivering*, is meant transfer of the *possession*. Such transfer does not require, in order to be effective, the actual physical handing over of the goods : it is sufficient if the buyer be put in control of the goods, as, for example, where the key of the warehouse in which the goods are stored is handed to the buyer. The transfer of a bill of lading is a valid transfer of the goods it represents.

Where nothing is said about payment, the law presumes that the delivery and the payment will take place at the same time. The seller cannot insist on payment unless he is ready and willing to deliver, and the buyer cannot insist on delivery unless he is ready and willing to pay the price.

The seller is not bound to send or carry the goods to the buyer ; it is sufficient if he affords the buyer reasonable facilities for taking possession of the goods. If nothing be said as to the *place* of delivery, it is assumed that the parties contemplate delivery at the place where the goods are at the time the contract is made, except when the goods are to be manufactured, and then the place of manufacture is regarded as the place of delivery.

It sometimes happens that the goods at the time of sale are in the possession of a third party : in such a case, care should be taken by the seller to obtain from such third party permission for the buyer to remove the goods, otherwise he may find himself unable to make delivery.

In many contracts, the seller undertakes to deliver the goods to the buyer. In such cases, if no time be fixed for delivery, the seller is bound to deliver within a reasonable

time.   What is a "reasonable time" depends on the facts
and circumstances of each case.

The seller ought to deliver the exact amount of goods
ordered, neither more nor less.   If he delivers more, the
whole may be rejected, inasmuch as the seller is not at
liberty to place on the buyer the duty of selecting, but the
buyer, if he chooses, may take the whole at the contract
rate, or may accept only the amount included in the contract, and reject the rest.   If the seller delivers less, the
buyer may reject or accept them.

The seller is not entitled to deliver the goods mixed with
goods of a different description : if he does so, and the buyer
cannot separate the goods bought from the other goods
without trouble and expense, he may reject the whole.

Where the seller is authorised by the contract to forward
the goods to the buyer, delivery to a common carrier or
a carrier named by the buyer is equivalent to a delivery to
the buyer, the carrier being, in contemplation of law, the
buyer to receive the goods.   The seller ought to take the
usual precautions for ensuring the safe delivery by the
carrier to the buyer.

§ 150. Lien of the Seller.—In order to protect a seller
of goods who has not been paid, the law gives him certain
rights that he can exercise, so long as they have not passed
into the actual possession of the buyer.

These rights are (1) lien, (2) stoppage *in transitu*, and
(3) resale.

The unpaid seller of goods, if he has not parted with
possession of them, is entitled to retain possession until
payment or tender of the price in the following cases :—

   (*a*) Where the goods have been sold without any
         stipulation as to credit.
   (*b*) Where the goods have been sold on credit, but the
         time for which credit was given has expired.
   (*c*) Where the buyer has become insolvent.
The lien will be lost—
   (*a*) If the goods be delivered to a carrier for transmission
         to the buyer, unless the seller has reserved the right
         of disposal.

(*b*) If the buyer or his agent obtains possession of the
goods.

(*c*) If the seller waives his right.

The delivery of part of the goods will not destroy the
lien on the remainder, unless such delivery amount to
waiver.

§ 151. Stoppage in Transitu.—Where the goods are
delivered to a carrier for transmission, the seller's lien is
gone ; but if the buyer becomes insolvent whilst the goods
are in transit, the seller may resume possession of them,
and may retain them until the payment or tender of the
price.   It has already been pointed out that (§ 149) a
carrier is an agent of the buyer to receive goods from the
seller, but such receipt of goods does not put an end to the
seller's right of stoppage ; an actual receipt by the buyer is
required for that purpose.

Goods are deemed to be *in transitu* not only while they
remain in the possession of the carrier, whether by water
or land, and although such carrier may have been named
and appointed by the consignee, but also when they are in
any place of deposit connected with the transmission and
delivery of them, and until they arrive at the actual or
constructive possession of the consignee.

No particular method of exercising the right has been
prescribed.   The seller may take actual possession, or he
may give a notice to the carrier or person in possession,
stating his claim, forbidding any delivery to the buyer,
or requiring that the goods shall be held subject to his
orders.

On receipt of such notice, the carrier or other person in
possession ought to deliver the goods to the seller, or hold
them at his orders.

If before the receipt of any such notice, the goods have
arrived at their destination and have been delivered to the
purchaser or his agent, or if the carrier hold them as warehouseman for the purchaser, and no longer as carrier, the
transitus and the right of stoppage are at an end.

§ 152. Resale.—The non-payment of the price does not
give the seller the right to rescind the contract, and if he

resells the goods, he is liable to an action for damages at the suit of the buyer. In order to protect himself, a seller ought in the contract to reserve to himself the right of resale in case the buyer makes default. There is some authority for saying that the seller would be justified in re-selling (1) where the goods are of a perishable nature, and (2) where he gives the buyer notice of his intention to resell, and the buyer does not within a reasonable time pay for the goods.

§ **153. Acceptance by the Buyer.**—The leading duties of the buyer are, first, to accept the goods, and, secondly, to pay the price.

In the absence of any special agreement, the buyer is not entitled to wait for delivery (§ 149), it is his duty to take possession within a reasonable time.

If the buyer has not previously examined the goods, he is entitled before accepting to a reasonable opportunity of inspecting the goods for the purpose of ascertaining if they are in conformity with the contract. The mere *receipt* of goods is not the same as *acceptance*, as the receipt may be merely for the purpose of examination (§ 135).

The buyer will be deemed to have *accepted* the goods—

1. When he informs the seller that he has accepted them ; or
2. When he has received the goods and does any act in relation to them inconsistent with the ownership of the seller ; or
3. When he allows a reasonable time to elapse without informing the seller that he has rejected them.

A buyer is not bound to accept delivery in instalments unless this has been agreed to, expressly or impliedly, by the contracting parties.

A buyer who rejects goods, having the right to do so (§ 139), may return them ; but, as a rule, it is sufficient if he notifies the seller of his refusal to accept them.

§ **154. Payment of the Price.**—If no credit be given, the buyer of goods is not entitled to them until he pays the price, and he should be ready to do so as soon as delivery is made. Where credit is given, the buyer is entitled to the goods at once, subject to the seller's right of stoppage whilst they are in transit, in case the buyer becomes insolvent (§ 151).

The contract may require the payment to be in one of two forms, viz. "cash" or "bill." Sometimes the buyer has an option, *e.g.* "bill with option of cash, less discount." Where the payment is to be in "cash," and there is a dispute as to the amount payable, care should be taken that any tender made by the buyer is in proper form. The money should be actually produced, and an opportunity given to the seller to examine and count it. Copper coins are a valid tender up to 1s. ; silver coins up to 40s. ; gold coins and Bank of England notes to any amount. The exact sum should be tendered, as the buyer is not entitled to tender a larger sum than is due with a demand for change. The buyer, if the amount paid is £2 and upwards, may tender a blank receipt, stamped, and the seller is bound to fill it up and pay for the stamp—a rule that practically throws on all creditors the duty of giving stamped receipts for sums amounting to £2 and upwards.

Where payment is made by "bill," it is always implied, in the absence of any agreement to the contrary, that if the bill be not honoured the vendor is entitled to sue for the price. But the parties may agree that the bill is to be taken in absolute discharge of the debt—in such a case, if the bill be not honoured, the seller may sue on the bill, but he cannot sue for the price of the goods.

Payment made to a duly authorised agent is the same as payment to the seller. A buyer ought, however, to assure himself that the agent is authorised *to receive payment*. A factor is an agent to receive payment, but a broker is not. A shopman is authorised to receive payment over the shop counter, but not elsewhere. An auctioneer, as a rule, can receive payment in cash. Payment to a wife is not a valid payment to her husband.

Where the seller prescribes a certain mode of payment, any payment made in such mode is good though the money never reach the seller. Hence if the seller requests a remittance by post, such a form of remittance will be good though the letter be lost or stolen.

§ 155. **The Transfer of Ownership.** — The object of the contract of sale is to transfer the right of property or the ownership of the goods from the seller to the buyer. In many cases this transfer takes place at the moment of time the contract is entered into, but in other cases the parties do not contemplate any immediate change in the ownership of the goods ; and if the contract be silent on the point, the law has to decide when ownership passes.

The practical importance of determining when the property passes lies in this, that, unless otherwise agreed, the moment the property passes to the buyer the goods are at his risk, whether delivery has been made or not. Any loss happening to the goods falls on the buyer. If, for example, they are destroyed by fire after the ownership has passed, the buyer is bound nevertheless to pay the price if he has not already done so.

A marked distinction is drawn between "ascertained" and "unascertained" goods. By the former is meant specific individual goods, *e.g.* a particular horse, a specific carriage, a particular bale of cotton. By the latter is meant goods not specifically ascertained, *e.g.* goods that have to be manufactured, measured, or weighed. The following principles may be laid down as regards ascertained goods :—

1. Where the sale relates to ascertained or specific goods in a deliverable state, and the contract is unconditional, the ownership passes immediately, *i.e.* at the time the contract is made, and it is immaterial whether payment or delivery, or both, be postponed. For example, on the 4th January, B. sold to A. a stack of hay for £145, payable on the 4th February, the hay to stand on the premises until the 1st May; the hay accidentally caught fire on the 20th January and was burned: it was held that the ownership in the hay passed to A. at the date of the contract, and therefore the loss fell upon him.

2. Where the seller has to do something to the goods

in order to put them into that state in which the purchaser would have to accept them, the property does not pass until such thing is done. Hence where a ship in progress of being built is purchased, and the contract shows that the parties contemplated the purchase of the ship when finished, the ownership will not pass until the vessel is completed.

3. Where the seller is bound to weigh, measure, or test the goods, or do some other act or thing with reference to the goods, so as to ascertain the price, the property does not pass until such has been done. Hence when a stack of bark was sold at £9 : 15s. per ton, and part was weighed and paid for, it was held that the ownership of the unweighed residue had not passed.

4. Where the goods are delivered by the buyer on "approval," or on "sale or return," the property passes when the buyer does any act adopting the transaction, or on the expiration of the time fixed for return of the goods, or if no time be so fixed, on the expiration of a reasonable time.

§ 156. Transfer of Ownership in unascertained Goods. —In the case of "unascertained" goods, the property does not pass until the goods are ascertained. Goods are "unascertained" if they have to be manufactured. Hence if a machine is ordered to be made, the property will not pass until the machine is finished. Goods are also "unascertained" when the contract relates to a quantity of a greater quantity, as, for example, where a buyer purchases 20 tons of oil out of the seller's stock : until the 20 tons are set aside or marked as the actual oil to be supplied, the property in the oil will not pass to the buyer.

The question sometimes arises as to the person who is to make the appropriation. In one type of case, *e.g.* where a merchant gives an order to another to send him a certain quantity of merchandise, it is assumed that the right of appropriation belongs to the seller. In a second type of case the appropriation is not regarded as complete until it has been assented to by the buyer. In a third type of case the buyer has, by the terms of the contract, the right of appropriation. It is obvious that when the contract is silent on the point, the questions as to who is to appropriate, and when the appropriation is to take place, depend largely on the circumstances of each case.

§ 157. Reservation of the Right of Disposition.— The seller may by the contract reserve to himself the right to dispose of the goods until certain conditions are fulfilled. In such a case, notwithstanding delivery, the property does not pass until the conditions are fulfilled. In some cases where the price is payable by instalments, the seller reserves this right, *e.g.* where goods are purchased on the three years' system of payment.

§ 158. Title acquired by the Buyer.—As a general rule, a buyer acquires no better right or title to the goods than that possessed by the seller. It follows from this principle that if the seller had stolen the goods, the buyer, even though he was unaware that the goods had been stolen, would not acquire the ownership.

In the interests of trade, and for the protection of dealers, certain exceptions to the above rule have been admitted by the law. The most important of these exceptions are as follows :—

1. Where goods, except horses, are sold in " market overt," according to the usage of the market, the buyer will acquire a good title, provided he buys them (*a*) in good faith, and (*b*) without any notice of the defect or want of title on the part of the seller.

In the city of London, every shop is a "market overt" for such foods as the owner usually trades in. Outside of London, a "market overt" means a particular spot of ground set apart for a market by grant or prescription. In London, every day except Sunday is a market-day, but in the country, markets are held on specified days. A buyer of stolen goods, in good faith, and without notice of the theft, in market overt acquires the property in the goods ; but by statute (24 and 25 Vic. c. 96, s. 100), if the thief be prosecuted to conviction, the property in the goods will revert on the original owner.

2. Where the seller has acquired the goods under such
circumstances that his right to them could be set
aside, a buyer from him will acquire the ownership
if he buys in good faith and without notice of the
defective ownership of the seller. For example, A.
bought a quantity of iron from B., giving bills pur-
porting to be accepted by C., who was really a
fictitious person. A. resold the iron to D., who
purchased *bona fide*, and it was held that D. obtained
the ownership of the goods, though before he bought
them B. could have had the contract of sale with
A. set aside.

§ 159. **Remedies of Seller and Buyer.**—Reference has
already been made to the remedies that the seller may
adopt where the buyer refuses to pay the price, and the
goods have either not left the seller's possession or are in
the course of transit (§§ 150, 151).

Where the goods have reached the buyer, and the property
has vested in him, the only remedy of the seller is to bring
an action for the price. Care must, however, be taken not
to bring any action before the time at which the price is
payable. Interest cannot be recovered where there is
no agreement for the payment of interest, or where the
debt was to be discharged by a negotiable instrument.[1]
If the buyer refuses to accept the goods, the seller may
bring an action for damages for non-acceptance. If
the seller refuses to deliver the goods, the buyer may
bring an action for damages for non-delivery. The damages
given will usually be the difference between the sale price
and the market price on the day the goods should have
been delivered, or if no time for delivery was fixed, the day
of the refusal to deliver. In certain cases the judge may
order the delivery of the goods.

In the case of a breach of warranty, so long as the buyer
has not accepted the goods and the property has not passed,
he may reject the goods.

But if he has accepted the goods, or if the property in

[1] Or in special cases coming under the 3 and 4 Will. IV. c. 42,
s. 28. See Mayne on Damages, p. 153.

the goods has passed to the buyer, he cannot reject them, but he may if sued for the price set up the warranty as a ground for reducing the same, or he may bring an action for damages.

§ **160. Authorities.**—Chalmers's *Digest of the Law of Sale* contains a concise digest of the law.   The well-known works of Lord Blackburn and Mr. Benjamin are standard treatises.   *The Law of Sale and Commercial Agency*, by Mr. Campbell, will also be found useful.

CHAPTER IV

§ 161. Definition.—By a contract of insurance one person undertakes, in consideration of a payment called the premium, to indemnify another against some risk or to pay a sum of money on death to a man's representatives. The system of insurance has been so extended during recent years that there is scarcely any form of risk that cannot be insured. But the leading kinds of insurance are Marine Insurance, Life Insurance, and Fire Insurance. The document in which the contract of insurance is contained is called the policy; the party who undertakes the risk is called the insurer, or where he subscribes the policy, the underwriter; the party indemnified against the loss is called the insured or assured.

§ 162. Fire and Marine Insurance based on Indemnity.—In a life insurance the insurer undertakes to pay a fixed sum on the death of the insured; but in fire and marine insurance, whatever sum be mentioned, the insurer is bound to make good the actual loss only, and under no circumstances is the insured entitled to a profit out of the loss. The result is that both parties have a common interest in the preservation of the thing insured. As a rule, the risks insured against are limited and defined in the instrument or policy embodying the terms of the contract. In some exceptional cases, *i.e.* in "valued policies," the value of the article is agreed, and such agreement is conclusive, but otherwise the insured is only entitled to be reimbursed his actual loss.

§ 163. **All material Facts must be disclosed.**—Whatever be the kind of insurance, complete disclosure is required of all facts relating to the risk to be undertaken by the insurer. If any information be kept back that would have affected the insurer in undertaking the risk, the policy will be void. A concealment will have the same effect as a misrepresentation. The insured is, however, only bound to disclose that which he knows, and where he has no information on any point raised he should say so. Statements as to "belief" are not statements of facts, and in such a case the insurer takes the risk.

§ 164. **The Insured must have an Interest in the Subject Matter.**—Any person may insure, provided he have an "insurable interest" in the event insured against. As far as life insurance is concerned, a man may insure his own life, but he cannot insure the life of another unless such other person has a claim upon him for support enforceable by law.

In the case of fire insurance the insured must possess an insurable interest, both at the date of the policy and at the time the fire happens. As regards buildings, any one having an interest in the property can insure, but he can only retain out of the insurance moneys the value of his own interest. Common carriers, factors, brokers, wharfingers, pawnbrokers, and commission agents have an insurable interest in the goods in their possession.

The same rule holds as regards marine insurance.

§ 165. **The Premium.**—The money payment in consideration of which the insurer undertakes the risk is called the premium. It is the universal practice of insurers, except in the case of marine insurance, to stipulate that the contract shall not take effect until the premium has been paid. The premium may consist of a lump sum or of periodical payments. Where the premiums are payable yearly the insurance is from year to year; if they are paid half-yearly or quarterly the insurance is from half-year to half-year or from quarter to quarter. In the case of an insurance extending over a number of years, a certain number of days, called days of grace, beyond the day fixed for the payment of premiums are allowed for payment.

Unless there is an agreement to the contrary, if a loss occur during these days of grace, the insured has no right of action on the policy. Strictly speaking, the premiums should be paid on the day appointed. Insurance companies, however, as a rule, provide that the policy shall be good and valid during the days of grace allowed.

It is a recognised rule that if the risk be not incurred the premium paid is recoverable,—no risk, no premium. The risk is regarded as the consideration for the premium, and if it be not incurred, the consideration fails and the premium must be returned. On the other hand, if the risk once commences no portion of the premium is returnable.

MARINE INSURANCE

§ 166. Underwriting.—Marine insurance takes place where a ship or cargo or freight is insured against loss during a fixed time or between one port and another. The insurance is generally effected with individuals who are called underwriters, from the custom of the insurer entering into the contract by writing under or at the foot of the policy his name and the amount of risk he undertakes. A well-known association of underwriters is known by the name of Lloyd's. The members meet and carry on their business in rooms over the London Royal Exchange. Lloyd's underwriters individually sign their names at the foot of the policy, and opposite thereto the sum insured by each, in figures and also in words, with the date of so doing. This is called underwriting the policy for so much, and each underwriter thereby enters into a separate contract with the insured for the amount set opposite to his name. Underwriting is also undertaken by companies, the form of underwriting depending on the articles of association or other instrument constituting the company. A number of shipowners sometimes join together for the mutual insurance of their respective vessels. Here there are no premiums, the losses in each year being made good by the members in proportion to the amount of ship property insured in the club. Insurance agents are often employed to negotiate a policy by both the insurer and the insured.

§ 167. **What may be insured.**—Not only may a ship or its cargo be insured, but also any special property in the same, such as the shipowner's interest in the freight. Freight is the price to be paid by a shipper of goods to the shipowner for the carriage of goods by ship. It is not due unless the goods are delivered at the port of destination. Many events might happen that would prevent such delivery, and in order to protect himself against possible loss the shipowner may insure his expected freight.

§ 168. **Kinds of Policies.**—The leading kinds of policies are valued and open policies, and time and voyage policies.

A *valued* policy is one in which the agreed value of the subject insured, as between the insured and the underwriter, is stated on the face of the policy. This value is conclusive, whether it be greater or less than the value in the open market. Ships and freights are generally insured in valued policies.

An *open* policy is one in which the value of the subject insured is not stated in the policy as between the insured and the underwriter, but is left to be proved by evidence in case of loss. Goods are generally insured by open policies, as their value can be ascertained by invoices, valuations, or other methods.

A *voyage* policy is one in which the risk is undertaken during a particular voyage between ports specified in the policy, *e.g.* from London to New York.

A *time* policy is one in which the risk is undertaken during a fixed time specified in the policy, *e.g.* from noon of the 1st January 1893 to noon of the 1st January 1894.

§ 169. **The Slip and the Policy.**—When a broker is requested to effect an insurance, he prepares a brief statement of the leading particulars of the risk to be insured. This statement, called the *slip*, is presented to the under-

writers, who initial it for the sum each proposes to under-
write.   In the case of companies a separate slip is presented
to each.   A policy embodying the terms contained in the
slip is subsequently prepared and underwritten, as the law
requires that every agreement for sea - insurance to be
valid must be expressed in a policy.   The slip by itself
cannot be enforced in the courts, but as it represents the
terms to which the parties have agreed, these identical terms
ought to be embodied in the policy.

The form of policy in use is very complex, but as every
clause has undergone a searching examination in the courts,
the meaning of the various clauses is well known.   The
policy is the only legal evidence of the terms of the contract,
and after it has been underwritten no material alteration can
be introduced without the consent of all parties.

§ 170. **Terms of the Policy.**—A policy usually contains
the name of the insured, the name of the ship, the subject
matter of the insurance, a statement of where the voyage is
to begin and end, the perils insured against, permission for
the insurer to take steps if necessary to protect the property,
the date, the amount of premium, and the sum underwritten
(see Appendix).   The policy must also be stamped.   Special
attention may be directed to warranties and to the clause
called the memorandum.

§ 171. **Warranties.** — Underwriters, for their own
protection, often stipulate for the insertion of certain express
warranties in the policy.   A warranty may be defined as a
stipulation upon the truth or fulfilment of which the validity
of the entire contract is to depend.   Express warranties
usually relate to the time of sailing, *e.g.* where it is alleged
that the ship has sailed or that it will sail on or before a
certain day, or to the neutral character of the ship and cargo
during a time of war.   Apart from these express warranties,
there are certain warranties implied by law that have the
same force as if they were formally set out in the policy
itself.

The leading implied warranties are : (1) that the ship is
seaworthy, (2) that the ship will not deviate, and (3) that
the voyage is legal.

1. *Seaworthiness.*—In the case of a voyage policy, *i.e.* where the insurance is in respect of a voyage from one port to another, the policy implies that the ship is seaworthy at the time the risk begins.

By seaworthy is meant "in a fit state as to repairs, equipments, crew, and all other respects, to encounter the ordinary perils of the risk." If the ship is lost, and it appears that she was unseaworthy, the underwriters are not liable on the policy. In the case of a "time" policy, which is usually effected when the ship is at sea, no warranty of seaworthiness is implied, as the owner has no means of knowing her condition.

2. *Not to deviate.*—A deviation from the proper course of the voyage releases the underwriters.

In almost all voyages usage has prescribed a certain course as the best, and it is risk to the vessel whilst pursuing this course that is insured against.

3. *Legality of voyage.*—An insurance on a ship engaged in a trade or venture illegal by the municipal law of the country in which the insurance is effected is void.

For instance, an insurance in England on a vessel engaged in smuggling goods into England is not binding.

§ 172. **The Memorandum.**—At the foot of the policy is found a clause that has for its object the protection of the underwriter against trifling claims and the exemption of certain perishable goods from the policy except under certain circumstances. The effect of the clause is as follows : The underwriter is not liable to make good (1) any partial loss in the case of corn, fish, salt, fruit, flour, and seed ; (2) any partial loss under 5 per cent in the case of sugar, tobacco, hemp, flax, hides and skins ; (3) any partial loss under 3 per cent in respect of other goods or of the ship and freight : except in all these cases where the loss is incurred (*a*) in order to save the vessel and cargo, *e.g.* by throwing goods overboard, or (*b*) by the ship being stranded.

Two terms are used in the memorandum that require

explanation. The word "average" is equivalent to "loss," hence, "free from average" means "free from loss." The term "general average" means a loss incurred for the benefit of the ship and cargo.

§ 173. **Total and Partial Loss.** — A ship may be totally lost or it may be injured only. A distinction is therefore drawn between *total* loss and *partial* loss.

A *total* loss is when there is in fact or in law a complete loss of the vessel; a *partial* loss is where the vessel sustains an injury only. In the former case the underwriter has to make good the loss, in the latter the injury. A *total* loss takes place when the ship wholly perishes. This is called *actual* total loss. But it also occurs where the ship is not wholly destroyed, but its destruction is so probable that recovery is exceedingly doubtful or too expensive to be worth undertaking : in such a case, if notice of abandonment be given, the vessel is regarded as wholly lost. This is called *constructive* total loss.

If the owner finds that it is impossible to save a vessel that is driven on the rocks by force of weather, and that there is every probability that she will become a complete wreck, he may before the completion of the wreck give notice orally or in writing to the underwriters that he abandons all interest in the vessel, and on doing so he is entitled to ask the underwriters to carry out their contracts as if the vessel had been totally destroyed. The notice must be unconditional and be given within a reasonable time after the owner hears of the loss. The notice has the effect of transferring the whole interest in the ship to the underwriters, who endeavour where possible to save the whole or part of the property.

In the case of a *partial* loss the damage has to be ascertained. Where the ship is damaged, two-thirds the costs of repairing are usually allowed. Where goods are damaged, the rule for ascertaining the loss is as follows : ascertain three things—(1) the value at the port of destination as if uninjured ; (2) the value at the same port as if injured ; (3) the original value. Then make the following calculation. As the value uninjured is to the value when damaged, so is their original value to the fourth quantity. This fourth quantity being subtracted from the original value, gives the amount to be paid by the underwriters. For instance, suppose goods valued £100 in London are shipped to Calcutta, where they would sell uninjured for £200, but owing to damage incurred on the voyage they bring £150.

$$200 : 150 :: 100.$$

The solution of this problem gives £75. Subtracting £75 from £100, we obtain £25 as the sum to be paid by the underwriters.

In this case the insured lost one-fourth the value of the goods at the port of destination, but the underwriter does not undertake to repay him more than one-fourth of the original value. The original value is regarded as the invoice price at the port of loading, plus the expenses of putting the goods on board, the premium for insurance, and commission.

LIFE INSURANCE

§ 174. **Not an Indemnity.**—A life insurance is a contract by which the insurer, in consideration of a premium usually paid yearly, undertakes to pay to the person insuring or his representatives a certain sum of money in case the insured dies within the period covered by the premium. The contract is an agreement to pay a given sum at death ; it is not a contract of indemnity. No question therefore arises as to whether any person suffers damage by the death of the party insured ; the death is the condition on which the sum is payable.

§ 175. **Insurable Interest.**—The person insuring must possess, as we have seen, an "insurable interest" on the life of the party insured. By an "insurable interest" is meant a pecuniary one. A man is regarded as having a pecuniary interest in his own life, a wife in that of her husband, and a creditor in the life of his debtor. A father, as such, has no insurable interest in the life of his son.

§ 176. **The Proposal and the Policy.**—The first step usually taken towards effecting an insurance is the filling up of a proposal giving particulars relating to the health and habits of the proposer. A declaration has also to be signed that the statements are to be taken as the basis of the contract, and that any untrue statement shall avoid it. This document is regarded as part of the policy. The greatest care should be taken in filling up the proposal, as any mis-statement will prevent the insurance moneys being received, even though the proposer passes the usual medical examination. The policy itself states the risks insured against, the time during which it is to be in force, and the names of the parties and the amount of the premium. The policy usually provides that it shall be forfeited by non-payment of the premiums, by residing outside certain specified limits, or by suicide, death by duelling, or the hands of justice, except so far as the *bona-fide* interests of third parties are concerned. This exception is introduced so as to protect the interest of any person who has purchased the policy or acquired any interest in it.

§ 177. **The Premium.**—The premium is usually made payable in annual, or half-yearly, or quarterly instalments. Sometimes a single payment is made to cover all premiums. Strictly speaking, the premium is payable on or before the day appointed, even though days of grace are allowed. But it is the general custom of companies, in the case of death after the day for payment, but before the days of grace have expired, to pay the amount of the policy, less the premium due. The insured should take care to see that such a clause is inserted in the policy.

§ 178. **Assignment.**—A policy of life insurance may be assigned or sold to a third party. The assignment should be in writing, and notice of the assignment should be given by the assignee to the insurance company. A policy may also be mortgaged to secure the repayment of a sum of money.

FIRE INSURANCE

§ 179. **Definition and Nature of the Contract.**—The contract of fire insurance is a contract by which one party, in consideration of the payment of a sum of money, undertakes to make good any loss or damage by fire, not exceeding a named amount, which may occur during a specified period. The contract is, as we have pointed out, one of indemnity—the sum named in the policy is not the measure of the loss, but the limit of what can be recovered. The insured must have an interest in the subject matter. As a rule, any subsisting right or interest in the property insured is an insurable interest. A trustee, for example, may insure the trust-estate, and so can the person entitled to the income of such estate. An insurance company in which property is insured has a sufficient "interest" to enable it to reinsure. A mere agent who has no possession of the property nor any claim upon it cannot insure on his own account. But any one who has possession and is responsible in case the property is destroyed by fire can insure, *e.g.* the pawnbroker. A factor, a warehouseman, or a wharfinger, as well as a common carrier, has an insurable interest in the property that comes into his possession in the ordinary course of trade.

§ 180. **The Risk undertaken.**—An insurance company that undertakes the risk to property through fire usually inserts stipulations in the policy with the object of defining the risk more clearly.

By "fire" is meant ignition of the property itself or some substance near it not used to create heat. Damage arising from excessive heat, the property not igniting, is not damage due to fire within the meaning of a policy. Something must catch fire, but so long as this occurs any resulting loss, *e.g.* by smoke or by water used to put out the fire, is recoverable though the insured property has not itself caught fire. In case a fire is due to an explosion, the company is liable, but not where the explosion of itself causes the damage. Clauses are frequently inserted in a policy with the object of defining the company's liability where there is an explosion, *e.g.* "The policy does not cover loss or damage by explosion, except loss or damage by explosion of gas in a building not forming part of any gas works, or by explosion of domestic boilers and domestic heating apparatus." Gas works are excepted as a specially hazardous risk.

Loss due to the natural heating that occurs sometimes
in hay, corn, seeds, and other property is usually excluded,
e.g. "The policy does not cover loss or damage by fire to
property occasioned by or happening through its own
spontaneous fermentation or heating."

It is also usual to except any loss by fire due "to
invasion, foreign enemy, riot, or civil commotion."

§ 181. The Property insured. — Certain kinds of
property are not included in the policy unless specifically
mentioned. The following is a usual clause :—

"The policy does not cover china, glass, looking-glasses,
jewels, clocks, watches, trinkets, medals, curiosities, manuscripts, government stamps, prints, paintings, drawings,
sculptures, musical, mathematical, or philosophical instruments, patterns, models, or moulds, unless specially
mentioned."

Certain other forms of property are completely excluded
e.g. "deeds, bonds, bills of exchange, promissory notes,
money, securities for money, or books of account." Care
should be taken to see that the ownership of the property
is correctly described. As a rule, "property held upon
trust or upon commission" is excluded unless expressly
described as such. An insurance by a husband of his own
property does not cover the property of his wife or of his
servants or his visitors.

§ 182. The Proposal.—Where it is desired to effect an
insurance against fire, it is necessary to make a proposal
stating particulars of the risk to be insured. In drawing
up this proposal care should be taken (1) to describe
accurately the property to be insured and the building, if
any, in which it is contained; (2) not to make any mis-
statement; (3) not to omit any known fact material in
estimating the risk. Not only does non-disclosure of
material facts known to the proposer vitiate the policy at
law; but a clause in the policy itself usually declares that
it is to be void if such non-disclosure exists. Misrepresentations have a similar effect.

§ 183. Conditions that are to avoid the Policy.—
A fire policy, as a rule, enumerates certain matters which

if they occur are to avoid the policy. The more important of these are as follows :—

1. Misdescription or omission of material facts in the proposal. This has been already referred to.

2. Increasing the risk subsequent to the policy by doing anything to the property or to any building in which it is contained.

3. Removing the property without the consent of the company.

4. Assigning the property otherwise than by will, unless the policy be assigned as well.

§ 184. The Premium.—The premium is usually payable at the time the insurance is effected ; the policy not being issued until such premium is paid.

Subsequent premiums are payable yearly, a certain number of days of grace being allowed by some offices. A clause is sometimes inserted to the effect that the policy is not to become void notwithstanding the occurrence of a loss by fire within the days of grace allowed, provided the premium be duly paid on or before the expiration of such days. Where no such clause is inserted, inquiry should be made as to the position of an insured during the running of the days of grace.

§ 185. Occurrence of a Loss.—A policy requires the insured when the loss occurs to give notice to the company and to deliver within a certain time a statement of the articles destroyed, with an estimate of their value at the time of fire, and to support such statement, if required, by proofs and explanations. A statutory declaration as to the truth of the statement may also be necessary.

Any fraudulent claim, as a rule, vitiates the policy.

An insurance company usually reserves to itself the right to reinstate or replace the property injured instead of paying the value of the damage sustained.

§ 186. Concurrent Policies. — An insurer may effect insurances on the same property in several offices. In such a case, apart from any stipulations in the policies, he might recover from any one office, but if one office pays, it is entitled to a contribution from the other offices. A clause

is usually inserted in a policy to restrict the liability of
each office to a proportionate amount of the loss, *e.g.* " If at
the time of any loss or damage by fire happening to any
property hereby insured there be any other subsisting
insurance or insurances, whether effected by the insured or
by any other persons, covering the same property, the
company shall not be liable to pay or contribute more
than its rateable proportion of such loss or damage."   The
apportionment of the loss between several companies is a
difficult matter.   As a rule, it is undertaken by the insurance
offices concerned or is referred to arbitration.

§ 187. Authorities. — *The Law of Insurance*, by Mr.
Porter, covers all forms—marine, fire, and life.   Marine
insurance is treated at length by Mr. Arnould, life insurance by Mr. Bunyan and Mr. Crawley, and fire insurance
by Mr. Bunyan.   Short chapters on the subject will be
found in Smith's *Mercantile Law*, and in Mr. Williams'
and Mr. Goodeve's works on Personal Property.

§ 188. Nature of a Guarantee. — A guarantee is a contract by which one person undertakes to be answerable for the payment of a debt or the performance of an act, in case another person who is primarily responsible fails to pay the debt or to perform the act. The person primarily liable is called the " principal," and the person who gives the guarantee the " surety."

As there cannot be an accessory without a principal, a guarantee implies that there is a contract on which a principal is primarily liable, the liability of the guarantee being secondary, *i.e.* arising only on the principal's default. The proper form of a guarantee is, " If A. will not pay you, I will." Here the writer clearly indicates that payment must be sought from A., and resort is to be had to himself only in case A. makes default. Expressions such as, " If you supply goods to A., I will pay you," are equivocal, since the words may mean either a guarantee or that a primary liability is undertaken. All the circumstances must then be examined in order to see to whom credit was really given. If, for example, the goods were debited to A., then it is clear that A. was treated as principal.

§ 189. Form of Guarantee. — The Statute of Frauds requires a guarantee to " answer for the debt, default, or mis-carriages of another person " to be in writing, signed by the guarantor or his authorised agent, otherwise no action can be brought upon it. Verbal guarantees are not, how-

ever, made void by the statute : if the principal or surety
discharges the promise the transaction is good.   But if the
principal does not discharge the promise, an action cannot
be brought against the guarantor.   The writing should
show the names of the parties and the promise, but the
consideration need not be stated in writing provided there
is an existing consideration.

§ 190. Liability of the Surety.—The surety is liable
on the default of the principal, but once the principal has
committed a default the surety may be sued at once.   In
other words, the creditor is not obliged to sue the principal
before sueing the surety, nor is he obliged to give the
surety notice of default having been made, nor need he
demand payment from the surety.   If the surety desires to
secure that the principal shall be sued first, and that he shall
have notice given him of any default, and that he is not to
be liable until a demand for payment is made, he must
secure that suitable provisions are inserted in the guarantee.

The extent of the surety's liability depends upon the
terms of the guarantee.   The instrument may contain
limitations as to amount or as to time.   As regards time,
a guarantee may be a "continuing" one or not.

§ 191. Continuing Guarantee.—A continuing guarantee
is one that is not restricted to a single dealing.   If A.
guarantees the payment of any debt B. may contract in his
business, not exceeding £100, A. makes himself liable for
any debts not exceeding £100 which B. may from time to
time contract in his business.   Hence if the guarantor
desires to be surety for a single dealing only, he should
take care to say so.

§ 192. Fidelity Guarantee.—Guarantees are frequently
given for the fidelity of a person engaged in an office, or in
some employment.   Care should be taken to state distinctly
whether the guarantee is intended to apply to an appointment to another but similar office.   As a rule, any material
alteration in the duties of an office or appointment to a
new office discharges the surety.

If a surety becomes bankrupt, his estate is liable under
the guarantee, and the creditor may prove against it.

§ 193. **Rights of the Surety.**—A surety who discharges the whole or part of the debt has a right of action against the principal for what he has paid with interest. This right of action does not arise directly out of the contract of guarantee, inasmuch as that contract is one entered into between the guarantor and the creditor: the principal is not a party to it. But when a guarantee is given by one man at the request of another, the law treats the payment of the debt by the surety as a payment at the request of the principal, and gives the surety an action against the principal for the amount paid. Where the surety pays the debt, he is entitled to the benefit of all securities which the principal may have given the creditor to secure payment.

Where there are several co-sureties, any one paying the debt has a right to compel the others to contribute their respective shares. This right arises the moment the surety has paid more than his share of the common debt. No contribution arises where the liability of each surety is limited to a given sum, inasmuch as in such a case each is bound to pay that sum and no more. The right exists only where the sureties are bound jointly or jointly and severally. The power of a surety to call on his co-sureties for contribution before he has paid anything, or where he has paid his share only, is doubtful : probably he could call upon them to give him an indemnity against having to pay more than his share.

§ 194. **Discharge of the Surety.**—The guarantee may be void *ab initio*, and have no legal effect. For instance, if the consideration for which it is given fails, or if the creditor alters the instrument of guarantee after its execution in a material point, the surety is discharged.

A guarantee often contains a clause that the surety may revoke it on notice to the creditor. In such a case, notice will always discharge the surety. If the guarantee contains no such clause, the right of the surety to revoke it, depends on the nature of the guarantee. The substitution of a new agreement for the guarantee before breach will discharge the surety from all liability under the old agreement. The death of the surety, though it does not affect the liability of his estate in respect of past transactions, will operate as a revocation, provided the guarantee could have been determined by notice. If, however, the surety could not have put an end to the guarantee by notice, his liability remains.

The conduct of the creditor may operate as a discharge of the surety. The general rule is, that if the creditor does any act to the prejudice of the surety, the guarantee is at an end. Hence any material variation from the terms of the contract made between the principal and the creditor discharges the surety, on the ground that the surety became surety on the faith of the original agreement. For instance, a building contract provided that three-quarters of the work as finished should be paid for every three months, and the remaining quarter on completion. Payments of more than three-quarters were made without the consent of the sureties before the work was completed, and it was held the sureties for the performance of the work were discharged.

The terms of the agreement between the principal and surety must also be carefully observed or fulfilled else the surety is not liable, e.g. a surety for moneys "to be received" by another is only liable for moneys actually received by that other.

A surety is discharged if the creditor without his consent extends the time originally fixed for payment, even though no injury actually accrues to the surety. The agreement to give time must, however, be one that the principal could enforce. We have seen that unless the extension of time given by a creditor to a debtor is supported by a consideration, the creditor is not bound to wait, but may sue at once. In such a case there is an agreement without a consideration, i.e. there is no contract. Even if the creditor agrees with the principal to give the surety an extension of time, the surety is discharged, because the right of the surety to pay the debt and sue the principal is affected. The surety by a contract made between himself and the creditor may secure time for payment provided he gives some consideration. Any negligence of the creditor in doing what he is legally bound to do, by reason of which the position of the surety is made worse, will discharge the surety : for instance, not presenting a bill of exchange for payment when it became due, and the parties liable to pay subsequently became insolvent. A surety, as we have seen, is on payment of the debt entitled to the securities held by the creditor. The creditor is bound to use due diligence in taking care of such securities, and if he lose them the surety is discharged.

The guarantee may also come to an end by payment of the debt by the principal and by release of the debt by the creditor.

When default is made by the principal, the surety should be sued within six years if the guarantee is not under seal, twenty years if it is under seal, otherwise the right of action is extinguished by the Statute of Limitations.

§ 195. **Authorities.** — Smith's *Mercantile Law;* De Colyar on Guarantees.

CHAPTER VI

CHARTER-PARTIES AND BILLS OF LADING

§ 196. Charter-parties and Bills of Lading.—A merchant who is shipping goods may either ship them as part of a cargo or may hire an entire vessel where the goods are sufficient to fill the vessel. In the latter case the goods may not be his own, as for example where he takes the risk of collecting a cargo from various exporters. Where an entire ship is hired, a formal document embodying the agreed terms is prepared, called a *charter-party*. Where goods are shipped as part of a cargo, the contract may be a verbal one or it may be collected from the notices issued by the shipping company; but on the delivery of the goods on board, a receipt, called a *bill of lading*, is given by the shipowner or his agent, and though this bill of lading is not the contract itself, it is evidence of the contract. A bill of lading contains the conditions upon which the shipowner receives the goods for carriage, and as the form of bill of lading used by every leading company is well known, shippers who send goods to be carried will usually be taken to have agreed to the bill of lading.

By a charter-party the charterer usually secures the use of the vessel and the services of a master and crew for a particular voyage. By a bill of lading the shipper secures a receipt for the goods, which may be endorsed and delivered to another party, who thereby takes the property in the goods and acquires the same rights and liabilities as if it were originally issued to him.

Before examining in detail the usual provisions found in charter-parties and bills of lading, reference may be made to certain general principles that apply to shipowners and shippers, unless there be an agreement to the contrary. This is the more necessary inasmuch as many of the provisions found in charter-parties and bills of lading have for their object the restriction of some legal liability that would be incurred in the absence of such provisions.

§ 197. Seaworthiness.—In all contracts for the carriage of goods it is implied that the vessel is seaworthy at the time of loading and at the time of sailing. By "seaworthy" is meant, fit to undertake the particular voyage in question (§ 171). Express stipulations are often introduced into charter-parties relating to seaworthiness, e.g. that the vessel is "staunch and strong and well provided with men and mariners" (§ 203).

§ 198. Despatch.—The shipowner also undertakes that the vessel will commence and complete the voyage with all reasonable despatch. If the voyage is rendered impossible by obstacles not known to the parties at the time of making the contract, which cannot be removed within a reasonable time, the contract may be repudiated.

In order to avoid liability from perils that cannot be foreseen, a clause is usually introduced specifying certain "excepted perils," and if delay occurs from such perils the shipowner is not to be liable.

§ 199. Deviation.—A shipowner is under an implied warranty that the ship will not deviate from the usual course of navigation except to save life or to protect the vessel or cargo from some imminent peril. Hence a vessel in the absence of the express consent of the shippers cannot deviate to save property or to tow another vessel. Any unauthorised deviation renders the shipowner liable for any resulting loss to the charterer or shipper. A vessel not authorised to deviate in order to tow another vessel did so and was wrecked when towing; the shipowner was held liable to the shippers for the loss of the cargo.

§ 200. Freight.—Freight is the amount payable to the shipowner for carriage and delivery of the goods. Freight is payable at the moment of delivery. The shipowner cannot claim it until he is ready to deliver the goods ; the consignee of the goods is not entitled to have them unless he is ready to pay freight.

No freight therefore is payable if the goods are lost on the voyage and are not delivered at the port of destination, but this general rule is usually restricted in charter-parties and bills of lading.

The master of the ship has a lien on the goods carried for the freight, *i.e.* he cannot be compelled to part with them until the freight is paid.

CHARTER-PARTIES

§ 201. **Form of Charter-party.**—The following is a form of charter-party : [1]—

LONDON, *5th November* 1886.

A. B. and Co. ——————— E.C.

OUTWARD.

This charter-party is mutually entered into between C. D. and Co. as agents for owners, and Messrs. A. B. and Co. as charterers of the good ship or vessel—

(*a*) 'Ajax'; captain, Anderson, now in Hull.
(*b*) The vessel is 1395 tons net, British register, guaranteed to be made tight, staunch, strong, coppered in 1886, and in every way fitted for the voyage. Class of vessel is $\frac{3}{8}$rds L 11 in French veritas, and is to be so continued throughout the voyage.
(*c*) The voyage to be, Liverpool to Yokohama and Hiogo, or so near thereto as the vessel can safely get, where cargo is to be delivered as per bills of lading in the customary manner, so ending the

---

[1] Smith's *Mercantile Law*, p. 323.

voyage. The vessel to proceed with all safe speed
direct to the port of discharge.

(*d*) Vessel's hold and cargo capacity are given to
charterers for cargo, except only what is customary
and necessary for the ship's stores for the above
voyage ; and owners hereby guarantee the vessel to
carry 1850 tons' (of 20 cwt.) weight of cargo (without being overladen), or if this be refused by owners
or captain, then charterers have power to deduct
the *pro rata* equivalent for such short carrying from
owners' account. The weight of cargo to be computed from invoices and from carriers' notes and
from bills of lading. Either these original documents or shippers' certificates of such weight to be
accepted as absolute proof by the owners.

(*e*) The cargo to be taken on board as customary, and
to be of lawful merchandise, including gunpowder
(in the river), charterers erecting the necessary
magazine ; specie, kerosine, or similar oils, acids on
deck at shippers' risk; also machinery which can
be shipped without cutting hatches. The vessel to
proceed to any crane as required in loading dock,
but any extra expense in loading or discharging
packages over three tons' weight to be borne by
charterers.

(*f*) Charter money to be paid owners is £2058, say
two thousand and fifty eight pounds sterling, in full
of all port charges, primages, etc. £1000 to be
payable abroad, at current rate of exchange, by
bills of lading or charterers' order (at their option),
to captain on final and true delivery of cargo ;
balance to be paid here in cash on sailing, less 5
per cent for interest and insurance. Captain to
have an absolute lien and charge for freight on
cargo, but to have no recourse on charterers for any
freight due abroad for bill of lading if not paid ;
charterers' responsibility to cease as soon as cargo
is signed for except for advance due here, and the
order (if any) for balance due abroad.

(g) Loading dock to be ordered by charterers, and to load in the river if required. Vessel to be made ready and proceed to her loading berth as soon as possible on signing of this charter. Provided there is not sufficient water to allow of her leaving the dock fully laden, the loading to be completed in the river.

(h) Loading days allowed charterers are thirty, with two clear days extra for cleaning; for any used for loading beyond these, £14 per day demurrage to be paid to owners by charterers. Sundays, customs or bank holidays or detention by frost are always excluded throughout this charter-party. Any day or days during which ballast is discharged not to count against charterers. Captain to notify in writing when vessel is in a proper loading berth, as above, with the hold clear and cleaned, vessel painted, rigged, and ready for cargo. When such are complied with, loading days to commence twenty-four hours after such notice has been received by charterers. Lay days not to count before 20th Nov. unless vessel and cargo both ready sooner : and charterers to have the option of cancelling this charter-party if vessel not arrived and ready to commence loading by 5th Dec.

(i) Mate's receipts to be signed for the cargo as taken on board. On production of these, the bills of lading are to be signed by the captain at charterers' request, at any rate of freight, such bills of lading to be without prejudice to this charter. Captain shall also sign for weight of coal, pig-iron, or cargo when weighed alongside or on board or delivered on official weighing-machine notes. Captain to attend at least once daily at the charterers' office to sign bills of lading.

(j) Stevedore to be appointed by the charterers. His men are to take on board and stow the cargo under the direction of the master. The master and owners alone to be responsible for stowage of cargo and trim of vessel. Charterers to charge owners for storage of cargo at the rate of 1s. 4d. per ton in account, owners to pay the usual advertising, printing, and measurer's charges, not exceeding eight guineas. Underwriters' surveyors to settle all disputes as to stowage or draught, and their recommendation or decision to be carried out by captain and owners. Dunnage or mats if required to be provided by the owners.

(k) Consignment of vessel to be placed in the hands of the agents appointed by the charterers, whom the owners also accept as agents of the vessel at her ports of discharge inwards, the owners paying $2\frac{1}{2}$ per cent inwards on amount of this charter, and charterers' agents to have the preference outwards. Should the vessel put into any port or ports on the way while under this charter, she is to be consigned to charterers' agents there.

(l) A brokerage of 5 per cent on this charter is due by owners to B. J. and Co. on signing of the same.

(m) If any disputes arise, the same to be settled by two London commercial men, each party naming one as an arbitrator, and if necessary the arbitrators to appoint a third. The decision of the majority shall be final, and any party attempting to revoke the submission to arbitration without the leave of a court shall be liable to pay to the other or others as liquidated damages the estimated amount of the chartered freight. It is further agreed that these presents may be made a rule of Her Majesty's High Court of Justice.

(n) It is also furthermore agreed that the said vessel shall by the owners thereof during the whole of the said voyage be kept tight, staunch, and strong, and well found and provided with men and mariners sufficient and able to navigate the said vessel, and with all manner of rigging, boats, tackle, provisions, and appurtenances whatsoever

(o) (restraints of princes and rulers, the dangers and

accidents of the seas, rivers, and navigation, fire,
pirates, enemies, throughout this charter-party always
excepted).

(*p*) In the event of war being declared between the
nation to which this vessel belongs and any other,
the charterers have the option of cancelling the
charter before the vessel proceeds to sea, upon
indemnifying the owners from all consequences of
re-delivering the cargo ; and in case the charter be
so cancelled, the charterers shall pay to the owners
£13 for each and every day which shall elapse
between the time of the vessel being in the loading
berth and the cancelling of such charter or the
final discharge of the cargo (if any) which may
have been received on board, whichever last shall
happen.   For the due performance of the agreement
and matters herein contained each of the said
parties bindeth himself and themselves, each of the
other, in the sum of estimated amount of freight.

(*q*) Vessel to call at a wharf in the Tees on her way
to dock to load some iron, provided the same can
be done with safety to vessel and no extra expense
be incurred ; if the latter, then the same to be paid
by the charterers.

An examination of the above form shows that the leading
terms may be classed under certain heads :—

§ 202. **The Name of the Ship.**—This must be correctly
stated (clause *a*).

§ 203. **Description of Ship.**—A description may be
given of the actual condition of the ship, *e.g.* "tight,
staunch, strong, coppered in 1886, and in every way fitted
for the voyage," or its actual condition may be implied by
reference to Lloyd's register.   For instance, a representation
that the ship is A1 implies that the ship is so classified at
Lloyd's.   Such a representation amounts to a condition
that the ship is so classified at the time the charter-party is
entered into (clause *b*).

§ 204. **The Voyage.**—The port of departure and the
port of destination require to be mentioned in order to

describe the voyage. Clauses are often inserted in order to provide for unforeseen circumstances likely to prevent the delivery of the cargo at the port of destination. A usual clause is to require delivery at the destination "or so near thereto as the vessel can safely get." The vessel must, in the first instance, proceed to the destination, but if after waiting a reasonable time she cannot get to the place for unloading, then she may proceed to another place as near thereto as possible. What is a reasonable time depends on circumstances, *e.g.* where the vessel arrives in a tidal river at low tide, she must wait until the tide rises; if a harbour is frozen, she must wait until the ice melts; and if a dock be full, she must wait a reasonable time for a vacancy.

The word "safely" in the clause means safely for the vessel having a cargo on board. Hence if the master finds that he cannot on account of the weight of the cargo reach the port without unloading a part, he is not bound to do so.

Other clauses are often introduced so as to cover any matters likely to prevent the vessel reaching its destination, such as blockades, quarantine, war, ice, an option being given to the master to land the goods at any other port he considers safe (clause *c*).

§ 205. Capacity of the Vessel.—Where a ship is registered her "tonnage" is registered at the same time. This term "tonnage" has no reference to weight; it refers to register tons of 100 cubic feet. When weight is referred to, the phrase "tons of 20 cwt." is generally used. A charter-party, as a rule, states the "tonnage" in order to give an idea of the size of the ship. In addition to this, a certain carrying capacity is usually guaranteed, *e.g.* "the owners hereby guarantee the vessel to carry 1850 tons of 20 cwt. weight of cargo without being overladen." The charterer generally stipulates that the weight shall be computed from invoices, carriers' notes, and bills of lading, in order to avoid the necessity of actually weighing the cargo.

The carrying capacity of a ship is often referred to as so many tons "dead weight." The primary meaning of "dead weight" is simply "weight," but in a charter-party it is often used to denote goods which measure less than 40 cubic feet per ton, and therefore pay freight by weight (clause *d*).

§ 206. **Nature of the Cargo.**—The charterer by law is bound not to ship dangerous goods without notice to the shipowner. Sometimes there is a stipulation to ship only "lawful merchandise," *i.e.* merchandise that can be lawfully shipped. If it is intended to ship any special kind of goods, such as machinery, it is desirable to refer to such goods in the charter-party, and to arrange by whom the extra expense (if any) of getting such goods on board is to be borne (clause *e*).

§ 207. **Freight.**—A charter-party specifies the amount of freight, for what it is payable, how it is payable, and usually gives the shipowner an express lien or charge on the goods carried for the freight.

On the shipment of goods certain charges are usually levied by the port, and a percentage on the freight, called "primage," is payable to the shipowner, who usually allows a part of it to the shipping agent—if the sum paid as freight is to include these or any other charges, a statement to that effect should be inserted. A portion of the freight is usually payable on the vessel sailing, and the remainder on delivery of the goods, either in cash or bills of exchange, *e.g.* "£1000 to be payable abroad, at current rate of exchange, by bills of lading or charterers' order (at their option), to captain on formal and true delivery of the cargo ; balance to be paid here in cash on sailing." The payment in advance may be either an advance of freight or a loan, and it is desirable that the charter-party should contain words to show clearly whether the advance is a loan or not, otherwise the rights of the parties will be doubtful. Where it is an advance of freight, such an advance can be insured, and frequently a deduction is made from the amount advanced on account of insurance, *e.g.* "less insurance."

The charterer may give the shipowner an express lien for the freight, *i.e.* a right to retain possession of the goods in case the freight be not paid. At common law a shipowner has always a lien for freight, and when an express lien is given in a charter-party the object usually is to limit the extent of the lien, *e.g.* where the lien is not to extend to any freight "due abroad per bill of lading" (clause *f*).

§ 208. **Place of Loading.**—The charter-party contains a statement of where the ship is at the time of making the charter (clause *a*), or mentions where she will be by a certain day. If such place be not the place of loading, there is inserted a clause requiring her "to proceed to a port and there load": in such a case it is the duty of the shipowner to send the vessel to such port with reasonable speed, and by the day named if one be fixed in the charter-party. The charterers may reserve the right to name the dock in which the cargo is to be taken on board or to load in a river (clause *g*).

§ 209. **Time for Loading.**—A certain time, *e.g.* thirty days, is allowed for loading. It is the interest of the charterer that the vessel should be ready to load by the time appointed, and of the shipowner that no delay should occur. The time for loading begins when the ship is ready to load at the place appointed, and the charterer has notice of this fact. The shipowner must always give notice to the charterers of the ship's readiness to load at the place agreed upon. The days allowed for loading are called "lay days" (clause *h*).

§ 210. **Mate's Receipt.**—On delivery of goods to a ship the shipper usually receives a document known as a "mate's receipt." Where goods are sent to the docks by land, the dock company give a "wharfage note" as a receipt, the dock company taking the "mate's receipt" from the ship. The "mate's receipts" are afterwards exchanged for bills of lading signed by the captain (clause *i*).

§ 211. **Expense of Loading.**—In the absence of any agreement to the contrary in the charter-party, the charterer bears the expense of bringing the cargo alongside the vessel. The shipowner's duty is to receive and properly stow the cargo. A person called a "stevedore" is often employed by the charterers to see to the proper stowage of the cargo, but this does not affect the liability of the shipowner for stowage. In some cases the charterer stows the cargo at the shipowner's risk and expense. Mats or other articles used to protect the cargo from the bottom and sides of the vessel are called "dunnage" (clause *j*).

§ 212. **Consignment of Vessel.**—The parties usually agree on some firm or person who is to act as agent for both the owners of the vessel and of the cargo in the ports to which the vessel proceeds. Sometimes the vessel is consigned to the charterers' agent, and the amount of commission to be paid such agent ought to be fixed by the charter-party (clause *k*).

§ 213. **Brokerage.**—On the signing of a charter-party, a commission is usually paid to the brokers who negotiate the charter-party. The amount is fixed by the charter-party (clause *l*).

§ 214. **Perils Excepted.**—The shipowner is liable, as we have seen, for any damage arising to the goods on the voyage. A charter-party usually excepts damage arising from "restraints of princes and rulers, the dangers and accidents of the seas, fire, pirates, and enemies," etc., and often makes provision for the case of war (clause *o*). The perils usually excepted will be discussed later on (§ 226).

§ 215. **Provision in Case of War.**—If war breaks out between the country to which a vessel belongs and a foreign state, the vessel is liable to capture. Hence if there is a probability of war, provision is often made for cancelling the charter-party (clause *p*).

§ 216. **Additional Clauses.**—Clauses are often inserted providing for arbitration in case of any dispute between the parties (clause *m*), for the payment of a fixed sum in case the charterers withdraw from the contract, and for cancelling the contract where misrepresentations as to the size or state of the vessel have been made by the owners.

BILLS OF LADING

§ 217. **Definition.**—A bill of lading is a receipt for goods shipped in a vessel signed by the person who contracts to carry them, and stating the terms on which the goods are to be carried. The bill of lading is not necessarily the contract itself, as that is made before the bill of lading is signed. As a rule, the conditions embodied in a bill of lading on which goods are to be carried by a particular line of vessels are well known, and when a shipper forwards goods for carriage he is supposed to contract with reference to such conditions. A bill of lading, though not the contract, is evidence of the contract.

§ 218. **Form of a Bill of Lading.**—Different trades use different bills of lading. A collection of various forms will be found in the work on Bills of Lading by E. Leggett. The following form used for general produce in the Mediterranean, Black Sea, and Baltic trades is taken from the appendix to Mr. T. E. Scrutton's work on Charter-parties and Bills of Lading.

(*a*) Shipped in good order and condition by ———

(*b*) in and upon the good steamship ———

(*c*) now lying in the Port of —— and bound for ——

(*d*) with liberty to call at any ports on the way for coaling or other necessary purposes

(*e*) being marked and numbered as per margin, and to be delivered in like good order and condition at the port of ——— unto ——— or to his or their assigns

(*f*) he or they paying freight on the said goods on delivery at the rate of ——— and charges as per margin.

(*g*) It is mutually agreed that the ship shall have liberty to sail without pilots; to tow and assist vessels in distress; to deviate for the purpose of saving life; to convey goods in lighters to and from the ship at the risk of the owners of the goods, but at the ship's expense; and in case the ship shall put into a port of refuge for repairs to tranship the goods to their destination by any other steamship.

(*h*) The Act of God, Perils of the Sea, Fire, Barratry of the Master and Crew, Enemies, Pirates, Robbers, Arrests and Restraints of Princes, Rulers, and People, and other Accidents of Navigation excepted. Strandings and collisions and all losses and damages caused thereby are also excepted, even when occasioned by negligence, default, or error in judgment of the Pilot, Master, Mariners, or other Servants of the Shipowner; but nothing herein contained shall exempt the shipowner from liability to pay for damage to cargo occasioned by bad stowage, by improper or insufficient dunnage or ventilation, or by improper opening of valves, sluices, and ports, or by causes other than those above excepted; and all the above exceptions are conditional on the Vessel being seaworthy when she sails on the voyage, but any latent Defects in the Machinery shall not be considered unseaworthiness provided the same do not result from any want of due diligence of the Owners or any of them or of the Ship's Husband or Manager.

(*i*) The Shipowner is not liable for Loss or Damage occasioned by Decay, Putrefaction, Rust, Sweat, Change of Character, Drainage, Leakage, Breakage, or any loss or damage arising from the nature of the goods or the insufficiency of packages:

(*j*) nor for Land Damage:

(*k*) nor for the obliteration or absence of Marks and Numbers

(*l*) nor for any loss or damage caused by the prolongation of the voyage.

(*m*) The Steamer while detained at any port for the purpose of coaling is at liberty to discharge and receive goods and passengers.

(*n*) The goods are to be applied for within 24 hours of ship's arrival and reporting at the Custom-House, otherwise the Master or Agent is to be at liberty to put into lighters or land the same at the risk and expense of the owners of the goods.

(*o*) In case of quarantine at any port, the goods destined for that port may be discharged into quarantine depot, hulk, or other vessel, as required for the

Ship's despatch.   Quarantine expenses upon the
said goods of whatever nature or kind shall be
borne by the Owners of the goods.

(*p*) In case any part of the within goods cannot be
found during the Ship's stay at the port of their
destination, they are to be sent back by first
steamer at the Ship's risk and expense, and subject
to any proved claim for loss of market.

(*q*) The Ship shall not be liable for incorrect delivery of
packages unless each of them shall have been
distinctly marked by the shippers before shipment.

(*r*) Should grain or seed be delivered in a heated or
damaged condition, and the receivers claim to
deduct half-freight upon such damaged or heated
portion, it shall be at the Master's option either to
allow the same or to be paid full freight upon the
quantity shipped according to the Bill of Lading,
provided always that no portion of the same has
been jettisoned or otherwise disposed of on the
voyage, and the quantity allowed exceeds the quantity
named in the Bill of Lading.

(*s*) General Average payable according to the York-
Antwerp Rules.

The Owner and Consignee of the goods and Shipowner
mutually agree to be bound by all of the above
stipulations, exceptions, and conditions, notwithstanding any custom of the ports of loading and
discharging to the contrary.

In witness whereof the master or duly authorised agent
of the said ship hath affirmed to the three Bills of Lading,[1]
all of this tenour and date, one of which Bills being accom-
plished, the others are to stand void.

Dated in ——— this ——— day of ——— 189 .

§ 219. "**Shipped in good order and condition.**"—This
clause exempts the master from any liability for misdescription
of the goods as regards either contents or weight.   It amounts
to an admission by the shipowner that the packages when
shipped were externally in good condition—it does not

---

[1] See Appendix.

amount to an admission that internally they were in good condition (clause *a*). The words " weight, quality, and contents unknown " are often inserted at the end in order to exclude any liability in respect of weight, quality, or condition.

§ 220. "In and upon the good steamship." — The name of the vessel must be described with substantial accuracy (clause *b*).

§ 221. "Now lying in the Port of ———, and bound for ———."—The port of departure and the destination are specified, so as to define whence, and to where the goods are to be carried. A false statement as to route or destination would probably, if discovered before the vessel sails, entitle the shipper to cancel the contract (clause *c*).

A subsequent clause (*m*) gives the vessel while detained at any port for the purpose of coaling, "liberty to discharge and receive goods and passengers."

§ 222. "With liberty to call at any ports on the way for coaling or other necessary purposes."—It is the duty of the master to proceed on the voyage without deviating from the usual course taken by vessels pursuing a similar voyage (§ 199). Deviation to save property is not allowed, but a master may deviate in order to save life, or to protect the vessel from any danger to the ship or the cargo. The deviation must not be greater than what is reasonably required.

With the object of giving power to deviate, clauses are introduced into bills of lading. The clause under consideration gives power to deviate in order to obtain a supply of coal or for other necessary purposes (clause *d*).

§ 223. "Being marked and numbered as per margin and to be delivered in good order and condition at the port of —— unto —— or to his or their assigns."

The packages are usually marked with letters and figures for the purpose of identification. The delivery is to be in good order and condition, *i.e.* in as good a state and condition as when they were received on board. The bill may provide that delivery is to be to the shipper himself, or to his agent, or to bearer, or to order, or to order or assigns. When it provides that the goods are to be delivered "to order," or "to order or assigns," the shipper may endorse the bill and send it to the person who is to receive delivery, inasmuch as endorsement and delivery transfer the right to receive the goods (clauses *e* and *q*).

§ 224. **"He or they paying freight on the said goods on delivery at the rate of ——, and charges as per margin "** (clause *f*).

Freight is payable at the moment of delivery. The shipowner cannot claim freight until he is ready to deliver the goods : the consignee of the goods is not entitled to have them unless he is ready to pay freight. A subsequent clause (*n*) provides that "the goods are to be applied for within 24 hours of the ship's arrival and reporting at the custom-house, otherwise the master or agent is to be at liberty to put into lighters or land the same at the risk and expense of the owners of the goods."

Sometimes the master is given a lien on the goods "for freight and payments made, if any, or liabilities incurred in respect of any charges stipulated herein to be borne by the owners thereof."

§ 225. **"It is mutually agreed that the ship shall have liberty to sail without pilots; to tow and assist vessels in distress; to deviate for the purpose of saving life; to convey goods in lighters to and from the ship at the risk of the owners of the goods, but at the ship's expense; and in case the ship shall put into a port of refuge for repairs, to tranship the goods to their destination by any other steamship."**

A pilot is a person taken on board at a particular place for the purpose of conducting a ship through a river, road, or channel, or to or from a port. The first part of the above clause exempts the master from taking a pilot on board as between himself and the shipper, but it must be remembered that in England vessels coming within certain districts are compelled by law to have a pilot on board.

The second part of the clause relating to the towing of vessels and deviation for the purpose of saving life has already been referred to. The next portion of the clause relating to the use of lighters may be very useful where the master is unable to reach a dock. The part of the clause, however, that calls for chief attention is that which relates to the master's power of transhipment (clause *g*).

§ 226. "**Excepted perils.**"—If the bill of lading were to stop at the end of clause *g*, it would amount to an undertaking to carry the goods at the shipowner's risk. If therefore the goods were lost or damaged, the shipowner would be liable, apart from losing his freight, for non-delivery of the goods.

In order to protect himself from such liability, the ship-owner stipulates that he is not to be liable for loss or injury from certain specified causes ; but even where such causes are specified, the shipowner must take reasonable care to avoid them.

The excepted perils vary in every trade and with every shipowner ; the tendency being to increase their number, so as to enable the shipowner to avoid as much liability as possible.

The perils excepted in clause *h* of the policy are :—

1. "*The act of God*," which includes any accident due to natural causes, and such as is not due to, and could not be prevented, by human intervention. A frost is an act of God ; but where a captain filled his boiler overnight, and a frost came on and burst the tubes, the goods being thereby damaged, it was held that the acci-dent might have been prevented, and was not due to the act of God.

2. "*Perils of the sea . . . and other accidents of naviga-tion.*"—Perils of the sea is a phrase used to cover any damage to the goods carried, by sea-water, storms, collisions, strandings, occurring to a vessel at sea and arising out of the sea. The damage must result directly from a peril connected with the sea, such as being wrecked, collision with an iceberg, rough weather, and not from perils which, though occurring when the vessel is at sea, are not peculiar to the sea, such as ordinary wear and tear or the bursting of boilers. The master is bound to take all reasonable care to avoid perils of the sea, and if he does not do so, the shipowner will be liable.

3. *"Fire."*—This exception will protect the shipowner from liability for damage caused by fire.

4. *"Barratry of the master and crew."* — Barratry is any criminal or fraudulent act on the part of the master of a ship, or the mariners, causing damage to the cargo, *e.g.* boring holes in a ship to scuttle it, breach of port rules resulting in detention of the ship, or fraudulent deviation from the course.

5. *"Enemies."*—This refers to damage by the enemies of the State to which the vessel belongs during a war.

6. *"Arrests or restraints of princes, rulers, and peoples."* —This exception does not refer to ordinary legal proceedings, but to the seizure of the vessel by a State, or the ships of a State. For instance, if the vessel is seized whilst running a blockade, it is liable to be confiscated by the squadron that is blockading the port. If France were at war with Germany, and France were to blockade a German port by prohibiting access to it through the presence of a French squadron, an English vessel trying to enter such port would be liable to capture and confiscation.

7. *"Strandings and collisions."*—Strandings and collisions may be perils of the sea, and therefore come under a former heading, but in some cases they would not be regarded as perils. The proviso exempts the shipowner from liability even when the stranding or collision is "occasioned by negligence, default, or error of judgment of the pilot, master, mariners, or other servants of the shipowners."

All the above exceptions are subject to the following limitations :—" Nothing herein contained shall exempt the shipowner from liability to pay for damage to cargo occasioned by bad stowage, by improper or insufficient dunnage[1] or ventilation, or by improper opening of valves, sluices, and ports, or by causes other than those above excepted ; and all the above exceptions are conditional on the vessel being seaworthy when she sails on the voyage."

§ 227. Damage excepted.

" Loss or damage occasioned by decay, putrefaction,

[1] Provision to protect the goods from damage by contact with the bottom or sides of the vessel.

K

rust, sweat, change of character,[1] drainage, leakage,[2] breakage, or any loss or damage arising from the nature of the goods or the insufficiency of packages " (clause *i*).

This clause protects the shipowner from liability arising from the nature of the goods, or the insufficiency of the packing, provided the goods have been stowed with reasonable care.

"*Land damage*," *i.e.* damage arising after the goods are landed, is also an exception (clause *j*).

§ 228. "**Obliteration of marks or numbers**" may cause the goods to go astray, their identity being, it may be, destroyed.   For this the shipowner takes no liability (clause *k*).

A further clause (*q*) provides that the ship shall not be liable for incorrect delivery of packages unless each of them shall have been distinctly marked by the shippers before shipment.

§ 229. "**Loss or damage caused by the prolongation of the voyage.**"—The shipowner cannot foresee what will be the length of the voyage, and therefore undertakes no liability for damage to perishable articles through the voyage being prolonged (clause *l*).

§ 230. **Quarantine.**—Provision is usually made to protect the shipowner from liability in case the ship is prevented from entering the port by quarantine regulations. A vessel coming from a port at which cholera or certain other infectious diseases prevail, is generally isolated for a certain time at any port at which she calls (clause *o*).

§ 231. **Demurrage.**—This term is used to denote an agreed sum that the charterer is to pay for any delay beyond the time stipulated for loading or unloading.   For example, the clause "ten days for loading, and demurrage at £20 per day afterwards," means that if a longer period than ten days be taken for loading or unloading, the charterer is to pay the shipowner £20 per day for every additional day.

[1] *e.g.* by fruit becoming over-ripe.
[2] But the shipowner will remain liable for damage to goods from the leakage of other goods.

Where no sum is agreed, the shipowner has a claim for damages for detention, though the term demurrage is often used to cover such claim for damages.

Demurrage begins to run when the days allowed, called lay-days, have expired. The lay-days begin when the ship arrives at the agreed place for loading or unloading, and is ready to load or discharge. It is usual to except from the lay-days Sundays and holidays, otherwise such days would count.

If no time be fixed for loading or unloading, the law implies that a reasonable time is allowed, and if such time be exceeded, either demurrage or damages for detention is payable. A bill of lading may contain a stipulation as to demurrage (clause *n*), and every bill of lading implies that the goods will be unloaded within a reasonable time.

§ 232. **General Average.**—Where an extraordinary loss is incurred for the preservation of the ship and cargo, all who are interested in such preservation must contribute to the loss. This claim gives rise to a general average contribution. When, for example, cargo is thrown overboard to save the ship, or is injured by water in putting out a fire, or sold to raise money to carry out necessary repairs, or where masts or tackle are cut away to right the ship, all parties concerned must contribute to the loss.

The parties interested are (1) the shipowner or charterer, who desires to save the ship and earn the freight, and (2) the cargo-owner. The master is the one to collect the contributions, but as a rule the amounts to be paid are adjusted at the termination of the voyage by specialists, called average adjustors. Certain rules, known as the York-Antwerp Rules, relative to general average are often incorporated in a bill of lading (clause *s*).

§ 233. **Salvage.**—Where a ship and cargo are saved from loss or damage by the efforts of another vessel, the captain and crew of such other vessel are entitled to a payment known as salvage. The ship and the cargo contribute separately, as the ship is not obliged to contribute for the salvage of the cargo, and *vice versa*. Where life is saved, the ship or the cargo, or both if also saved, may have to contribute life salvage. Where the amount to be paid cannot be agreed upon, it will be fixed by the Admiralty Court.

§ 234. **Bottomry.**—Money is sometimes advanced to the master of a ship upon the security of the cargo, upon the condition that it is only to be repaid if the ship reaches its destination safely. The document embodying such an arrangement is called a bottomry bond. The master has no power to raise money in this way unless no other course is open. If, for example, he could borrow on his own personal credit or on that of the shipowner, he is not justified in resorting to a bond. The money must be borrowed in the interests of the cargo, *e.g.* to enable the cargo to be carried in safety: the bond, in other words, must be one that is beneficial to the cargo-owner. If communication with the cargo-owner is possible, the master must wait his instructions; but if no instructions are sent within a reasonable time, he may raise the money. No more must be borrowed than is necessary, as the nature of the contract necessitates the payment of a high rate of interest.

§ 235. **Powers and Duties of the Master.**—Reference has been made in the preceding sections to the acts of the master of a vessel. It may be convenient to bring together some of his more important powers.

Primarily the master is the agent of the shipowner: necessity may make him the agent of the cargo-owner. In the absence of express instructions, the master ought always to communicate with the shipowner or the cargo-owner and take their instructions: when this is impossible he can act himself. But under such circumstances whatever he does he must be prepared to justify on the ground of necessity, it is not sufficient that he act in good faith.

The master of a ship as the agent of the shipowner is bound to do everything necessary to carry out the contract or contracts made between the shipper or shippers and the shipowner. From this principle flow both his powers and his duties.

As agent of the shipowner the master may—

1. Deviate from the usual course in order to protect the ship and cargo from imminent peril.
2. Tranship the goods into another vessel where he is prevented through excepted perils from completing the voyage.
3. Throw overboard a part of the cargo in case of necessity.
4. Make a salvage agreement on behalf of the ship.

As agent of the cargo-owner the master may—
1. Sell damaged goods where this is the wisest course, provided he cannot communicate with the cargo-owner.
2. Borrow money on the security of the cargo in case of necessity.
3. Make a salvage agreement on behalf of the cargo.

§ 236. **Authorities.**—*Charter-parties and Bills of Lading*, by T. E. Scrutton, contains a concise digest of the law. The standard treatises on shipping by Mr. Abbott and Mr. Maclaghlan discuss the subject in detail. A shorter account will be found in Smith's *Mercantile Law*.

CHAPTER VII

BILLS, NOTES, CHEQUES, AND I.O.U.s

§ 237. Mercantile Instruments.—The greater portion of mercantile transactions are carried out by means of credit. Whenever a seller of goods, instead of taking cash at once in payment, gives time for payment, he is said to give credit. Custom has made usual the use of documents or instruments by which the buyer promises to pay the debt. The chief credit instruments are bills of exchange and cheques, but promissory notes and I.O.U.s are also met with.

BILLS OF EXCHANGE

§ 238. Form.—A bill of exchange is a written promise to pay a sum of money on demand or at the expiration of a given time.[1] The person who gives the promise is called the acceptor, the person to whom the promise is given is called the drawer. Every bill of exchange may, like other contracts, be resolved into a proposal and an acceptance. The proposal takes the following form :—

---

[1] The following definition is given in the Bills of Exchange Act 1882 : "A bill is an unconditional order given in writing, addressed by one person to another, signed by the person granting it, requiring the person to whom it is addressed to pay on demand, or at a fixed or determinable future time, a certain sum in money to the order of a specified person or to bearer."

LONDON, *1st January* 1893.

£1000

One month after date pay to my order One Thousand Pounds.

To C. D.   A. B.

This form is merely a request or proposal made by A. B. to C. D., asking C. D. to pay £1000 one month after the 1st January 1893. C. D. by writing the word "accepted" across the bill and signing his name and delivering the bill to the drawer, undertakes to comply with the request, and if the bill be duly stamped, a valid contract arises between the parties.

§ 239. Inland and Foreign Bills.—Bills of exchange are either inland or foreign. An inland bill is one which is or purports to be both drawn and payable within the British Islands. Any other bill is a foreign bill. A foreign bill usually consists of a set of three bills, each bill being numbered and containing a reference to the other bills. These bills being transmitted separately, the risk of losing the bill is greatly diminished, as any one bill of the set being paid, the other two bills of the set are of no use.

The following is a form of a foreign bill :—

LONDON, *1st January* 1893.

For Rs. 550.

At sixty days after sight of this first of exchange (second and third unpaid), pay to the order of C. D. Five hundred and fifty rupees value received of them, and place the same to account.

To E. F.   A. B.

§ 240. Amount.—The amount is usually specified in figures on the upper left-hand corner, and in writing in the body of the instrument.

§ 241. Stamp.—A bill, if drawn and made payable in the

United Kingdom, should be stamped with the proper stamp, *i.e.*—

Where it does not exceed £5	.	.	.	1d.
Where it exceeds £5 and does not exceed £10	.			2d.
,, £10 ,, £25	.			3d.
,, £25 ,, £50	.			6d.
,, £50 ,, £75	.			9d.
,, £75 ,, £100	.			1s.
For every £100, and also for every fractional part of £100	. . . . . .		.	1s.

If the bill is payable on demand, and the amount of the stamp is 1d., an adhesive stamp may be used : in all other cases an impressed stamp is required. A bill drawn abroad requires no stamp, unless it is expressed to be payable, or is endorsed or paid, in the United Kingdom. Any person issuing, endorsing, transferring, or paying a bill not being duly stamped, is liable to a penalty of £10, and the person taking the bill cannot recover on it.

§ 242. **Date.**—A bill should be dated, but if not dated it is not invalid, as it is regarded as dating from the time it was issued, *i.e.* from the date of delivery of the bill by the acceptor to the drawer.

§ 243. **The Time for Payment.**—The parties may, in the bill, fix a time for payment, which may be at the expiration of a given time from the date of the bill, as in the first example above given. The time may be fixed with reference to the presentation of the bill to C. D. for payment, or it may be when payment is demanded. If no time be fixed, the bill is payable on demand.

Though a bill need not be presented for payment in order to charge the acceptor, it must be so presented to charge the drawer or an endorser. If the bill be payable on demand, it should be presented within a reasonable time after its issue ; if not payable on demand, then presentment should be made on the day it is due, three days of grace being added to the time of payment, the bill being regarded as due on the last of these days. If the last day of grace falls on Sunday, Christmas Day, or Good Friday, the bill is payable on the previous day : if the last day is on a bank holiday (other than Christmas Day and Good Friday), or if the last day of grace is a Sunday, and the previous day is a bank holiday, the bill is payable on the succeeding business day.

§ 244. **The Place of Payment.**—It is desirable that the parties should specify the place of payment. If no place be specified, but the acceptor's address is given in the bill, it is payable at such address. The acceptor may fix the place of payment when accepting, but in order to do so he must not only accept the bill to pay at a particular place, but state that it is to be paid there and nowhere else.

If no place of payment or address be given in the bill, the place of payment is the place of business of the acceptor, if known, but if not known, then his ordinary residence. If neither his place of business nor his ordinary residence be known, the place of payment is wherever he can be found, or his last known place of business or residence.

§ 245. **The Position of the Acceptor.**—The acceptor engages to pay the bill. If, however, he has accepted with certain qualifications, *e.g.* as to time, or place, or amount, he is only bound to pay subject to such qualifications. As far as the acceptor's liability is concerned, he is not entitled to any presentation of the bill for payment, or any demand of the money due. It is, however, usual and desirable to present a bill for payment when due. If the bill be not paid by the acceptor, it is said to be dishonoured.

§ 246. **Transfer.**—A bill of exchange may be transferred by the holder unless it contains words prohibiting any transfer. A bill payable to bearer is transferred by delivery : a bill payable to order is transferred by endorsement of the holder, followed by delivery. The transfer of a bill payable to bearer by delivery without endorsement imposes no liability on the transferrer, but a transfer by endorsement and delivery imposes important duties on the parties, and it is therefore necessary to examine the position of the drawer, of the endorser, and of the holder.

§ 247. **Position of the Drawer.**—Where the amount is payable to the drawer, he has only to receive the amount. But if the amount is payable to a third party, the drawer, in case the bill be not paid by the acceptor, is liable to pay the amount to the third party or the holder. The drawer may also, by endorsing a bill, become liable to the holder. His liability, however, is in every case subject to the conditions that the bill be presented for payment, and that if not paid, notice of such non-payment (called notice of dishonour) be duly given to him. Presentation of the bill for payment, though, as we have seen, it cannot be required by the acceptor, is all important as regards the position of a third party, into whose hand the bill comes. A holder (other than the drawer) cannot, in case of non-payment by the acceptor, make the drawer liable unless he has presented the bill for payment to the acceptor. Not only must the holder present the bill for payment to the acceptor, but if it is not duly paid he must at once give notice of the non-payment to the drawer. Such notice must be given within a reasonable time. If the parties live in the same place, the notice should reach the drawer the day after the day of dishonour : if the parties live in different places, notice should be posted the day after the day of dishonour.

§ 248. **Position of an Endorser.**—The person to whom the drawer endorses a bill may in turn transfer it by endorsement and delivery to some one else. The question then arises what is the position of an endorser. The rule is that every endorser of a bill is in the nature of a new drawer, and is liable to every subsequent holder in default of payment by the acceptor. This liability is subject to the rules already referred to relating to presentation for payment and notice of dishonour.

§ 249. **Position of the Holder.**—The holder is the person in possession of the bill. The law presumes that a bill is given for a sufficient consideration, but it is open to any party sued on a bill to show that there was no consideration given. For example, if A. by way of doing B. a favour accepts a bill drawn by B., and B. brings an action against A., it is open to A. to show that B. gave him no consideration for the bill, and in such a case B. cannot recover. If, however, the holder took the bill before it was due in good faith, and gave value for it, and had no notice of any defects in title, it will be immaterial that the bill was given originally without any consideration. For instance, if B. in the above case discounts the bill with C., then C. can sue A. for its amount. The holder cannot sue on a forged bill. In order to protect himself, the holder must be careful to present the bill when due at the proper place, and if it be dishonoured, to give notice to the drawer and every endorser. In the case of a foreign bill the dishonour should be noted by protest. The protest should be made by a notary public at the place where the dishonour occurs. The protest is a solemn declaration signed by the notary containing a copy of the bill and specifying amongst other things the reason of protesting, and place and date of protest, as well as the name of the person at whose request the bill is protested. The protest will be good evidence of the dishonour of the bill in case an action is brought in a foreign court.

§ 250. **Example.**—An example summing up the different rules may now be given.

A. B. is the drawer.

C. D. the acceptor.

E. F. the person to whom A. B. transfers the bill.

G. H. the person to whom E. F. transfers the bill.

G. H. becomes the holder, and if the bill has been transferred by endorsement and delivery, A. B., C. D., and E. F. are endorsers.

C. D. is bound to pay the bill whether it be presented or not.

A. B. is bound to pay G. H. the holder if C. D. does not pay, provided G. H. has presented the bill for payment and has given A. B. notice of non-payment.

E. F. is also liable to pay G. H. in case of non-payment by C. D., provided the bill was duly presented for payment and notice of dishonour given to him.

G. H. if not paid by C. D. may proceed against either C. D., A. B., or E. F., provided he has presented the bill for payment and given notice of dishonour, but he can only recover the amount of the bill and the costs to which he has been put. As a rule he will sue all parties at one and the same time.

§ 251. **Definition.**—A cheque is an order given to a bank by a customer requesting the bank to pay a sum of money to the person named or to the bearer on demand.[1]

A cheque differs from a bill of exchange in several points.

A bill requires to be accepted in order to charge the acceptor ; a cheque is never accepted by a bank, and the holder has no remedy against the bank in case of dishonour. A bill must be presented for payment in due time, otherwise the drawer is discharged ; failure to present a cheque in due time does not discharge the drawer unless the bank fails. In the case of a bill, notice of dishonour must usually be given ; in the case of a cheque this is rarely necessary, as the want of effects excuses such notice.

§ 252. **"And Co." "not negotiable."**—It is not unusual to write across a cheque the words "and Co." between two transverse lines ; these words amount, though two tranverse lines without any words are sufficient, to a direction by the drawer to his bank to pay the cheque only when it is presented for payment by another bank. If a bank be specified, payment can be obtained only through that bank.

The words "not negotiable" may also be written across a cheque. Where a crossed cheque bears the words "not negotiable" the holder takes no better title than the person had from whom he took it.

The holder of an uncrossed cheque may cross it, and the holder of a crossed cheque may add the words "not negotiable."

§ 253. **Duty of Bank.**—A bank is bound to honour a customer's cheques so long as there is a balance to the credit of such customer's account. This results from the implied contract entered into between the bank and the customer when an account is opened. Notice of the death

---

[1] The Bills of Exchange Act 1882 defines a cheque as a bill of exchange drawn on a banker payable on demand.

of a customer determines the authority of a bank to pay cheques drawn by such customer before his death.

§ 254. **Presentation of Cheques.**—A cheque should be presented for payment within a reasonable time, as the holder by delay takes the risk as regards the drawer of the failure of the bank, and an endorser after unreasonable delay will be discharged from liability. By reasonable time is meant the day after the cheque has been received. Where it has to be sent by post to an agent for collection, it should be posted not later than the day after it is received, and the agent should present it not later than the day after he receives it.

§ 255. **Promissory Notes.**—A promissory note is a promise in writing by which one person undertakes to pay another a certain sum of money. Delivery of the note by the maker to the other person is essential to make the note complete, and the note should be stamped with the proper stamp. The money may be made payable on demand or at a fixed time. The person to whom the money is to be paid may be a specified person or the bearer. The following is a form :—

LONDON, 1st January 1893.

£100

On demand [*or* at sight, *or*   days after sight, *or* days after date, *or* on the   day of   ] I promise to pay C. D. [*or* C. D. or order, *or* C. D. or bearer, *or* bearer] one hundred pounds.   A. B.

A bank-note is an example of a promissory note in which the promise is given by a bank.

The maker of the note promises to pay it : no presentation for payment is necessary to charge him, but such presentation is necessary to charge an endorser if the note has been endorsed.

§ 256. **I.O.U.s**—An I.O.U. is an acknowledgment of a debt, such acknowledgment implying a promise to repay the money.

The following is the usual form :—

                                        1st January 1893.
A. B.
                    I.O.U. £100.
                                                A. B.

No stamp is·required, but if any words are added to show that the money is to be paid on a given day or even on demand, the I.O.U. becomes a promissory note, and a stamp is necessary.

An I.O.U. is not negotiable.

§ 257. **Authorities.** — The law relating to bills of exchange has been embodied in an Act of Parliament. Byles on Bills, or Chalmers on Bills, contains the Act with notes. *Practical Banking*, by T. B. Moxon, can be recommended to those engaged in banks.

PART IV

BANKRUPTCY

§ 258. **Principle involved.**—The law of bankruptcy is based on the principle that if a person is unable to pay his debts in full, his property should be taken to satisfy his creditors as far as it will go, he himself being discharged from any further liability in respect of such debts. The first English statute on the subject was directed against fraudulent debtors. Subsequently bankruptcy was restricted to traders, but now any person (with some exceptions), whether a trader or not, may take advantage of the bankruptcy laws.

§ 259. **The Board of Trade.**—The Board of Trade is entrusted with very important powers and duties in all cases of bankruptcy. All moneys received by a trustee are paid into an account kept by the Board with the Bank of England, called " The Bankruptcy Estates Account," except when the committee of inspection (§ 269) or the Board of Trade think it desirable to have the money paid to a local bank. Any local account has to be kept in the name of the debtor's estate.

The Board of Trade appoints the official receivers (§ 264) and other officers. It has also power to issue general orders of an administrative character; and may alter the form of all official documents not of a judicial nature.

§ 260. Acts of Bankruptcy.

§ 260. Acts of Bankruptcy. — Proceedings in bankruptcy are commenced by a creditor presenting a petition in the proper court alleging that the debtor has committed an "act of bankruptcy." The following are acts of bankruptcy :—

1. Where the debtor departs out of or remains out of England, or departs from his dwelling-house, or otherwise absents himself, or begins to keep house, with the object of defeating or delaying his creditors.
2. When he assigns his property to trustees for the benefit of his creditors generally ; or
3. Assigns his property or part thereof with the object of defrauding or defeating or delaying his creditors.
4. Where he assigns his property or part thereof, or creates any charge with the object of fraudulently benefiting one or more of his creditors at the expense of the others.
5. Where he files in court a declaration of inability to pay debts.
6. Where he permits an execution to be levied by seizure of his goods under an order of the court, and the goods are sold or held by the sheriff for twenty-one days.

   When judgment is recovered in an action, if the amount claimed be not paid, the creditor issues execution, *i.e.* he sets the sheriff in motion, and the sheriff seizes the goods of the debtor, and holds them until the debt is paid or sells them.
7. A creditor who obtains judgment may serve the debtor with a notice requiring him to pay, and if he does not do so within a given time, he commits an act of bankruptcy.
8. Where the debtor gives notice to any of his creditors that he has suspended or is about to suspend payment of his debts.

§ 261. Who may be made Bankrupt. — Any person who can enter into a binding contract may, as a rule, be made bankrupt. A person under twenty-one years cannot be made bankrupt since he cannot make binding contracts except for necessaries. A married woman may be made bankrupt where she can contract as if she were a single woman, *e.g.* where she carries on trade in the city of London. And a married woman carrying on trade in respect of her separate estate (§ 45) may be made bankrupt in respect of such separate estate. But if she is not carrying on trade, she cannot be made bankrupt though she possesses separate estate.

§ 262. **Who can petition.**—A person may petition to have himself adjudicated a bankrupt, but as a rule a petition is presented by a creditor who cannot obtain payment of his debt. The following conditions must be fulfilled in order to enable a creditor to petition :—

(*a*) The debt due must be at least £50.

(*b*) The debt must be an ascertained amount. The price of goods bought is ascertained, but a claim for damages is unascertained.

(*c*) The debt must be payable immediately or at some certain future time.

(*d*) The act of bankruptcy must have occurred within three months before the presentation of the petition.

(*e*) The debtor must reside in England, or within a year before the presentation of the petition have resided or had a place of business in England.

§ 263. **Order of Adjudication.**—When the petition is presented by a creditor, the court requires proof of the debt and of the act of bankruptcy. It must also be shown that the debtor had notice of the petition. If the court is satisfied that an act of bankruptcy has been committed, it will make a "receiving order," which has the immediate effect of making the official called the "official receiver" the receiver of all the property of the debtor, with certain exceptions, and deprives the creditors of power to bring any actions against the bankrupt for their debts.

§ 264. **The Official Receiver.**—The Board of Trade has appointed a number of official receivers, who have important duties to discharge. The debtor is always examined by an official receiver, who makes a report to the

court on the debtor's conduct, and especially as to whether
the debtor has done any act that would justify the court in
refusing, suspending, or modifying an order for discharge
(§ 275).

Pending the appointment of a trustee (§ 268) or special
manager, he has charge of all the property of the debtor ;
he summons and presides at meetings of creditors ; and he
makes a report to the creditors on any proposal of the
debtor regarding the payment of the debts.

§ 265. Special Manager.—Where it is necessary in the
interests of the estate that a special manager should be
appointed, the official may make such appointment on the
application of any creditor. The special manager has to
give security for the performance of his duties, and may be
removed by the official receiver. The creditors may
require his removal. If it is necessary for the special
manager to raise money to carry on the business, he must
get the assent of the official receiver.

§ 266. Public Examination of the Debtor.—When the
court makes a receiving order, it appoints a day for the
examination of the debtor, and the debtor is required to
attend. The debtor is also required to furnish the official
receiver with a statement of affairs showing the particulars
of the debtor's liabilities, debts, assets, the names and
addresses of the creditors, the securities (if any) held by
them, and any other information the official receiver may
require. At the public examination questions may be put
by the official receiver or by any creditor who has tendered
a proof of a debt (§ 270). The evidence of the debtor is
taken on oath, and the examination cannot be declared
closed until after the first meeting of creditors.

§ 267. First General Meeting.—Within fourteen days
after the receiving order is made, a general meeting of
creditors, at which the debtor must be present, is called by
the official receiver. Each creditor is entitled to have sent
him a summary of the debtor's statement of affairs,
accompanied by any observations the official receiver may
think fit to make. The creditors at this meeting may
resolve that the debtor be adjudged a bankrupt, or may agree

to accept a scheme put forward by the debtor (§ 279). The resolution in favour of bankruptcy must be carried by a majority "in value" of the creditors present, personally or by proxy, *i.e.* each vote is estimated at the amount of the debt due to the voter. The court will subsequently adjudge the debtor bankrupt, and thereupon his property becomes available for the payment of his debts.

§ 268. **The Trustee.**—When the creditors have resolved that the debtor be adjudged bankrupt, the creditors may appoint a fit person to be trustee of the property of the bankrupt, but they may leave the appointment to the committee of inspection (§ 269). Until the trustee is appointed the official receiver acts as trustee. If the creditors do not appoint a trustee, the Board of Trade may appoint, but a trustee subsequently appointed by the creditors will displace the trustee appointed by the Board of Trade.

On his appointment all the property of the bankrupt passes to the trustee. The chief duties of the trustee are to take possession or get in all the debtor's property liable for payment of his debts, to keep books and accounts, to pay all moneys received into the Bank of England, and to declare and pay dividends from time to time.

The chief powers of the trustee are to get in all the property of the bankrupt, to sell any part of such property, to hold property, to make contracts, to give receipts, to prove in bankruptcy when the bankrupt is a creditor, and to summon meetings of the creditors. The powers he can exercise with the consent of the committee of inspection are enumerated in another section (§ 269).

§ 269. **The Committee of Inspection.**—The creditors may appoint a committee of their own number qualified to vote, of not less than three and not more than five, to be a "committee of inspection." The duty of such committee is to superintend the administration of the bankrupt's estate by the trustee, and to give directions to the trustee subject to the views of the creditors assembled in general meeting.

The committee are entitled to see the record and cash books kept by the trustee, and once in every three months it is to audit the cash-book. The trustee requires the

consent of the committee to employ a solicitor, to mortgage the property of the bankrupt, to carry on the business,
to sue for debts, to refer disputes to arbitration, to compromise any debt or claim between the bankrupt and third
parties, to compromise debts and claims provable, or to
divide property amongst the creditors in specie.

§ 270. **Proof of Debts.**—Before a claim is admitted
against the estate of the bankrupt, the creditor must prove
it by sending to the official receiver an affidavit or sworn
declaration that the debt is due, full particulars of such
debt being given. The official receiver hands over all
proofs to the trustee to examine. Within twenty-eight
days after receiving a proof, the trustee must state in writing
whether he admits or rejects it. A creditor whose proof is
rejected may appeal to the court, and when a proof is
accepted the trustee, and in some cases a creditor, may
ask the court to expunge it. Only debts proved are
entitled to be paid out of the assets, and, as a rule, only
creditors who have proved their debts can vote at meetings.

§ 271. **Secured Debts.**—A creditor may have his debt
"secured." For instance, the debt may be £1000, and the
creditor may have a mortgage on part of the debtor's
property. Where a secured creditor proves his debt, he
must give particulars of the security he holds and state its
value. The trustee may call on the creditor to give up
his security for the benefit of the estate, on being paid its
estimated value with an addition of 20 per cent. At
meetings he is entitled to vote only in respect of the
balance, if any, due to him after deducting the value of the
security. Suppose, for example, in the above case the
mortgage is only worth £750, then the creditor's voting
power is represented by £250.

§ 272. **Property available for paying Debts.**—

1. All the bankrupt's moveable property, wherever
   situate, except the tools of his trade, the wearing
   apparel and bedding of himself, his wife, and his
   children, not exceeding £20 on the whole.
2. All the bankrupt's immoveable property, *e.g.* land,
   or leaseholds, situate in Her Majesty's dominions.

Immoveable property situate in foreign countries will pass to the trustee when the bankrupt makes a conveyance to him.

3. All goods that belong to other persons, but which at the commencement of the bankruptcy are in the possession, order, or disposition of the bankrupt under the following conditions :—

(a) The goods must be in his possession in the course of his trade or business.

(b) They must be in his possession by consent of the owner.

(c) The possession must be under such circumstances that the bankrupt is the reputed owner.

The principle on which such goods are made liable is that persons are led to give credit to the bankrupt because he is supposed to be owner of the goods.

4. Property that the bankrupt has professed to assign away to others previous to the bankruptcy, in a manner not recognised by law, where bankruptcy ensues. Where property is conveyed by a person who receives no consideration for it, and such person becomes bankrupt within two years, the trustee may recover the property for the creditors ; and if he becomes bankrupt subsequently within ten years from the date of the conveyance, the trustee can recover the property, unless the bankrupt shows that at the time of the conveyance he was perfectly solvent. Any settlement of property outside of such ten years may be set aside if it was fraudulent, *i.e.* made to delay or defeat creditors.

§ 273. **Disclaimer of onerous Property.**—If any portion of the bankrupt's property is burthened with onerous covenants, or consists of stocks or shares in companies, or of unprofitable contracts, or of any other property that is unsaleable by reason of its binding the possessor to the performance of onerous acts, the trustee may, instead of accepting the same, disclaim it, and thereupon he is discharged from any liability in respect of the property. A lease, for example, binds the lessee to pay rent, to repair, to insure, etc., and the trustee who accepts the lease will find himself bound to perform all these covenants. The disclaimer must take place within three months after the trustee is appointed, or within two months after he first becomes aware of the existence of the property. In the case of leases, the consent of the court is necessary for disclaimer, except in certain cases.

§ 274. **Payment of Dividends.**—The first charge on the estate of a bankrupt is the expense of administering the estate, and it is the duty of the trustee to retain out of the assets an amount sufficient to meet such expense. Subject to this, the trustee is required to declare and distribute dividends amongst the creditors who have proved their debts.

The first dividend should be distributed within four months after the conclusion of the first meeting of creditors, unless the committee of inspection are satisfied that there is good ground for postponing such distribution. Subsequent dividends are to be declared and distributed at intervals of not more than six months.

When all the property has been realised, a final dividend is declared. Notice of the intention to pay a final dividend is given to those creditors who have not established their claim, and if they fail to establish their claim to the satisfaction of the trustee within a fixed time, they are excluded from the distribution.

§ 275. **Discharge of Bankrupt.**—A bankrupt may at any time apply to the court for his discharge. The court, on hearing the application, will take into account the report of the official receiver on the conduct of the bankrupt. In this report the official receiver is required to state whether the bankrupt has committed any criminal act under the Debtors Act of 1869, or any act that would justify the court in refusing, suspending, or qualifying the order of discharge. The court is bound to refuse the discharge if any such criminal act has been committed ; and it is bound, except where for special reasons it otherwise determines, either (a) to refuse the discharge, or (b) to suspend it for not less than two years, or (c) to suspend it until a dividend of at least 10s. in the £ be paid, or (*d*) to require the bankrupt to consent to judgment being entered against him for any balance of debts not paid at the date of the discharge, such balance to be payable out of future earnings, in the following cases :—

1. Where the assets are not sufficient to pay 10s. in the £, unless this is due to circumstances for which he is not responsible.
2. Where he omitted to keep proper books of account during the three years preceding his bankruptcy.
3. Where he continued to trade knowing he was insolvent.
4. Where he contracted a debt without having reasonable ground of expecting to be able to pay.
5. Where the bankruptcy was due to rash and hazardous speculation, or to unjustifiable extravagance in living.
6. Where he put any creditor to unnecessary expense by a frivolous or vexatious defence to an action.
7. Where he, within three months of the date of the receiving order, being unable to pay his debts, gave an undue preference to any of his creditors.
8. Where he has been bankrupt previously, or made a composition with his creditors.
9. Where he made a fraudulent settlement of his property.

§ 276. **Effect of an Order of Discharge.**—The order of discharge releases the bankrupt from all debts provable in the bankruptcy, with certain exceptions, such as debts due to the Crown, or debts incurred by fraud to which he was a party. In respect of all discharged debts no action can be brought against him. The discharge will not affect his liability to any criminal prosecution, and he is liable to be prosecuted for any of the offences mentioned in the Bankruptcy Acts. An undischarged bankrupt who obtains credit to the extent of £20 from any person without informing such person that he is an undischarged bankrupt is liable to be prosecuted.

§ 277. **Disabilities of a Bankrupt.**—Bankruptcy disqualifies the bankrupt from holding the office of mayor, alderman, councillor, guardian, member of a sanitary authority, school board, or vestry. He cannot sit or vote in the House of Lords, or be elected to the House of Commons. If a member of the House of Commons becomes bankrupt, and the disqualification is not removed within six months, the seat becomes vacant. These disqualifications cease (1) where the adjudication of bankruptcy is annulled, (2) when the court, on granting his discharge, certifies that the bankruptcy was caused by misfortune.

A bankrupt cannot act as a trustee, but may act as an executor.

§ 278. **Annulment of Adjudication.**—The court will always annul an adjudication where the order ought not to have been made, and if a debtor pays his debts in full, or the creditors accept a scheme of arrangement, the adjudication may be annulled.

All acts done by the official receiver or trustee previous to the annulment are valid.

§ 279. **Composition or Scheme of Arrangement.**—Before the court orders a person to be adjudicated a bankrupt, the creditors may agree to a scheme of arrangement of the debtor's affairs. The debtor may, for example, offer to pay by instalments 10s. or 15s. in the £ to his creditors, and may give security for payment of the same. If such scheme be accepted, the receiving order (§ 263) will be rescinded. The resolution accepting the scheme must be adopted not only by a majority in number, but by three-fourths in value of the creditors present, personally or by proxy, and voting at the meeting, and be subsequently confirmed by a resolution passed by a majority in number representing three-fourths in value all the creditors who have proved and been approved by the court. Before the court will give its approval the official receiver must make his report on the scheme. After approval the receiving order is rescinded, and the debtor is put into possession of the property. A composition or scheme duly accepted and approved binds all the creditors, so far as any debt provable in bankruptcy is concerned, but it does not release the bankrupt from liability in certain cases, *e.g.* under a judgment as co-respondent in a divorce, unless the court makes an order to that effect.

After a man is adjudicated bankrupt, the creditors may resolve to adopt a scheme of arrangement, and if such scheme of arrangement be approved by the court, the court may annul the bankruptcy.

§ 280. **Private Arrangements with Creditors.**—A debtor may arrange with his creditors privately that each shall accept part payment in satisfaction of the whole debt due.   Such an arrangement only binds those creditors who are parties to it.   It is not necessary that the agreement should be under seal, inasmuch as the forbearance of each to sue is a consideration sufficient to make the agreement a binding contract.   Usually a deed is prepared by which, in consideration of the payment of a composition, the creditors release and discharge the debtor from the debts due.   It is important that all the creditors should join.   If one refuses, he may take bankruptcy proceedings, inasmuch as the making the composition is an act of bankruptcy (§ 260).   If bankruptcy ensue, the deed takes no effect. It must be registered, otherwise it is void under the Deeds of Arrangement Act 1887.

§ 281. **Authorities.**—The law of bankruptcy is regulated by the Bankruptcy Act of 1883, with its amending Acts of 1884, 1887, 1888, and 1890.   The student may refer with advantage to the treatises by Mr. Baldwin, Mr. Williams, and Mr. Robson.

PART V

THE APPLICATION OF LAW

§ 282. Introductory.—It has hitherto been assumed that all commercial disputes in England are governed by English law. As a general rule, the laws of a state apply to all persons and to all transactions within the state. But cases often occur where mercantile transactions are entered into in one country, but are to be performed in another country. For instance, A. and B. enter into a contract in England that is to be performed in France. Suppose a breach of this contract to take place, ought the action for damages to be brought in England or in France, and is the liability under the contract to be governed by English or by French law?

Prima facie the law of the place where the action is brought will be applied by the courts, but as a matter of commercial convenience every civilised country recognises and enforces to some extent the laws of other states.

§ 283. What is Foreign Law?—By foreign law is meant not merely the laws of foreign states, but the laws of different parts of the Empire. Ireland and Scotland have different laws from England. Each of the colonies has its own system of law. Irish, Scotch, and colonial law is, in England, regarded as foreign law.

§ 284. Land.—Land is always subject to the law of the place where it is situated. Such law governs—

1. The legal incidents that attach to its ownership;
2. The capacity of the owner to transfer it, as well as the form of transfer;
3. The capacity of the owner to leave it by will, the formalities of the will, as well as the effects of the will on the land;
4. Who is to take the land in case the owner dies without making a will.

Hence if an Englishman buys land in France, such land will in all important respects be governed by the law of France.

As is well known, a man by English law cannot marry the sister of his deceased wife; if he goes through the ceremony of marriage, any children resulting from the marriage are illegitimate. In some of the colonies such marriages are legal, and hence a child of the marriage is legitimate. But by English law such child cannot succeed to any land that his father may own in England, in case the father dies without making a will. To this extent colonial marriages with a deceased wife's sister are not recognised by the law of this country.

§ 285. Moveable Property.—The law of the " domicile " of a man at the time of his death determines—

1. His capacity to make a will, the formalities of the will, and the legal effects of the will;
2. The person who is to take out letters of administration in case of intestacy, and how the property is to be divided;
3. The duties to be paid by those who receive the property.

A distinction is drawn between (*a*) probate duty and (*b*) legacy and succession duty. The former is regarded as a part of the expense of getting in the assets, and is payable in respect of the authority given by the state to enable the assets to be collected. In the case of a will, the authority consists of the probate of the will; in the case of intestacy, it consists of letters of administration, granted in England by the Court of Probate. The duty payable on the grant is payable in the country where the assets are collected.

Legacy duty is payable on all legacies, and succession duty on all successions to land. Such duties are regarded as a tax on the succession to property, and are payable according to the law of the domicile. For instance, if an Englishman domiciled in England dies, leaving personal property in France, probate duty will be payable in France, and legacy or succession duty in England.

§ 286. **Domicile.**—Reference has been made to the law of the domicile. Two elements are required in domicile : (1) actual residence in a country, and (2) an intention to remain in such country. If an Englishman goes to France, and hires a house for twelve months, intending to return to England, he does not acquire a French domicile ; but if he takes the house intending to reside permanently in France, then he acquires for the time being a French domicile, even though he should subsequently change his mind and return to England.

Every man at his birth acquires the domicile of his father, and such domicile remains until he acquires a new one.

§ 287. **Contracts relating to Immoveables.**—All contracts relating to immoveable property, *e.g.* land, as we have seen (§ 284), is governed by the law of the state where the land is situated. The word land includes all interests in land, for example, leaseholds. The purchaser of land in a foreign country must therefore be careful to see that he observes the rules relating to the transfer of land in such country, otherwise he will not obtain a good title. He must also remember that he cannot dispose of such land except in accordance with the law of the foreign state. If, for example, the land be in France and the owner die intestate, the land will not descend to the eldest son, according to English law, but will be divided amongst all the children, according to French law.

§ 288. **Contracts relating to Moveables.**—As a general rule, a contract relating to moveable property is valid everywhere if valid by the law of the place where the contract is made. A contract is regarded as being made in the place where the offer is accepted. The validity of the contract may be considered in detail with reference to (*a*) capacity to contract; (*b*) formalities; (*c*) rights and liabilities; and (*d*) performance.

(*a*) *Capacity to Contract.*—It is doubtful in the case of mercantile contracts whether the capacity of the parties is to be referred to the law of the place where the contract is made or to the law of the domicile. The older authorities adopt the former rule, whilst the modern English authorities tend to adopt the latter law, referring all questions of capacity to the law of the domicile of the party.

(*b*) *Formalities of the Contract.* — *Prima facie* the formalities required are those of the country in which the contract is made; but there is nothing to prevent Englishmen abroad from entering into contracts according to the formalities required by English law, provided it appears that the parties contracted with reference to such law. In other words, the formalities of a contract depend on the law contemplated by the parties; but in the absence of any evidence to the contrary, the parties are presumed to contract with reference to the law of the place where the contract is entered into.

If the law contemplated requires a stamp as a part of the formalities, the contract must bear such stamp.

The formalities of a contract must be distinguished from the evidence required to prove a contract in a court of justice. The rules that govern evidence are those embodied in the law of the country where legal proceedings are taken. Hence if an action be brought in England on a foreign contract that by English law must be evidenced in writing, such written evidence must be given, though it is not required by the law of the place where the contract is made.

(*c*) *Rights and Liabilities.*—The rights and liabilities of the parties depend on the law contemplated by the parties, but there is a *prima facie* presumption in favour of the law of the place where the contract is made. A., a merchant in London, sold to B., another merchant in London, 20,000 tons of Algerian esparto, to be shipped by a French company at an Algerian port. Default was made in delivery, and B. brought an action for damages against A. It was urged that as the contract was to be performed at Algiers, the French law, which is the law of Algiers, applied, and under that law A. would not have been liable. The court held that as the contract was made in England, and as there was no evidence that the French law was contemplated by the parties, the liability of A. was to be governed by English law. "What is to be the law by which a contract, or any part of it, is to be governed or applied, must always be a matter of construction of the contract itself, as read by the light of the subject-matter and of the surrounding circumstances . . . the broad rule is that the law of the country where a contract is made presumably governs the nature, obligation, and the interpretation of it, unless the contrary appears to be the express intention of the parties."

Charter-parties and bottomry bonds are exceptions to the rule. The rights and liabilities of the parties are governed by the law of the flag, *i.e.* the law of the country to which the ship belongs.

§ 289. Bills of Exchange.—A bill of exchange may be drawn in one country and be accepted or made payable in another. The Bills of Exchange Act 1882 contains the following rules relating to such bills :—

(*a*) As far as form is concerned, the bill will be valid in England if the English law or the law of the place of issue be followed (§ 242).

(*b*) The absence of a stamp required by the foreign place of issue will not invalidate the bill.

(*c*) The holder, in presenting for acceptance or for payment, or in protesting, or in giving notice of dishonour, should observe the law of the place where the act is done, or the bill is dishonoured.

(*d*) An acceptance or endorsement should be according to the law of the place where the bill is accepted or endorsed.

(*e*) The date depends on the law of the place where the bill is payable.

§ 290. Jurisdiction in the Case of Contracts.—The

question often arises whether or not an action for breach of a contract made abroad can be brought in this country.   As a general rule, if the contract was to be performed in England and it is broken in England, the action can be brought. It is immaterial that the defendant resides in a foreign country, as the writ can, by leave of the court, be served on him in such foreign country.   If the defendant is domiciled or ordinarily resident in Scotland or in Ireland, proceedings should be taken in the country in which he resides.   Where the contract was to be performed abroad, but the defendant is resident in England, proceedings for breach can be taken against him in England.

§ 290. **Foreign Judgment.**—In some cases it may be necessary to bring an action in another country.   Suppose judgment is obtained, but the defendant's property is in England, can the foreign judgment be enforced in England ?   If the defendant appeared, and the foreign judgment was a final one, and the foreign court had jurisdiction in the case, the party who obtained judgment in his favour may bring an action in England to enforce it.   All that he requires to prove is that the foreign court had jurisdiction, and that the judgment was a final one.   He will then obtain judgment in England that can be enforced.

Instead of adopting this mode of procedure, the plaintiff may, in case the English court has jurisdiction, bring an action on the original cause of action apart from the foreign judgment.

§ 291. **Authorities.**—*Private International Jurisprudence*, by J. A. Foote ; *Private International Law*, by J. Westlake.

APPENDIX

GLOSSARY

Alien. He who is not a subject of the Crown is an alien. The status of aliens is regulated by the Naturalisation Act 1870.

Annuity. An annual payment granted to a person for life or other period. It is personal property. Frequently, however, its payment is secured by charging it on land, and then the land is a security for its payment.

Artificial Person. A number of individuals may be so united by law as to form an "artificial person," capable of acquiring legal rights and of being subject to legal duties, *e.g.* a corporation, a company, a college, a society. An artificial person is created by a charter granted by the Crown, or by Act of Parliament.

Assets. The property of a deceased person applicable to the payment of debts and legacies. The term is also used to denote the stock-in-trade and property of a trader.

Bill of Sale. A deed assigning chattels personal. The term is usually applied to mortgages of personal property. Such mortgages must be in a certain form, and be registered.

Carrier. A person who carries goods for hire. If the carrier undertakes to carry the goods of all comers, he is a "common carrier," and is answerable for the safety of the goods.

Chancery Division. The High Court of Justice is divided into two divisions; the one called the Queen's Bench Division, and the other the Chancery Division.

Charge. A charge is a burden placed on property. If A. charges his land with £100, the £100 can be raised out of the value of the land.

Charter. The Crown by a writing under seal, called a charter, can grant certain privileges to an individual, or incorporate a company.

Chattel. The term chattel covers all forms of property that do not amount to an estate for life. Chattels are divided into two classes —chattels real and chattels personal. The former is restricted to chattel interests in land, *e.g.* leaseholds ; the latter covers all other chattels.

Chose in Action. A right to bring an action.

High Court of Justice. The High Court of Justice and the Court of Appeal are the two branches of the Supreme Court of Judicature. The High Court is divided into three divisions—viz. the Chancery Division, the Queen's Bench Division, and the Probate, Admiralty, and Divorce Division.

Imprisonment for Debt. Direct imprisonment for debt has been abolished, but if a Court orders a person to pay a sum of money and he neglects to do so, he may be imprisoned for disobedience to the order of the Court.

Incorporation. The formation of an artificial person or corporation.

Judicial Separation. A husband and wife may be judicially separated without the marriage being dissolved. In this case neither party can remarry.

Law. "Every one is supposed to know the law," is a maxim acted on by the courts, on the ground that to permit a man to deny he did not know the law would encourage fraud.

Letters Patent. A writing sealed with the Great Seal. The Crown grants the monopoly of a new invention by letters patent.

Lien. The right of one person to retain property of another in his possession until a debt due is discharged.

Mortgage. The conveyance of an interest in land to secure the repayment of a sum of money.

Ownership. See *Property*.

Property. The word is often used to denote that which is the subject of ownership, but at times it means the right of ownership.

Prerogative. The Crown has certain privileges and a limited right of legislation that are referred to its prerogative, *e.g.* in virtue of its powers the Crown can incorporate a company.

Personal Representatives. The personal representatives of a deceased person are his executors where he has made a will and appointed executors, or the administrator appointed by the Court of Probate where he has made no will.

M

Resolution. Under the Companies Acts a special resolution is a resolution passed at one meeting and confirmed at another. The majority required at the first meeting is a three-fourths, and at the second meeting a simple majority of the members present in person or by proxy.

An extraordinary resolution is one passed by three-fourths of those present personally or by proxy.

Security. Anything that makes the payment of money due more assured is a security in the wide sense of the term, *e.g.* a bill of exchange. In a narrower sense of the term the word is used to denote that the payment of money is secured by being charged on property.

Set of Bills. Bills of lading as well as bills of exchange are usually issued in sets of three ; that is to say, three copies are issued : one copy being used, the remaining copies are void.

Title. As applied to mercantile property, this term is used to denote the right to property as regards the method of transfer or the capacity of the grantor to transfer it.

Trustee. A person who holds property for the benefit of another is called a trustee.

Ultra vires. Where a company exceeds its powers it is said to act *ultra vires.*

Underwriting. Reference has been made in the text to the use of this term in insurance. It is also used to denote a guarantee that if the public do not take up all the shares in a company that is being brought out, the person giving the guarantee will take up a certain portion of the shares.

Winding-up. The process by which the existence of a company is terminated. It is initiated by a petition.

Wrong. The terms "wrong," "wrongful act," and "tort," are each used to denote the infringement of certain legal rights not arising out of contract. The injured party has an action for damages.

PROPOSAL FOR LIFE INSURANCE

If any change has taken place in the Name it should be stated.	Name, Residence, Profession or Occupation of the Person whose Life is to be Assured ?	
Proof should be furnished in order that the Policy may be Indisputable.	Place and Date of Birth ?	
	Has the Life been proposed to any other Office ? If so, name the Office and the result of the Proposal	
	Name and Residence of usual Medical Attendant; how long has he known you ?	
	Name and Residence of any other Medical Gentleman consulted within the past seven years ?	
If no Medical Attendant, a second Private Reference should be named.	Name and Residence of an intimate Private Friend ; how long has he known you ?	
	Sum to be assured ? With or without Profits ? Term for which Assurance is required ?	
This question need only be answered when the Proposal is on the Life of another person.	Name, Residence, and Occupation of the Person in whose favour the Policy is to be granted ?	

I declare the above statements are true ; that the Private and Medical Referees named are competent to give information as to past and present state of health and habits of life ; and I agree that such Statements, together with those made *or to be made to the Medical Officers of the Society and signed* by me, shall be the basis of the proposed contract of Assurance.

Signature of the Person whose }
Life is to be Assured. }

Witness

Date

The Policy, on the age being admitted, will be indisputable except on the ground of fraud.

FORM OF LIFE POLICY

No.

Sum Assured £   *Premium £*

WHEREAS
(hereinafter called The Life Assured), whose age is admitted not to exceed   years, has this day paid to the
                ASSURANCE SOCIETY the sum of
                as a first Premium on this Policy and
                        the like Premium is to be paid on the same day in every future year during the whole survivorship of The Life Assured in order to keep this Policy on foot :

Now these Presents witness, That on the death of The Life Assured and on due proof given of the death and of title, the Society will pay to the executors, administrators, or assigns, of The Life Assured the sum of   pounds, together with any BONUS which according to the provisions of the Deed of Settlement of the Society may at the time of such death be attached to this Policy :

Provided That this Policy is granted upon the following conditions, that is to say :—

(1) That payment of every Premium, which is to be paid as above mentioned, be made within Thirty Days from the day fixed for payment thereof ; and if so made, this Policy shall remain in force notwithstanding the death of The Life Assured during such thirty days.

(2) That, if The Life Assured commit suicide within one year from the date of this Policy, all money which would otherwise have become payable for the benefit of his estate under this Policy shall be forfeited and belong to the Society ; but this condition shall not prejudice the interest in such money of any Assignee for value.

Provided also That the Society's Assurance Fund for the time being, and the Proprietors' Fund on the first day of
(which then amounted to the sum of £   ), and so much of the Capital of the Society, held in Shares by the Proprietors and others, as on the said first day of   had not been paid up or according to the provisions of the Deed of Settlement been considered as paid up (such Proprietors' Fund and Capital amounting together to the sum of *One Million Pounds Sterling*), shall alone be liable to any claim or demand in respect of this Policy ; and no

Director signing this Policy, nor any other Proprietor, shall be liable to any claim or demand in respect thereof beyond the unpaid portion of the Capital held by him. And as to the Proprietors' Fund, nothing herein contained is to be construed to give to any person entitled to the benefit of this Policy any charge or claim on any accumulation thereof made, or to be made, after the thirty-first day of

In witness whereof We, Three of the Directors of the said Society, have hereunto set our hands this   day of One thousand eight hundred and

Examined

Entered

NOTICE

All Notices of Assignment of the Policy must be sent *direct to Street, London*, the principal place of business of the Society. No Agent of the Society is authorised, under any circumstances whatever, to receive, acknowledge, or transmit such Notice.

GUARANTEE OF SURRENDER VALUE

The within written Policy will acquire a Surrender Value so soon as three full annual Premiums have been paid, and the Society then guarantees the following sums as the Surrender Value, namely :—

(1) One-third of so much of the Premiums received as would represent ordinary Premiums on the same Policy according to the true age at the date of issue thereof.

(2) The full Cash Value calculated according to the published Bonus Table of the Profits (if any) attached to the Policy at the time of surrender.

PROTECTION AGAINST FORFEITURE FOR NON-PAYMENT OF PREMIUMS IN CERTAIN CASES AND FOR A LIMITED TIME

When a Policy has a Surrender Value, then, notwithstanding an omission to pay any subsequent Premium or Premiums, the Policy will remain in force unless and until the Surrender Value of the Policy, as at the date when the first unpaid Premium is payable, becomes exceeded by the total of the amount due in respect of Premiums, and in respect of any loan made on the Policy by the Society and of the accumulated compound interest with half-yearly rests on the amount of Premiums and loan (if any) at the rate for the time being charged on loans made by the Society on the security of their Policies.

The Premium or Premiums due, if paid with accumulated compound interest at the before-mentioned rate while the Policy remains in force under this Provision, will be accepted by the Society.

Own Life.   *Age Proved.*

FORM OF MARINE POLICY

£

BE IT KNOWN THAT

as well in   own Name, as for and in the Name and
Names of all and every other Person or Persons to whom
the same doth, may, or shall appertain in part or in all, doth
make assurance, and cause   and them and
every of them, to be insured, lost or not lost, at and from

upon any kind of Goods and Merchandises, and also upon
the Body, Tackle, Apparel, Ordnance, Munition, Artillery,
Boat and other Furniture, of and in the good Ship or Vessel
called the
whereof is Master, under God, for this present voyage,
                              or whosoever else shall go for
Master in the said Ship, or by whatsoever other Name or
Names the said Ship or the Master thereof is or shall be
named or called, beginning the Adventure upon the said
Goods and Merchandises from the loading thereof aboard
the said Ship
upon the said Ship, &c.
and shall so continue and endure, during her Abode there,
upon the said Ship, &c., and further, until the said Ship,
with all her Ordnance, Tackle, Apparel, &c., and Goods
and Merchandises whatsoever, shall be arrived at
                              upon the said Ship, &c.,
until she hath moored at Anchor Twenty-four Hours in good
Safety, and upon the Goods and Merchandises, until the
same be there discharged and safely landed ; and it shall be
lawful for the said Ship, &c., in this Voyage to proceed and
sail to and touch and stay at any Ports or Places whatsoever

without Prejudice to this Insurance. The said Ship, &c.,
Goods and Merchandises, &c., for so much as concerns the
Assured, by Agreement between the Assured and Assurers
in this Policy, are and shall be valued at

Touching the Adventures and Perils which we the Assurers are con-
tented to bear and do take upon us in this Voyage, they are, of the
Seas, Men-of-War, Fire, Enemies, Pirates, Rovers, Thieves, Jettisons,
Letters of Mart and Countermart, Surprisals, Takings at Sea, Arrests,

Restraints and Detainments of all Kings, Princes, and People, of what Nation, Condition, or Quality soever, Barratry of the Master and Mariners, and of all other Perils, Losses, and Misfortunes that have or shall come to the Hurt, Detriment, or Damage of the said Goods and Merchandises and Ship, &c., or any Part thereof; and in case of any Loss or Misfortune, it shall be lawful to the Assured, their Factors, Servants, and Assigns, to sue, labour, and travel for, in, and about the Defence, Safeguard and Recovery of the said Goods and Merchandises, and Ship, &c., or any Part thereof, without Prejudice to this Insurance ; to the Charges whereof we, the Assurers, will contribute, each one according to the Rate and Quantity of his Sum herein assured. And it is agreed by us the Insurers, that this Writing or Policy of Assurance shall be of as much Force and Effect as the surest Writing or Policy of Assurance heretofore made in Lombard Street, or in the Royal Exchange, or elsewhere in London. And so we the Assurers are contented, and do hereby promise and bind ourselves, each one for his own Part, our Heirs, Executors, and Goods, to the Assured, their Executors, Administrators, and Assigns, for the true Performance of the Premises, confessing ourselves paid the Consideration due unto us for this Assurance by the Assured
at and after the Rate of

In witness whereof, we the Assurers have subscribed our Names and Sums assured in

N.B.—Corn, Fish, Salt, Fruit, Flour, and Seed are warranted free from Average, unless general, or the Ship be stranded ; Sugar, Tobacco, Hemp, Flax, Hides, and Skins are warranted free from Average under Five Pounds per Cent ; and all other Goods, also the Ship and Freight, are warranted free from Average under Three Pounds per Cent, unless general, or the Ship be stranded.

QUESTIONS

1. Can a married woman carry on a trade?

2. Define a partnership.

3. What is meant by a limited liability company; how is it formed?

4. Describe a "memorandum of association," stating what it contains.

5. What are "articles of association"?

6. What is meant by a "share"? A. applies for shares in a company, when will he be bound to take them; up to what time can he withdraw his application?

7. When will the court order a company to be wound up?

8. What is meant by saying that moveable property is the subject of absolute ownership?

9. What special characteristics attach to the ownership of British ships?

10. Distinguish stock from shares. What is meant by "$2\frac{1}{2}$ per cent consols"?

11. What is a debenture; how does it differ from debenture stock?

12. What is copyright; how long does copyright in a book last?

13. What is a design; how can the right to the exclusive use of a design be obtained?

14. What is a patent; how is it obtained, and for how long does it last?

15. How is the exclusive user of a trademark obtained? how is a trademark assigned?

§§ 26 to 37

1. What is a contract ; how does it differ from an agreement ?

2. " Every agreement can be analysed into an offer and an acceptance." Explain this statement.

A firm of auctioneers advertise that they will sell furniture by auction on a certain day : B. goes to the auction-rooms at the time advertised, and is informed that the auction will not take place, has he any claim for his expenses against the auctioneer ?

3. A. makes an offer by post, and B. accepts by telegram, when is the acceptance complete ?

4. A. gets into a tramcar, travels a certain distance, pays his fare, and then gets out. Show that there was a contract between the tramcar company and A., pointing out the offer and the acceptance.

5. State the chief rules relating to the revocation of offers.

6. A. advertises that he will give £100 to any person who, suffering from a cold, uses an article sold by A. and is not cured. B., who is suffering from cold, buys the article and is not cured, can he recover the £100?

7. At what moment of time is the revocation of an offer complete ?

8. When does an agreement amount to a contract ?

THE CAPACITY OF PARTIES TO CONTRACT

§§ 38 to 57

1. To what extent can an infant enter into contracts binding on him ?

2. A., being under 21 years of age, purchases a horse for £150, on credit ; when he comes of age he writes a letter to the vendor admitting that the £150 is due for the horse ; can the vendor sue him and recover the £150?

3. Can a money-lender recover money lent to a person under 21 years of age ?

4. What is meant by "necessaries"? Are books necessaries? How is the question as to what are necessaries determined ?

5. Distinguish "void" from "voidable" contracts : what contract of an infant falls under each class ?

6. When can a married woman enter into a contract binding on her?

7. What is separate estate? A married woman owning separate estate incurs a large debt at her dressmaker's, can she be sued for the debt?

8. A married woman is sued for a debt; it turns out she had no separate estate at the time she contracted the debt, but acquired separate estate afterwards; is such estate liable to pay the debt?

9. What power has a married woman to contract as agent of her husband?

10. How does a corporation enter into a contract?

11. When may a corporation contract without using its seal?

12. Is a contract entered into by a lunatic binding on him?

13. A. contracts with B., a lunatic, not knowing that he is insane, what is the position of the parties?

14. A., whilst drunk, enters into a contract with B., is such contract binding?

THE FORM OF AND CONSIDERATION FOR CONTRACTS

§§ 58 to 73

1. How many classes of contracts are recognised by English law?

2. What is a record; what are contracts by record?

3. What are the requisites of a contract under seal?

4. What is a deed; from what time does it date? Distinguish a deed from an escrow.

5. What contracts usually require a deed?

6. When ought a trading corporation to contract under seal?

7. Define a simple contract?

8. What simple contracts are required to be in writing?

9. A. engages a servant at the rate of £20 a year, wages to be paid monthly, ought the contract to be in writing?

10. When ought contracts for the sale of goods to be in writing?

11. What is a consideration?

12. Distinguish an executed from an executory consideration.

13. A., being in want of money, sells B. a picture that is worth £500 for £100; can A. afterwards set aside the sale on the ground that B. did not give him the full value of the picture?

14. A. owes B. £100, and B. threatens legal proceedings; A.

writes B. asking for a month's time to pay ; B. replies saying he will wait for a month.   Is B. legally bound to wait the month?

15. What is a past consideration ; will it support a simple contract ?

LEGALITY AND POSSIBILITY OF PERFORMANCE

§§ 74 to 87

1. A. lends B. money for an illegal purpose ; can he recover it ?
2. Can A. insure B.'s life ?
3. Can a father insure his son's life ?
4. What restrictions exist as to trading on Sunday? Is a contract made on a Sunday binding ?
5. What special rules exist regarding the sale of game, coal, and bread ?
6. What is meant by an agreement in restraint of trade ? To what extent is such an agreement lawful ?
7. A. sells his business and the goodwill thereof to B., can A. set up a similar business in the same street ?
8. What conditions must be fulfilled in order that the court may uphold an agreement in restraint of trade ?
9. A. threatens to make B. a bankrupt, B. offers A. £10 not to do so, and A. accepts the offer, is the agreement binding?
10. Enumerate and describe the different kinds of " impossibility of performance."
11. When will impossibility of performance avoid a contract ?
12. A., a married man, proposes marriage to B., who knows he is married ; B. afterwards brings a breach of promise against A.; is A. liable for damages ?
13. A. sells B. shares that he (A.) does not possess, and fails to deliver them to B., has B. any remedy ?

MISTAKE, MISREPRESENTATION, AND FRAUD

§§ 88 to 97

1. What is meant by unreality of consent ?
2. When will mistake avoid a contract ?
3. A. buys from B. a piece of old china which he (A.) believes to be Dresden, but which B. knows is not Dresden, is the sale binding?

4. A. sells B. a piece of china, both believe it to be Dresden, but it is not, is the sale binding?

5. What amounts to a misrepresentation? Distinguish misrepresentation from fraud.

6. When will misrepresentation be a ground for avoiding a contract?

7. A. reads the prospectus of a company and applies for shares, which are allotted to him. Afterwards, he finds that some of the statements in the prospectus are untrue : can he rescind the contract to take shares?

8. What remedies are open to a person who has been induced to enter into a contract by misrepresentation or by fraud?

ASSIGNMENT OF CONTRACTS

§§ 98 to 101

1. Can the liability under a contract be assigned?

2. A. owes B. £10, can B. assign the right to receive the money to C. ? If so, how must the assignment be made?

3. A. has bought 1000 pieces of cloth, can he assign to C. the right to receive the cloth?

4. How is a bill of exchange assigned?

5. Illustrate the assignment of rights and liabilities by operation of law.

PERFORMANCE, BREACH, AND DISCHARGE

§§ 102 to 110

1. In what form must tender of money be made in order to amount to " legal tender "?

2. A. owes B. £20, and B. gives him a bill of exchange for £20, is the debt discharged?

3. When can a party to a contract refuse performance where there has been a breach on the other side?

4. A. commits a breach of a contract made with B., what are B.'s remedies?

5. How can a contract be discharged?

6. A. enters into a written contract with B. ; they desire to rescind it. How can this be effected?

1. Define a partnership. A. becomes a partner on condition that he is to have no share in the profits, is such an arrangement binding?

2. Is sharing profits conclusive evidence of partnership?

3. What power has a partner to bind the firm?

4. To what extent is a partner liable for the debts of the firm?

5. How does the law of Scotland differ from that of England as to liability?

6. What is the position of a person who holds himself out to be a partner?

7. What effect has the purchase of land for partnership purposes upon the legal characteristics of such land?

8. State the chief duties of partners as between themselves.

9. Suppose the partners differ as to the management of the business, how is the matter decided?

10. What effect has the death of a partner on the partnership?

11. How is a partnership dissolved?

12. What are the effects of a dissolution?

13. Is the private property of a partner liable for the debts of a firm?

PRINCIPAL AND AGENT

1. Distinguish a factor from a broker.

2. What is a *del credere* agent?

3. Distinguish a "general" from a "special" agent.

4. How may an agent be appointed?

5. What is meant by ratification? What conditions are required for a valid ratification?

6. What power has an agent to bind his principal?

7. When can an agent appoint a sub-agent? What relation exists between the sub-agent and the principal?

8. Describe the chief duties of an agent.

9. What degree of diligence must an agent show in discharge of his duties?

10. What remedies has an agent for his commission?

11. What are the chief duties of the principal as regards the agent?

12. The principal directs his agent to do a wrongful act, is the agent bound to do it? Is the principal or the agent liable for the wrong done?

13. An agent contracts with a third party without disclosing the name of his principal, what is the legal position of the parties?

14. When is an agent personally liable on a contract?

15. What is the result where an agent falsely pretends to be an agent and enters into a contract?

16. What special powers are possessed by (a) factors, (b) brokers?

17. What are the powers of an auctioneer?

18. The principal revokes the authority of an agent, who after such revocation enters into a contract on behalf of the principal, is the contract binding on the principal?

19. In what way is the relation of principal and agent terminated?

The Sale of Goods

§§ 134 to 159

1. Distinguish a sale from an agreement to sell.

2. Distinguish sale from "gift" and from "barter."

3. What is meant by price? Suppose the parties do not agree on the price, is there a valid sale?

4. What form is required for a contract for the sale of goods under £10?

5. State the form requisite for a sale of goods over £10 in value.

6. What is meant by "acceptance and receipt"? A. orders a package of sponges from B. at 11s. per lb. On the arrival of the package A. examines the sponges, and finding them worth only 6s. a lb. returns them to B. Was there an acceptance and receipt of the goods sufficient to satisfy the Statute of Frauds?

7. Distinguish "earnest" from "part payment."

8. Under what circumstances can a contract in writing be gathered from a series of letters?

9. Where a contract of sale of goods over £10 in value is reduced to writing, what ought the memorandum to contain?

10. Can a written offer be accepted orally; will such acceptance satisfy the Statute of Frauds where the goods sold are over £10 in value?

11. State the chief rules relating to the signature of contracts so as to satisfy the Statute of Frauds.

12. How are the provisions of the Statute of Frauds fulfilled in the case of a public auction?

13. Explain the nature of a "bought" and a "sold" note.

14. What are the powers and functions of a "broker"?

15. Explain the rule *caveat emptor*.

16. What is a warranty?

17. When does the law imply a warranty?

18. What warranties are implied in a sale by sample?

19. A. orders goods from B. of his own manufacture; B. supplies similar goods made by C.; is A. bound to accept them?

20. What are the chief duties of a seller of goods?

21. Is a seller of goods bound to send them to the purchaser?

22. What is meant by lien? What lien has a seller over the goods sold?

23. What is stoppage *in transitu?* When and how is it exercised?

24. When can a seller resell goods not paid for by the buyer?

25. Mention some acts that amount to acceptance of goods by the buyer.

26. How should the price be tendered so as to be a "legal tender"?

27. A. owes B. £5:6:8 for goods bought; he tenders a £10 note, which B. refuses; is the tender good?

28. A. buys £100 worth of goods from B., and gives B. a bill of exchange. The bill is not paid when due. Can B. sue A. on the original contract, apart from the bill?

29. Can an agent of the seller receive payment? A. owes B. £10 for goods bought. He meets a clerk from A.'s shop in the street, and pays him the £10. The clerk runs away and B. demands payment. Can A. successfully resist the demand?

30. A. writes B. to ask him to remit the amount of a debt by cheque by post. B. posts a cheque for the amount, but the letter never reaches A. The bank on which the cheque was drawn suspends payment. A. writes B. saying he has not received the cheque. B. replies he sent it as requested. Can B. be compelled to pay A.?

31. A. enters B.'s shop and selects a box of cigars. C. seizes the cigars and runs away with them. Who has to bear the loss, A. or B.?

32. A. orders 20 lbs. of sugar from B. at 2d. a lb. of a certain quality, when will the ownership of the 20 lbs. pass to A.?

33. When does the ownership pass to the buyer when goods are sent on approval?

34. When will the ownership of unascertained goods pass to the buyer? What is meant by unascertained goods?

35. Can a seller reserve the right to dispose of goods after he has made delivery?

36. A thief sells B. goods stolen from A., can A. claim the goods from B.?

37. What is the effect of a sale in market overt? What is market overt?

38. Can an unpaid seller claim interest on the price from the buyer?

39. What is the remedy of a buyer where the seller refuses to deliver goods bought from him?

40. When can a buyer refuse to take delivery of goods?

INSURANCE

§§ 161 to 186

1. What is insurance?

2. What is meant by saying that fire and marine insurance are based on the principle of indemnity?

3. What conditions must be observed by any one who is making a proposal for insurance?

4. What is an insurable interest?

5. A person insured omits to pay the premium when it is due, but pays it during the days of grace, what is the effect on the policy?

6. What is meant by underwriting?

7. Distinguish a valued from an open policy.

8. Distinguish a voyage from a time policy.

9. What is the slip; has it any legal effect?

10. What is a warranty? What warranties are implied in a marine policy?

11. What amounts to seaworthiness?

12. Explain the terms "average," "free from average," and "general average."

13. What amounts to a total loss? A vessel is wrecked, what steps should the owner take so as to be able to claim for a total loss?

14. How is a partial loss calculated?

15. When can A. insure B.'s life?

16. The proposer for a life insurance makes an untrue statement in the proposal, what effect has this on the policy?

17. Can a policy of life insurance be assigned?

18. What is meant by fire in a fire policy?

19. What losses are usually excepted in a fire policy?

20. What conditions, if they occur, will usually avoid a fire policy?

21. What steps ought to be taken when a loss occurs by fire?

22. Suppose the articles are insured in different offices, can the insured recover from each?

GUARANTEES

§§ 188 to 194

1. Describe the nature and objects of a guarantee.

2. In what form must a guarantee be made?

3. State the position of the party guaranteeing; can he be sued before the principal?

4. What is a continuing guarantee?

5. What is the position of a surety who pays the whole debt as regards the principal debtor?

6. A. B. and C. are sureties for D.; D. fails to pay, and A. is sued. Is A. liable for the whole debt? Suppose he pays the whole, what right has he against B. and C.?

7. A. B. and C. are sureties; A. is sued for the whole debt; can he, before paying anything, call on B. and C. to contribute their shares?

8. Distinguish joint from several liability.

9. When can a surety withdraw from a guarantee?

10. What conduct on the part of the creditor will discharge the surety?

11. A. is surety for B. paying a debt to C. on the 1st January. C. extends the time to the 1st February, but before the 1st February B. becomes bankrupt; is A. liable to C.?

CHARTER-PARTIES AND BILLS OF LADING

§§ 196 to 235

1. What is a charter-party?

2. What warranties are implied in a charter-party?

3. What is freight; when is it earned?

4. Mention some of the chief provisions found in charter-parties.

5. What is tonnage?

6. On sailing, a captain is paid a portion of the freight, when

will such payment be an advance, and when a loan? What is the importance of the distinction?

7. What are lay-days?

8. What is the mate's receipt?

9. What perils are usually excepted in a charter-party?

10. What is a bill of lading? how is it transferred?

11. What is the duty of the captain as regards deviation?

12. To whom are goods comprised in a bill of lading to be delivered?

13. What perils are usually excepted in a bill of lading?

14. What is meant by "act of God"?

15. What perils are covered by the phrase "perils of the sea"?

16. What is barratry?

17. How far is the shipowner liable for bad stowage?

18. How does a shipowner protect himself from liability for deterioration to the cargo due to the nature of the goods?

19. What is demurrage?

20. What is general average? who must contribute to it?

21. What is salvage?

22. What is the nature and object of a bottomry bond?

23. What powers has the master as regards the shipowner?

24. To what extent is the master the agent of the cargo-owner?

Bills of Exchange

§§ 237 to 256

1. What is a bill of exchange? Write out an example.

2. Distinguish an inland from a foreign bill.

3. What are the requisites of a bill of exchange?

4. What is presentation for payment? When is it necessary?

5. What are days of grace?

6. Where is a bill payable? If an acceptor desires to pay at a given place, how should he accept?

7. Who is the acceptor? What is his legal position?

8. How can a bill be transferred?

9. Who is the drawer? What is his legal position?

10. Who is an endorser? When is he liable to a subsequent holder?

11. What course ought the holder of a bill to take if the bill be dishonoured?

12. Distinguish a cheque from a bill of exchange.

13. What is the effect of crossing a cheque?

14. What is the effect of writing "not negotiable" across a crossed cheque?

15. Has the holder of a dishonoured cheque any remedy against the bank?

16. What advantage does the holder of a cheque derive by presenting the cheque within a reasonable time after he receives it? What is a reasonable time?

17. What is a promissory note?   Is presentation necessary?

18. What is an I.O.U.?   Can it be transferred?

BANKRUPTCY

§§ 258 to 280

1. What is meant by an act of bankruptcy?

2. Enumerate the chief kinds of acts of bankruptcy.

3. When can a creditor present a petition in bankruptcy?

4. What is an order of adjudication?   What is its effect?

5. Can a married woman be made bankrupt?

6. What are the chief duties of the official receiver?

7. What is the object of the first general meeting?

8. What is a scheme of arrangement?   How must it be passed to be binding?

9. How is the trustee appointed?   What are his chief duties and powers?

10. What is the committee of inspection?   How is it appointed?

11. How are debts proved in bankruptcy?

12. What is a secured debt?   What is the position of a creditor whose debt is secured?

13. What property belonging to the bankrupt is not available for paying his debts?

14. What property belonging to others is liable for a bankrupt's debts?

15. When are goods said to be in the order or disposition of a bankrupt?

16. A bankrupt made a settlement of part of his property before his bankruptcy, is such settlement perfectly valid?

17. What is onerous property?   What powers has the trustee over such property?

18. How does a bankrupt get his discharge?

19. What are the effects of a discharge?

20. When will a discharge be withheld or suspended?

21. What disabilities is a bankrupt under?

22. When will an adjudication be annulled?

23. What conditions must be fulfilled before a scheme of arrangement is binding?

24. What is the effect of a private arrangement with creditors?

THE APPLICATION OF LAW

§§ 282 to 290

1. By what law is the ownership of land governed? A. is a Scotchman residing in England, and owning land in Scotland. He dies without a will. What law will govern the descent of the land?

2. What is domicile?

3. An Englishman, domiciled in England, owns shares in an Australian bank; he wishes to leave them by will: ought the will to be in accordance with English or Australian law?

4. By what law is the validity of a contract governed?

5. A bill of exchange is drawn in France according to French law, and is payable in England, is the bill valid according to English law?

6. How can a foreign judgment be enforced in England?

INDEX

The figures refer to the pages

Printed by R. & R. CLARK, *Edinburgh.*

MACMILLAN'S COMMERCIAL CLASS BOOKS.

MACMILLAN'S ELEMENTARY COMMERCIAL CLASS BOOKS.
Edited by JAMES GOW, Litt.D., Headmaster of the High
School, Nottingham. Globe 8vo.

THE HISTORY OF COMMERCE IN EUROPE. By H. DE B.
GIBBINS, M.A. 3s. 6d.

COMMERCIAL GEOGRAPHY. By E. C. K. GONNER, M.A.,
Professor of Political Economy in University College, Liverpool. [*In preparation.*

COMMERCIAL ARITHMETIC. By S. JACKSON, M.A. 3s. 6d.

ADVANCED BOOKKEEPING. By J. THORNTON. [*In the Press.*

INTRODUCTION TO COMMERCIAL GERMAN. By F. C.
SMITH, B.A., formerly Scholar of Magdalene College, Cambridge. 3s. 6d.

COMMERCIAL FRENCH. By JAMES B. PAYNE, King's
College School, London. [*In preparation.*

COMMERCIAL SPANISH. By Prof. DELBOS, Instructor
H.M.S. *Britannia*, Dartmouth. [*In preparation.*

COMMERCIAL LAW. By J. E. C. MUNRO, LL.D., late
Professor of Law and Political Economy in the Owens College,
Manchester. Globe 8vo.

INTRODUCTION TO THE STUDY OF POLITICAL ECONOMY.
Being an entirely rewritten third edition of the Guide to the
Study of Political Economy by LUIGI COSSA, Professor in the
Royal University of Pavia. Translated by LOUIS DYER.
Crown 8vo.

POLITICAL ECONOMY FOR BEGINNERS, WITH QUESTIONS.
By Mrs. HENRY FAWCETT. 7th Ed. Pott 8vo. 2s. 6d.

A MANUAL OF POLITICAL ECONOMY. By the Right Hon.
HENRY FAWCETT, F.R.S. 7th Ed., revised. Cr. 8vo. 12s.

AN EXPLANATORY DIGEST of above. By C. A. WATERS, B.A.
Cr. 8vo. 2s. 6d.

PRIMER OF POLITICAL ECONOMY. By W. STANLEY
JEVONS, F.R.S. Pott 8vo. 1s.

THE THEORY OF POLITICAL ECONOMY. By the same
Author. 3rd Ed., revised. 8vo. 10s. 6d.

PRINCIPLES OF ECONOMICS. By ALFRED MARSHALL, M.A.,
Professor of Political Economy in the University of Cambridge.
2 vols. 8vo. Vol. I. 2nd Ed. 12s. 6d. net.

Works by FRANCIS A. WALKER, M.A.

FIRST LESSONS IN POLITICAL ECONOMY. Cr. 8vo. 5s.

A BRIEF TEXT-BOOK OF POLITICAL ECONOMY. Cr. 8vo.
6s. 6d.

POLITICAL ECONOMY. 2nd Ed., revised and enlarged. 8vo.
12s. 6d.

THE WAGES QUESTION. Ex. Cr. 8vo. 8s. 6d. net.

MONEY. Ex. Cr. 8vo. 8s. 6d. net.

MACMILLAN AND CO., LONDON.

A SERIES OF

ELEMENTARY COMMERCIAL CLASS-BOOKS

EDITED BY

JAMES GOW, Litt.D.,

HEADMASTER OF NOTTINGHAM SCHOOL, BARRISTER-AT-LAW, LATE FELLOW
OF TRINITY COLLEGE, CAMBRIDGE.

THIS series is designed, in the first instance, for the use of young students who are preparing for any of the Commercial Examinations now held by Chambers of Commerce, various University Boards and Syndicates, the College of Preceptors, and the Society of Arts. Special attention, however, has been paid to the requirements of those schools which, if they are to give commercial teaching at all, must do so with no special staff and with very little disturbance to other subjects of instruction.

Experience seems to show that ordinary schools, though they can hardly expect to teach much of commercial technique, can teach many subjects from the commercial point of view, and that this innovation is in reality a considerable educational improvement. History and Geography, for instance, gain very greatly in interest by being studied with a definite reference to familiar things, such as roads and ships and steam-engines and raw material. In the same way, though not to the same degree, foreign languages are more attractive to most boys when taught through a commercial vocabulary than they are when confined to observations on the family, the house, and the garden. Indeed, it may be said generally that there has been, of late years, a noticeable tendency in educational writers to enliven the drudgery of beginners by giving them, very early, some glimpse of the utility of their studies. It is believed, therefore, that school-masters will receive with welcome a systematic attempt to apply this principle on a larger scale, and to provide a series of elementary manuals which, though they are primarily intended for commercial classes, may be used with advantage by other classes as well.

The following volumes are arranged for :—

THE HISTORY OF COMMERCE IN EUROPE. By H. DE B. GIBBINS, M.A. Globe 8vo. 3s. 6d. [*Ready.*

COMMERCIAL GERMAN. By F. C. SMITH, B.A., formerly Scholar of Magdalene College, Cambridge. 3s. 6d. [*Ready.*

COMMERCIAL ARITHMETIC. By S. JACKSON, M.A., Head Master of Victoria College, Congleton. 3s. 6d. [*Ready.*

COMMERCIAL GEOGRAPHY. By E. C. K. GONNER, M.A., Professor of Political Economy in University College, Liverpool. [*In preparation.*

COMMERCIAL FRENCH. By JAMES B. PAYNE, King's College School, London. [*In preparation.*

COMMERCIAL SPANISH. By L. DELBOS, M.A. Paris; Instructor, H. M. Ship "Britannia." [*In preparation.*

COMMERCIAL GEOGRAPHY. By E. C. K. GONNER, M.A., Professor of Political Economy in University College, Liverpool. [*In preparation.*

COMMERCIAL LAW. By J. E. C. MUNRO, LL.D., formerly Professor of Law and Political Economy in the Owens College, Manchester. [*In preparation.*

ADVANCED TEXT-BOOK OF BOOK-KEEPING. By J. THORNTON. [*In preparation.*

MACMILLAN & CO., BEDFORD STREET, STRAND, LONDON.

5.3.93.

June 1893

A Catalogue

OF

Educational Books

PUBLISHED BY

Macmillan & Co.

BEDFORD STREET, STRAND, LONDON

For books of a less educational character on the subjects named below, see Macmillan and Co.'s Classified Catalogue of Books in General Literature.

CONTENTS

B

GREEK AND LATIN CLASSICS.

Elementary Classics; Classical Series; Classical Library, (1) Texts, (2) Translations; Grammar, Composition, and Philology; Antiquities, Ancient History, and Philosophy.

*ELEMENTARY CLASSICS.

18mo, Eighteenpence each.

The following contain Introductions, Notes, and **Vocabularies**, and in some cases **Exercises**.

ACCIDENCE, LATIN, AND EXERCISES ARRANGED FOR BEGINNERS.—By W. WELCH, M.A., and C. G. DUFFIELD, M.A.

AESCHYLUS.—PROMETHEUS VINCTUS. By Rev. H. M. STEPHENSON, M.A.

ARRIAN.—SELECTIONS. With Exercises. By Rev. JOHN BOND, M.A., and Rev. A. S. WALPOLE, M.A.

AULUS GELLIUS, STORIES FROM.—Adapted for Beginners. With Exercises. By Rev. G. H. NALL, M.A., Assistant Master at Westminster.

CÆSAR.—THE HELVETIAN WAR. Selections from Book I., adapted for Beginners. With Exercises. By W. WELCH, M.A., and C. G. DUFFIELD, M.A.
   THE INVASION OF BRITAIN. Selections from Books IV. and V., adapted for Beginners. With Exercises. By the same.
   SCENES FROM BOOKS V. AND VI. By C. COLBECK, M.A.
   THE GALLIC WAR. BOOK I. By Rev. A. S. WALPOLE, M.A.
   BOOKS II. AND III. By the Rev. W. G. RUTHERFORD, M.A., LL.D.
   BOOK IV. By CLEMENT BRYANS, M.A., Assistant Master at Dulwich College.
   BOOK V. By C. COLBECK, M.A., Assistant Master at Harrow.
   BOOK VI. By C. COLBECK, M.A.
   BOOK VII. By Rev. J. BOND, M.A., and Rev. A. S. WALPOLE, M.A.
   THE CIVIL WAR. BOOK I. By M. MONTGOMREY, M.A.

CICERO.—DE SENECTUTE. By E. S. SHUCKBURGH, M.A.
   DE AMICITIA. By the same.
   STORIES OF ROMAN HISTORY. Adapted for Beginners. With Exercises. By Rev. G. E. JEANS, M.A., and A. V. JONES, M.A.

CURTIUS (Quintus). — SELECTIONS. Adapted for Beginners. With Notes, Vocabulary, and Exercises. By F. COVERLEY SMITH.   [*In preparation.*

EURIPIDES.—ALCESTIS. By Rev. M. A. BAYFIELD, M.A.
   MEDEA. By Rev. M. A. BAYFIELD, M.A.
   HECUBA. By Rev. J. BOND, M.A., and Rev. A. S. WALPOLE, M.A.

EUTROPIUS.—Adapted for Beginners. With Exercises. By W. WELCH, M.A., and C. G. DUFFIELD, M.A.
   BOOKS I. and II. By the same.

HERODOTUS, TALES FROM. Atticised. By G. S. FARNELL, M.A.

HOMER.—ILIAD. BOOK I. By Rev. J. BOND, M.A., and Rev. A. S. WALPOLE, M.A.
   BOOK VI. By WALTER LEAF, Litt.D., and Rev. M. A. BAYFIELD.
   BOOK XVIII. By S. R. JAMES, M.A., Assistant Master at Eton.
   ODYSSEY. BOOK I. By Rev. J. BOND, M.A., and Rev. A. S. WALPOLE, M.A.

HORACE.—ODES. BOOKS I.-IV. By T. E. PAGE, M.A., Assistant Master at the Charterhouse. Each 1s. 6d.

LIVY.—BOOK I. By H. M. STEPHENSON, M.A.
   BOOK V. By M. ALFORD.
   BOOK XXI. Adapted from Mr. Capes's Edition. By J. E. MELHUISH, M.A.

BOOK XXII. By J. E. MELHUISH, M.A.
SELECTIONS FROM BOOKS V. and VI. By W. CECIL LAMING, M.A.
THE HANNIBALIAN WAR. BOOKS XXI. and XXII. adapted by G. C. MACAULAY, M.A.
BOOKS XXIII. and XXIV. adapted by the same. [*In preparation.*
THE SIEGE OF SYRACUSE. Being part of the XXIV. and XXV. BOOKS OF LIVY, adapted for Beginners. With Exercises. By G. RICHARDS, M.A., and Rev. A. S. WALPOLE, M.A.
LEGENDS OF ANCIENT ROME. Adapted for Beginners. With Exercises. By H. WILKINSON, M.A.

LUCIAN.—EXTRACTS FROM LUCIAN. With Exercises. By Rev. J. BOND, M.A., and Rev. A. S. WALPOLE, M.A.

NEPOS.—SELECTIONS ILLUSTRATIVE OF GREEK AND ROMAN HISTORY. With Exercises. By G. S. FARNELL, M.A.

OVID.—SELECTIONS. By E. S. SHUCKBURGH, M.A.
EASY SELECTIONS FROM OVID IN ELEGIAC VERSE. With Exercises. By H. WILKINSON, M.A.
METAMORPHOSES.—BOOK I.—By CHARLES SIMMONS, M.A. [*In preparation.*
STORIES FROM THE METAMORPHOSES. With Exercises. By Rev. J. BOND, M.A., and Rev. A. S. WALPOLE, M.A.
TRISTIA.—BOOK I. By E. S. SHUCKBURGH, M.A. [*In preparation.*
BOOK II. By E. S. SHUCKBURGH, M.A. [*In preparation.*

PHÆDRUS.—SELECT FABLES. Adapted for Beginners. With Exercises. By Rev. A. S. WALPOLE, M.A.

THUOYDIDES.—THE RISE OF THE ATHENIAN EMPIRE. BOOK I. CHS. 89-117 and 228-238. With Exercises. By F. H. COLSON, M.A.

VIRGIL.—SELECTIONS. By E. S. SHUCKBURGH, M.A.
BUCOLICS. By T. E. PAGE, M.A.
GEORGICS. BOOK I. By T. E. PAGE, M.A.
BOOK II. By Rev. J. H. SKRINE, M.A.
ÆNEID. BOOK I. By Rev. A. S. WALPOLE, M.A.
BOOK I. By T. E. PAGE, M.A.
BOOK II. By T. E. PAGE, M.A.
BOOK III. By T. E. PAGE, M.A.
BOOK IV. By Rev. H. M. STEPHENSON, M.A.
BOOK V. By Rev. A. CALVERT, M.A.
BOOK VI. By T. E. PAGE, M.A.
BOOK VII. By Rev. A. CALVERT, M.A.
BOOK VIII. By Rev. A. CALVERT, M.A.
BOOK IX. By Rev. H. M. STEPHENSON, M.A.
BOOK X. By S. G. OWEN, M.A.

XENOPHON.—ANABASIS. Selections, adapted for Beginners. With Exercises. By W. WELCH, M.A., and C. G. DUFFIELD, M.A.
BOOK I. With Exercises. By E. A. WELLS, M.A.
BOOK I. By Rev. A. S. WALPOLE, M.A.
BOOK II. By Rev. A. S. WALPOLE, M.A.
BOOK III. By Rev. G. H. NALL, M.A.
BOOK IV. By Rev. E. D. STONE, M.A.
BOOK V. By Rev. G. H. NALL, M.A.
BOOK VI. By Rev. G. H. NALL, M.A.
SELECTIONS FROM BOOK IV. With Exercises. By Rev. E. D. STONE, M.A.
SELECTIONS FROM THE CYROPÆDIA. With Exercises. By A. H. COOKE, M.A.
TALES FROM THE CYROPÆDIA. With Exercises. By CHARLES H. KEENE.
[*In preparation.*

The following contain Introductions and Notes, but no Vocabulary:—

CICERO.—SELECT LETTERS. By Rev. G. E. JEANS, M.A.
HERODOTUS.—SELECTIONS FROM BOOKS VII. AND VIII. THE EXPEDITION OF XERXES. By A. H. COOKE, M.A.

HORACE.—SELECTIONS FROM THE SATIRES AND EPISTLES. By Rev. W.
J. V. Baker, M.A.
SELECT EPODES AND ARS POETICA. By H. A. Dalton, M.A.
PLATO.—EUTHYPHRO AND MENEXENUS. By C. E. Graves, M.A.
TERENCE.—SCENES FROM THE ANDRIA. By F. W. Cornish, M.A., Assistant
Master at Eton.
THE GREEK ELEGIAC POETS.—FROM CALLINUS TO CALLIMACHUS.
Selected by Rev. Herbert Kynaston, D.D.
THUCYDIDES.—BOOK IV. Chs. 1-41. THE CAPTURE OF SPHACTERIA. By
C. E. Graves, M.A.

CLASSICAL SERIES
FOR COLLEGES AND SCHOOLS.
Fcap. 8vo.

ÆSCHINES.—IN CTESIPHONTA. By Rev. T. Gwatkin, M.A., and E. S.
Shuckburgh, M.A. 5s.
ÆSCHYLUS.—PERSÆ. By A. O. Prickard, M.A., Fellow and Tutor of New
College, Oxford. With Map. 2s. 6d.
SEVEN AGAINST THEBES. SCHOOL EDITION. By A. W. Verrall, Litt.D.,
and M. A. Bayfield, M.A. 2s. 6d.
ANDOCIDES.—DE MYSTERIIS. By W. J. Hickie, M.A. 2s. 6d.
ATTIC ORATORS.—Selections from ANTIPHON, ANDOCIDES, LYSIAS, ISO-
CRATES, and ISAEUS. By R. C. Jebb, Litt.D., Regius Professor of Greek
in the University of Cambridge. 5s.
*CÆSAR.—THE GALLIC WAR. By Rev. John Bond, M.A., and Rev. A. S.
Walpole, M.A. With Maps. 4s. 6d.
CATULLUS.—SELECT POEMS. By F. P. Simpson, B.A. 3s. 6d. The Text of this
Edition is carefully expurgated for School use.
*CICERO.—THE CATILINE ORATIONS. By A. S. Wilkins, Litt.D., Professor of
Latin, Owens College, Manchester. 2s. 6d.
PRO LEGE MANILIA. By Prof. A. S. Wilkins, Litt.D. 2s. 6d.
THE SECOND PHILIPPIC ORATION. By John E. B. Mayor, M.A., Professor
of Latin in the University of Cambridge. 3s. 6d.
PRO ROSCIO AMERINO. By E. H. Donkin, M.A. 2s. 6d.
PRO P. SESTIO. By Rev. H. A. Holden, Litt.D. 3s. 6d.
PRO MILONE. By F. H. Colson, M.A.
SELECT LETTERS. By R. Y. Tyrrell, M.A. 4s. 6d.
DEMOSTHENES.—DE CORONA. By B. Drake, M.A. 7th Edition, revised by
E. S. Shuckburgh, M.A. 3s. 6d.
ADVERSUS LEPTINEM. By Rev. J. R. King, M.A., Fellow and Tutor of Oriel
College, Oxford. 2s. 6d.
THE FIRST PHILIPPIC. By Rev. T. Gwatkin, M.A. 2s. 6d.
IN MIDIAM. By Prof. A. S. Wilkins, Litt.D., and Herman Hager, Ph.D., the
Owens College, Victoria University, Manchester. [In preparation.
EURIPIDES.—HIPPOLYTUS. By Rev. J. P. Mahaffy, D.D., Fellow of Trinity
College, and Professor of Ancient History in the University of Dublin, and J.
B. Bury, M.A., Fellow of Trinity College, Dublin. 2s. 6d.
MEDEA. By A. W. Verrall, Litt.D., Fellow of Trinity College, Cambridge.
2s. 6d.
IPHIGENIA IN TAURIS. By E. B. England, M.A. 3s.
ION. By M. A. Bayfield, M.A., Headmaster of Christ College, Brecon. 2s. 6d.
BACCHAE. By R. Y. Tyrrell, M.A., Regius Professor of Greek in the University
of Dublin. 3s. 6d.
HERODOTUS.—BOOK III. By G. C. Macaulay, M.A. 2s. 6d.
BOOK V. By J. Strachan, M.A., Professor of Greek, Owens College, Man-
chester. [In preparation.
BOOK VI. By the same. 3s. 6d.
BOOK VII. By Mrs. Montagu Butler. 3s. 6d.

HOMER.—ILIAD. In 4 vols. Edited by W. LEAF, Litt.D., and Rev. M. A. BAYFIELD, M.A. [In preparation.
ILIAD. BOOKS I., IX., XI., XVI.-XXIV. THE STORY OF ACHILLES. By the late J. H. PRATT, M.A., and WALTER LEAF, Litt.D., Fellows of Trinity College, Cambridge. 6s.
ODYSSEY. BOOK IX. By Prof. JOHN E. B. MAYOR. 2s. 6d.
ODYSSEY. BOOKS XXI.-XXIV. THE TRIUMPH OF ODYSSEUS. By S. G. HAMILTON, M.A., Fellow of Hertford College, Oxford. 2s. 6d.
HORACE.—*THE ODES. By T. E. PAGE, M.A., Assistant Master at the Charter-house. 6s. (BOOKS I. II. and IV. separately, 2s. each.)
THE SATIRES. By ARTHUR PALMER, M.A., Professor of Latin in the University of Dublin. 6s.
THE EPISTLES AND ARS POETICA. By Prof. A. S. WILKINS, Litt.D. 6s.
ISAEOS.—THE ORATIONS. By WILLIAM RIDGEWAY, M.A., Professor of Greek, Queen's College, Cork. [In preparation.
JUVENAL.—*THIRTEEN SATIRES. By E. G. HARDY, M.A. 5s. The Text is carefully expurgated for School use.
SELECT SATIRES. By Prof. JOHN E. B. MAYOR. XII.-XVI. 4s. 6d.
LIVY.—*BOOKS II. and III. By Rev. H. M. STEPHENSON, M.A. 3s. 6d.
*BOOKS XXI. and XXII. By Rev. W. W. CAPES, M.A. With Maps. 4s. 6d.
*BOOKS XXIII. and XXIV. By G. C. MACAULAY, M.A. With Maps. 3s. 6d.
*THE LAST TWO KINGS OF MACEDON. EXTRACTS FROM THE FOURTH AND FIFTH DECADES OF LIVY. By F. H. RAWLINS, M.A., Assistant Master at Eton. With Maps. 2s. 6d.
LUCRETIUS.—BOOKS I.-III. By J. H. WARBURTON LEE, M.A., late Assistant Master at Rossall. 3s. 6d.
LYSIAS.—SELECT ORATIONS. By E. S. SHUCKBURGH, M.A. 6s.
MARTIAL.—SELECT EPIGRAMS. By Rev. H. M. STEPHENSON, M.A. 5s.
*OVID.—FASTI. By G. H. HALLAM, M.A., Assistant Master at Harrow. 3s. 6d.
*HEROIDUM EPISTULÆ XIII. By E. S. SHUCKBURGH, M.A. 3s. 6d.
METAMORPHOSES. BOOKS I.-III. By C. SIMMONS, M.A. [In preparation.
BOOKS XIII. and XIV. By the same. 3s. 6d.
PLATO.—LACHES. By M. T. TATHAM, M.A. 2s. 6d.
THE REPUBLIC. BOOKS I.-V. By T. H. WARREN, M.A., President of Magdalen College, Oxford. 6s.
PLAUTUS.—MILES GLORIOSUS. By R. Y. TYRRELL, M.A., Regius Professor of Greek in the University of Dublin. 2nd Ed., revised. 3s. 6d.
AMPHITRUO. By Prof. ARTHUR PALMER, M.A. 3s. 6d.
CAPTIVI. By A. R. S. HALLIDIE, M.A. 3s. 6d.
PLINY.—LETTERS. BOOKS I. and II. By J. COWAN, M.A., Assistant Master at the Manchester Grammar School. 3s.
LETTERS. BOOK III. By Prof. JOHN E. B. MAYOR. With Life of Pliny by G. H. RENDALL, M.A. 3s. 6d.
PLUTARCH.—LIFE OF THEMISTOKLES. By Rev. H. A. HOLDEN, Litt.D. 3s. 6d.
LIVES OF GALBA AND OTHO. By E. G. HARDY, M.A. 6s.
LIFE OF PERICLES. By Rev. H. A. HOLDEN, Litt.D. [In preparation.
POLYBIUS.—THE HISTORY OF THE ACHÆAN LEAGUE AS CONTAINED IN THE REMAINS OF POLYBIUS. By Rev. W. W. CAPES, M.A. 6s.
PROPERTIUS.—SELECT POEMS. By Prof. J. P. POSTGATE, Litt.D. 2nd Ed. 6s.
SALLUST.—*CATILINA and JUGURTHA. By C. MERIVALE, D.D., Dean of Ely. 3s. 6d. Or separately, 2s. each.
*BELLUM CATULINÆ. By A. M. COOK, M.A. 2s. 6d.
JUGURTHA. By the same. [In preparation.
TACITUS.—THE ANNALS. BOOKS I. and II. By J. S. REID, Litt.D. [In prep.
BOOK VI. By A. J. CHURCH, M.A., and W. J. BRODRIBB, M.A. 2s.
THE HISTORIES. BOOKS I. and II. By A. D. GODLEY, M.A. 3s. 6d.
BOOKS III.-V. By the same. 3s. 6d.
AGRICOLA and GERMANIA. By A. J. CHURCH, M.A., and W. J. BRODRIBB, M.A. 3s. 6d. Or separately, 2s. each.
AGRICOLA AND GERMANIA (separately). By F. J. HAVERFIELD, M.A., Student of Christ Church, Oxford. [In preparation.
TERENCE.—HAUTON TIMORUMENOS. By E. S. SHUCKBURGH, M.A. 2s. 6d. With Translation. 3s. 6d.

PHORMIO. By Rev. JOHN BOND, M.A., and Rev. A. S. WALPOLE, M.A. 2s. 6d.
ADELPHI. By Prof. S. G. ASHMORE. [In the Press.
THUCYDIDES.—BOOK I. By CLEMENT BRYANS, M.A. [In preparation.
BOOK II. By E. C. MARCHANT, M.A., Fellow of St. Peter's Coll., Cam. 3s. 6d.
BOOK III. By E. C. MARCHANT, M.A. [In preparation.
BOOK IV. By C. E. GRAVES, M.A., Classical Lecturer at St. John's College,
Cambridge. 3s. 6d.
BOOK V. By C. E. GRAVES, M.A. 3s. 6d.
BOOKS VI. AND VII. By Rev. PERCIVAL FROST, M.A. With Map. 3s. 6d.
BOOK VI. By E. C. MARCHANT, M.A. [In preparation.
BOOK VII. By E. C. MARCHANT, M.A. 3s. 6d.
BOOK VIII. By Prof. T. G. TUCKER, Litt.D. 3s. 6d.
TIBULLUS.—SELECT POEMS. By Prof. J. P. POSTGATE, Litt.D. [In preparation.
VIRGIL.—ÆNEID. BOOKS II. AND III. THE NARRATIVE OF ÆNEAS.
By E. W. HOWSON, M.A., Assistant Master at Harrow. 2s.
XENOPHON.—*THE ANABASIS. BOOKS I.-IV. By Profs. W. W. GOODWIN
and J. W. WHITE. Adapted to Goodwin's Greek Grammar. With Map. 3s. 6d.
BOOKS V.-VII. By Rev. G. H. NALL, M.A. [In preparation.
HELLENICA. BOOKS I. AND II. By H. HAILSTONE, B.A. With Map. 2s. 6d.
HELLENICA. BOOK III.-VII. 2 vols. By H. G. DAKYNS, M.A.
[III.-IV. in the Press.
CYROPÆDIA. BOOKS VII. AND VIII. By A. GOODWIN, M.A. 2s. 6d.
MEMORABILIA SOCRATIS. By A. R. CLUER, B.A., Balliol College, Oxford. 5s.
HIERO. By Rev. H. A. HOLDEN, Litt.D. 2s. 6d.
OECONOMICUS. By the same. With Lexicon. 5s.

CLASSICAL LIBRARY.

Texts, Edited with Introductions and Notes, for the use of
Advanced Students ; **Commentaries and Translations.**

ÆSCHYLUS.—THE SUPPLICES. A Revised Text, with Translation. By T.
G. TUCKER, Litt.D., Professor of Classical Philology in the University of Mel-
bourne. 8vo. 10s. 6d.
THE SEVEN AGAINST THEBES. With Translation. By A. W. VERRALL,
Litt.D., Fellow of Trinity College, Cambridge. 8vo. 7s. 6d.
AGAMEMNON. With Translation. By A. W. VERRALL, Litt.D. 8vo. 12s.
THE CHOEPHORI. With Translation. By A. W. VERRALL, Litt.D. 8vo. 12s.
AGAMEMNON, CHOEPHORI, AND EUMENIDES. By A. O. PRICKARD,
M.A., Fellow and Tutor of New College, Oxford. 8vo. [In preparation.
THE EUMENIDES. With Verse Translation. By B. DRAKE, M.A. 8vo. 5s.
ÆSCHYLUS. Translated into English Prose by Prof. T. G. TUCKER. Cr. 8vo.
[In preparation.
ANTONINUS, MARCUS AURELIUS.—BOOK IV. OF THE MEDITATIONS.
With Translation. By HASTINGS CROSSLEY, M.A. 8vo. 6s.
ARISTOPHANES.—THE BIRDS. Translated into English Verse. By B. H.
KENNEDY, D.D. Cr. 8vo. 6s. Help Notes to the Same, for the Use of
Students. 1s. 6d.
SCHOLIA ARISTOPHANICA; being such Comments adscript to the text of
Aristophanes as are preserved in the Codex Ravennas, arranged, emended, and
translated. By Rev. W. G. RUTHERFORD, M.A., LL.D. 8vo. [In the Press.
ARISTOTLE.—THE METAPHYSICS. BOOK I. Translated by a Cambridge
Graduate. 8vo. 5s.
THE POLITICS. By R. D. HICKS, M.A., Fellow of Trinity College, Cambridge.
8vo. [In the Press.
THE POLITICS. Translated by Rev. J. E. C. WELLDON, M.A., Headmaster of
Harrow. Cr. 8vo. 10s. 6d.
THE RHETORIC. Translated by the same. Cr. 8vo. 7s. 6d.
AN INTRODUCTION TO ARISTOTLE'S RHETORIC. With Analysis, Notes,
and Appendices. By E. M. COPE, Fellow and late Tutor of Trinity College,
Cambridge. 8vo. 14s.
THE NICOMACHEAN ETHICS. Translated by Rev. J. E. C. WELLDON, M.A.
Cr. 8vo. 7s. 6d.

THE SOPHISTICI ELENCHI. With Translation. By E. POSTE, M.A., Fellow of Oriel College, Oxford. 8vo. 8s. 6d.

ON THE CONSTITUTION OF ATHENS. By J. E. SANDYS, Litt.D. 8vo. 15s.

ON THE CONSTITUTION OF ATHENS. Translated by E. POSTE, M.A. 2nd Ed. Cr. 8vo. 3s. 6d.

ON THE ART OF POETRY. A Lecture. By A. O. PRICKARD, M.A., Fellow and Tutor of New College, Oxford. Cr. 8vo. 3s. 6d.

ATTIC ORATORS.—FROM ANTIPHON TO ISAEOS. By R. C. JEBB, Litt.D., Regius Professor of Greek in the University of Cambridge. 2 vols. 8vo. 25s.

BABRIUS.—With Lexicon. By Rev. W. G. RUTHERFORD, M.A., LL.D., Headmaster of Westminster. 8vo. 12s. 6d.

CATULLUS. By Prof. ARTHUR PALMER. [In preparation.

CICERO.—THE ACADEMICA. By J. S. REID, Litt.D., Fellow of Caius College, Cambridge. 8vo. 15s.

THE ACADEMICS. Translated by the same. 8vo. 5s. 6d.

SELECT LETTERS. After the Edition of ALBERT WATSON, M.A. Translated by G. E. JEANS, M.A., Fellow of Hertford College, Oxford. Cr. 8vo. 10s. 6d.

EURIPIDES.—MEDEA. By A. W. VERRALL, Litt.D. 8vo. 7s. 6d.

IPHIGENEIA AT AULIS. By E. B. ENGLAND, Litt.D. 8vo. 7s. 6d.

*INTRODUCTION TO THE STUDY OF EURIPIDES. By Professor J. P. MAHAFFY. Fcap. 8vo. 1s. 6d. (Classical Writers.)

HERODOTUS.—BOOKS I.-III. THE ANCIENT EMPIRES OF THE EAST. By A. H. SAYCE, Deputy-Professor of Comparative Philology in the University of Oxford. 8vo. 16s.

BOOKS IV.-IX. By R. W. MACAN, M.A., Reader in Ancient History in the University of Oxford. 8vo. [In preparation.

THE HISTORY. Translated by G. C. MACAULAY, M.A. 2 vols. Cr. 8vo. 18s.

HOMER.—THE ILIAD. By WALTER LEAF, Litt.D. 8vo. Books I.-XII. 14s. Books XIII.-XXIV. 14s.

COMPANION TO THE ILIAD FOR ENGLISH READERS. By the same. Cr. 8vo. 7s. 6d.

THE ILIAD. Translated into English Prose by ANDREW LANG, M.A., WALTER LEAF, Litt.D., and ERNEST MYERS, M.A. Cr. 8vo. 12s. 6d.

THE ODYSSEY. Done into English by S. H. BUTCHER, M.A., Professor of Greek in the University of Edinburgh, and ANDREW LANG, M.A. Cr. 8vo. 6s.

*INTRODUCTION TO THE STUDY OF HOMER. By the Right Hon. W. E. GLADSTONE. 18mo. 1s. (Literature Primers.)

HOMERIC DICTIONARY. Translated from the German of Dr. G. AUTENRIETH by R. P. KEEP, Ph.D. Illustrated. Cr. 8vo. 6s.

HORACE.—Translated by J. LONSDALE, M.A., and S. LEE, M.A. Gl. 8vo. 3s. 6d.

JUVENAL.—THIRTEEN SATIRES OF JUVENAL. By JOHN E. B. MAYOR, M.A., Professor of Latin in the University of Cambridge. Cr. 8vo. 2 vols. 10s. 6d. each.

THIRTEEN SATIRES. Translated by ALEX. LEEPER, M.A., LL.D., Warden of Trinity College, Melbourne. Revised Ed. Cr. 8vo. 3s. 6d.

KTESIAS.—THE FRAGMENTS OF THE PERSIKA OF KTESIAS. By JOHN GILMORE, M.A. 8vo. 8s. 6d.

LIVY.—BOOKS I.-IV. Translated by Rev. H. M. STEPHENSON, M.A. [In prep.

BOOKS XXI.-XXV. Translated by A. J. CHURCH, M.A., and W. J. BRODRIBB, M.A. Cr. 8vo. 7s. 6d.

*INTRODUCTION TO THE STUDY OF LIVY. By Rev. W. W. CAPES, M.A. Fcap. 8vo. 1s. 6d. (Classical Writers.)

LONGINUS.—ON THE SUBLIME. Translated by H. L. HAVELL, B.A. With Introduction by ANDREW LANG. Cr. 8vo. 4s. 6d.

MARTIAL.—BOOKS I. AND II. OF THE EPIGRAMS. By Prof. JOHN E. B. MAYOR, M.A. 8vo. [In the Press.

MELEAGER.—FIFTY POEMS OF MELEAGER. Translated by WALTER HEADLAM. Fcap. 4to. 7s. 6d.

PAUSANIAS.—DESCRIPTION OF GREECE. Translated with Commentary by J. G. FRAZER, M.A., Fellow of Trinity College, Cambridge. [In prep.

PHRYNICHUS.—THE NEW PHRYNICHUS; being a Revised Text of the Ecloga of the Grammarian Phrynichus. With Introduction and Commentary by Rev. W. G. RUTHERFORD, M.A., LL.D., Headmaster of Westminster. 8vo. 18s.

PINDAR.—THE EXTANT ODES OF PINDAR. Translated by ERNEST MYERS, M.A. Cr. 8vo. 5s.

THE OLYMPIAN AND PYTHIAN ODES. Edited, with an Introductory Essay, by BASIL GILDERSLEEVE, Professor of Greek in the Johns Hopkins University, U.S.A. Cr. 8vo. 7s. 6d.

THE NEMEAN ODES. By J. B. BURY, M.A., Fellow of Trinity College, Dublin. 8vo. 12s.

THE ISTHMIAN ODES. By the same Editor. 8vo. 12s. 6d.

PLATO.—PHÆDO. By R. D. ARCHER-HIND, M.A., Fellow of Trinity College, Cambridge. 8vo. 8s. 6d.

PHÆDO. By Sir W. D. GEDDES, LL.D., Principal of the University of Aberdeen. 8vo. 8s. 6d.

TIMAEUS. With Translation. By R. D. ARCHER-HIND, M.A. 8vo. 16s.

THE REPUBLIC OF PLATO. Translated by J. LL. DAVIES, M.A., and D. J. VAUGHAN, M.A. 18mo. 2s. 6d. net.

EUTHYPHRO, APOLOGY, CRITO, AND PHÆDO. Translated by F. J. CHURCH. 18mo. 2s. 6d. net.

PHÆDRUS, LYSIS, AND PROTAGORAS. Translated by J. WRIGHT, M.A. 18mo. 2s. 6d. net.

PLAUTUS.—THE MOSTELLARIA. By WILLIAM RAMSAY, M.A. Ed. by G. G. RAMSAY, M.A., Professor of Humanity, University of Glasgow. 8vo. 14s.

PLINY.—CORRESPONDENCE WITH TRAJAN. C. Plinii Caecilii Secundi Epistulæ ad Traianum Imperatorem cum Eiusdem Responsis. By E. G. HARDY, M.A. 8vo. 10s. 6d.

POLYBIUS.—THE HISTORIES OF POLYBIUS. Translated by E. S. SHUCK-BURGH, M.A. 2 vols. Cr. 8vo. 24s.

SALLUST.—CATILINE AND JUGURTHA. Translated by A. W. POLLARD, B.A. Cr. 8vo. 6s. THE CATILINE (separately). 3s.

SOPHOCLES.—ŒDIPUS THE KING. Translated into English Verse by E. D. A. MORSHEAD, M.A., Assistant Master at Winchester. Fcap. 8vo. 3s. 6d.

TACITUS.—THE ANNALS. By G. O. HOLBROOKE, M.A., Professor of Latin in Trinity College, Hartford, U.S.A. With Maps. 8vo. 16s.

THE ANNALS. Translated by A. J. CHURCH, M.A., and W. J. BRODRIBB, M.A. With Maps. Cr. 8vo. 7s. 6d.

THE HISTORIES. By Rev. W. A. SPOONER, M.A., Fellow and Tutor of New College, Oxford. 8vo. 16s.

THE HISTORY. Translated by A. J. CHURCH, M.A., and W. J. BRODRIBB, M.A. With Map. Cr. 8vo. 6s.

THE AGRICOLA AND GERMANY, WITH THE DIALOGUE ON ORATORY. Translated by the same. With Maps. Cr. 8vo. 4s. 6d.

*INTRODUCTION TO THE STUDY OF TACITUS. By A. J. CHURCH, M.A., and W. J. BRODRIBB, M.A. Fcap. 8vo. 1s. 6d. (*Classical Writers.*)

THEOCRITUS, BION, AND MOSCHUS. Translated by A. LANG, M.A. 18mo. 2s. 6d. net. Also an Edition on Large Paper. Cr. 8vo. 9s.

THUCYDIDES.—BOOK IV. A Revision of the Text, Illustrating the Principal Causes of Corruption in the Manuscripts of this Author. By Rev. W. G. RUTHERFORD, M.A., LL.D., Headmaster of Westminster. 8vo. 7s. 6d.

BOOK VIII. By H. C. GOODHART, M.A., Professor of Latin in the University of Edinburgh. [*In the Press.*]

VIRGIL.—Translated by J. LONSDALE, M.A., and S. LEE, M.A. Gl. 8vo. 8s. 6d.

THE ÆNEID. Translated by J. W. MACKAIL, M.A., Fellow of Balliol College, Oxford. Cr. 8vo. 7s. 6d.

XENOPHON.—Translated by H. G. DAKYNS, M.A. In four vols. Cr. 8vo. Vol. I. "The Anabasis" and "The Hellenica I. and II." 10s. 6d. Vol. II. "Hellenica" III.-VII. "Agesilaus," the "Politics," and "Revenues." 10s. 6d.

GRAMMAR, COMPOSITION, & PHILOLOGY.
Latin.

*BELCHER.—SHORT EXERCISES IN LATIN PROSE COMPOSITION AND EXAMINATION PAPERS IN LATIN GRAMMAR. Part I. By Rev. H. BELCHER, LL.D., Rector of the High School, Dunedin, N.Z. 18mo. 1s. 6d.

KEY, for Teachers only. 18mo. 3s. 6d.
*Part II., On the Syntax of Sentences, with an Appendix, including EXERCISES
IN LATIN IDIOMS, etc. 18mo. 2s. KEY, for Teachers only. 18mo. 3s.
*BRYANS.—LATIN PROSE EXERCISES BASED UPON CÆSAR'S GALLIC
WAR. With a Classification of Cæsar's Chief Phrases and Grammatical Notes
on Cæsar's Usages. By CLEMENT BRYANS, M.A., Assistant Master at Dulwich
College. Ex. fcap. 8vo. 2s. 6d. KEY, for Teachers only. 4s. 6d.
CORNELL UNIVERSITY STUDIES IN CLASSICAL PHILOLOGY. Edited by
I. FLAGG, W. G. HALE, and B. I. WHEELER. I. The CUM-Constructions: their
History and Functions. By W. G. HALE. Part 1. Critical. 1s. 8d. net. Part
2. Constructive. 3s. 4d. net. II. Analogy and the Scope of its Application
in Language. By B. I. WHEELER. 1s. 8d. net.
*EICKE.—FIRST LESSONS IN LATIN. By K. M. EICKE, B.A., Assistant Master
at Oundle School. Gl. 8vo. 2s. 6d.
*ENGLAND.—EXERCISES ON LATIN SYNTAX AND IDIOM. ARRANGED
WITH REFERENCE TO ROBY'S SCHOOL LATIN GRAMMAR. By E.
B. ENGLAND, Assistant Lecturer at the Owens College, Manchester. Cr. 8vo.
2s. 6d. KEY, for Teachers only. 2s. 6d.
GILES.—A SHORT MANUAL OF PHILOLOGY FOR CLASSICAL STUDENTS.
By P. GILES, M.A., Reader in Comparative Philology in the University of Cam-
bridge. Cr. 8vo. [In the Press.
HADLEY.—ESSAYS, PHILOLOGICAL AND CRITICAL. By JAMES HADLEY,
late Professor in Yale College. 8vo. 16s.
HODGSON.—MYTHOLOGY FOR LATIN VERSIFICATION. Fables for render-
ing into Latin Verse. By F. HODGSON, B.D., late Provost of Eton. New Ed.,
revised by F. C. HODGSON, M.A. 18mo. 3s.
JANNARIS.—HISTORICAL GRAMMAR OF THE GREEK LANGUAGE. By
Prof. A. N. JANNARIS. 8vo. [In preparation.
LUPTON.—*AN INTRODUCTION TO LATIN ELEGIAC VERSE COMPOSI-
TION. By J. H. LUPTON, Sur-Master of St. Paul's School. Gl. 8vo. 2s. 6d.
KEY TO PART II. (XXV.-C.), for Teachers only. Gl. 8vo. 3s. 6d.
*AN INTRODUCTION TO LATIN LYRIC VERSE COMPOSITION. By the
same. Gl. 8vo. 3s. KEY, for Teachers only. Gl. 8vo. 4s. 6d.
*MACMILLAN.—FIRST LATIN GRAMMAR. By M. C. MACMILLAN, M.A.
Fcap. 8vo. 1s. 6d.
MACMILLAN'S LATIN COURSE.
*FIRST PART. By A. M. COOK, M.A., Assistant Master at St. Paul's School.
Gl. 8vo. 3s. 6d.
*SECOND PART. By A. M. COOK, M.A., and W. E. P. PANTIN, M.A. New and
Enlarged Edition. Gl. 8vo. 4s. 6d.
*MACMILLAN'S SHORTER LATIN COURSE.—By A. M. COOK, M.A. Abridgment
of "Macmillan's Latin Course," First Part. Gl. 8vo. 1s. 6d. [2nd Part in prep.
KEY, for Teachers only. 4s. 6d.
*MACMILLAN'S LATIN READER.—A LATIN READER FOR THE LOWER
FORMS IN SCHOOLS. By H. J. HARDY, M.A., Assistant Master at Win-
chester. Gl. 8vo. 2s. 6d.
NIXON.—PARALLEL EXTRACTS, Arranged for Translation into English and
Latin, with Notes on Idioms. By J. E. NIXON, M.A., Fellow and Classical
Lecturer, King's College, Cambridge. Part I.—Historical and Epistolary.
Cr. 8vo. 3s. 6d.
PROSE EXTRACTS, Arranged for Translation into English and Latin, with
General and Special Prefaces on Style and Idiom. By the same. I. Oratorical.
II. Historical. III. Philosophical. IV. Anecdotes and Letters. 2nd Ed.,
enlarged to 280 pp. Cr. 8vo. 4s. 6d. SELECTIONS FROM THE SAME. 2s. 6d.
Translations of about 70 Extracts can be supplied to Schoolmasters (2s. 6d.),
on application to the Author: and about 40 similarly of "Parallel Extracts."
1s. 6d. post free.
*PANTIN.—A FIRST LATIN VERSE BOOK. By W. E. P. PANTIN, M.A
Assistant Master at St. Paul's School. Gl. 8vo. 1s. 6d.
KEY, for Teachers only. 4s. net.

*PEILE.—A PRIMER OF PHILOLOGY. By J. Peile, Litt.D., Master of Christ's College, Cambridge. 18mo. 1s.

*POSTGATE.—SERMO LATINUS. A short Guide to Latin Prose Composition. By Prof. J. P. Postgate, Litt.D., Fellow of Trinity College, Cambridge. GL 8vo. 2s. 6d. KEY to "Selected Passages." Gl. 8vo. 3s. 6d.

POTTS.—*HINTS TOWARDS LATIN PROSE COMPOSITION. By A. W. Potts, M.A., LL.D., late Fellow of St. John's College, Cambridge. Ex. fcap. 8vo. 3s.

*PASSAGES FOR TRANSLATION INTO LATIN PROSE. Edited with Notes and References to the above. Ex. fcap. 8vo. 2s. 6d. KEY, for Teachers only. 2s. 6d.

*PRESTON.—EXERCISES IN LATIN VERSE OF VARIOUS KINDS. By Rev. G. Preston. Gl. 8vo. 2s. 6d. KEY, for Teachers only. Gl. 8vo. 5s.

REID.—A GRAMMAR OF TACITUS. By J. S. Reid, Litt.D., Fellow of Caius College, Cambridge. [In preparation.
A GRAMMAR OF VIRGIL. By the same. [In preparation.

ROBY.—Works by H. J. Roby, M.A., late Fellow of St. John's College, Cambridge.
A GRAMMAR OF THE LATIN LANGUAGE, from Plautus to Suetonius. Part I. Sounds, Inflexions, Word-formation, Appendices. Cr. 8vo. 9s. Part II. Syntax, Prepositions, etc. 10s. 6d.
*SCHOOL LATIN GRAMMAR. Cr. 8vo. 5s.

ROBY—WILKINS. AN ELEMENTARY LATIN GRAMMAR. By H. J. Roby, M.A., and Prof. A. S. Wilkins, Litt.D. Gl. 8vo. 2s. 6d.

*RUSH.—SYNTHETIC LATIN DELECTUS. With Notes and Vocabulary. By E. Rush, B.A. Ex. fcap. 8vo. 2s. 6d.

*RUST.—FIRST STEPS TO LATIN PROSE COMPOSITION. By Rev. G. Rust, M.A. 18mo. 1s. 6d. KEY, for Teachers only. By W. M. Yates. 18mo. 3s. 6d.

SHUCKBURGH.—PASSAGES FROM LATIN AUTHORS FOR TRANSLATION INTO ENGLISH. Selected with a view to the needs of Candidates for the Cambridge Local, and Public Schools' Examinations. By E. S. Shuckburgh, M.A. Cr. 8vo. 2s.

*SIMPSON. — LATIN PROSE AFTER THE BEST AUTHORS : Cæsarian Prose. By F. P. Simpson, B.A. Ex. fcap. 8vo. 2s. 6d. KEY, for Teachers only. 5s.

STRACHAN — WILKINS. — ANALECTA. Selected Passages for Translation. By J. S. Strachan, M.A., Professor of Greek, and A. S. Wilkins, Litt.D., Professor of Latin, Owens College, Manchester. Cr. 8vo. In two parts, 2s. 6d. each. Indexes to Greek and Latin passages, 6d. each.

THRING.—A LATIN GRADUAL. By the Rev. E. Thring, M.A., late Headmaster of Uppingham. A First Latin Construing Book. Fcap. 8vo. 2s. 6d.
A MANUAL OF MOOD CONSTRUCTIONS. Fcap. 8vo. 1s. 6d.

*WELCH—DUFFIELD.—LATIN ACCIDENCE AND EXERCISES ARRANGED FOR BEGINNERS. By W. Welch and C. G. Duffield. 18mo. 1s. 6d.

WRIGHT.—Works by J. Wright, M.A., late Headmaster of Sutton Coldfield School.
A HELP TO LATIN GRAMMAR; or, the Form and Use of Words in Latin, with Progressive Exercises. Cr. 8vo. 4s. 6d.
THE SEVEN KINGS OF ROME. An Easy Narrative, abridged from the First Book of Livy by the omission of Difficult Passages; being a First Latin Reading Book, with Grammatical Notes and Vocabulary. Fcap. 8vo. 3s. 6d.
FIRST LATIN STEPS; OR, AN INTRODUCTION BY A SERIES OF EXAMPLES TO THE STUDY OF THE LATIN LANGUAGE. Cr. 8vo. 3s.
A COMPLETE LATIN COURSE, comprising Rules with Examples, Exercises, both Latin and English, on each Rule, and Vocabularies. Cr. 8vo. 2s. 6d.

Greek.

BLACKIE.—GREEK AND ENGLISH DIALOGUES FOR USE IN SCHOOLS AND COLLEGES. By John Stuart Blackie, Emeritus Professor of Greek in the University of Edinburgh. New Edition. Fcap. 8vo. 2s. 6d.
A GREEK PRIMER, COLLOQUIAL AND CONSTRUCTIVE. Cr. 8vo. 2s. 6d.

BRYANS.—GREEK PROSE EXERCISES based upon Thucydides. By C. Bryans, M.A. [In preparation.

GILES.—See under Latin.

GOODWIN.—Works by W. W. GOODWIN, LL.D., D.C.L., Professor of Greek in Harvard University.
SYNTAX OF THE MOODS AND TENSES OF THE GREEK VERB. New Ed., revised and enlarged. 8vo. 14s.
*A GREEK GRAMMAR. Cr. 8vo. 6s.
*A GREEK GRAMMAR FOR SCHOOLS. Cr. 8vo. 3s. 6d.

HADLEY.—See under Latin.

HADLEY—ALLEN.—A GREEK GRAMMAR FOR SCHOOLS AND COLLEGES. By JAMES HADLEY, late Professor in Yale College. Revised by F. DE F. ALLEN, Professor in Harvard College. Cr. 8vo. 6s.

*JACKSON.—FIRST STEPS TO GREEK PROSE COMPOSITION. By BLOMFIELD JACKSON, M.A. 18mo. 1s. 6d. KEY, for Teachers only. 18mo. 3s. 6d.
*SECOND STEPS TO GREEK PROSE COMPOSITION, with Examination Papers. By the same. 18mo. 2s. 6d. KEY, for Teachers only. 18mo. 3s. 6d.

KYNASTON.—EXERCISES IN THE COMPOSITION OF GREEK IAMBIC VERSE. By Rev. H. KYNASTON, D.D., Professor of Classics in the University of Durham. With Vocabulary. Ex. fcap. 8vo. 5s. KEY, for Teachers only. Ex. fcap. 8vo. 4s. 6d.

MACKIE.—PARALLEL PASSAGES FOR TRANSLATION INTO GREEK AND ENGLISH. With Indexes. By Rev. E. C. MACKIE, M.A., Classical Master at Heversham Grammar School. Gl. 8vo. 4s. 6d.

MACMILLAN'S GREEK COURSE.—Edited by Rev. W. G. RUTHERFORD, M.A., LL.D., Headmaster of Westminster. Gl. 8vo.
*FIRST GREEK GRAMMAR—ACCIDENCE. By the Editor. 2s.
*FIRST GREEK GRAMMAR—SYNTAX. By the same. 2s.
ACCIDENCE AND SYNTAX. In one volume. 3s. 6d.
*EASY EXERCISES IN GREEK ACCIDENCE. By H. G. UNDERHILL, M.A., Assistant Master at St. Paul's Preparatory School. 2s.
*A SECOND GREEK EXERCISE BOOK. By Rev. W. A. HEARD, M.A., Headmaster of Fettes College, Edinburgh. 2s. 6d.
*EASY EXERCISES IN GREEK SYNTAX. By Rev. G. H. NALL, M.A., Assistant Master at Westminster School. 2s. 6d.
MANUAL OF GREEK ACCIDENCE. By the Editor. [In preparation.
MANUAL OF GREEK SYNTAX. By the Editor. [In preparation.
ELEMENTARY GREEK COMPOSITION. By the Editor. [In preparation.

*MACMILLAN'S GREEK READER.—STORIES AND LEGENDS. A First Greek Reader, with Notes, Vocabulary, and Exercises. By F. H. COLSON, M.A., Headmaster of Plymouth College. Gl. 8vo. 3s.

*MARSHALL.—A TABLE OF IRREGULAR GREEK VERBS, classified according to the arrangement of Curtius's Greek Grammar. By J. M. MARSHALL, M.A., Headmaster of the Grammar School, Durham. 8vo. 1s.

MAYOR.—FIRST GREEK READER. By Prof. JOHN E. B. MAYOR, M.A., Fellow of St. John's College, Cambridge. Fcap. 8vo. 4s. 6d.

MAYOR.—GREEK FOR BEGINNERS. By Rev. J. B. MAYOR, M.A., late Professor of Classical Literature in King's College, London. Part I., with Vocabulary, 1s. 6d. Parts II. and III., with Vocabulary and Index. Fcap. 8vo. 3s. 6d. Complete in one Vol. 4s. 6d.

NALL.—A SHORT LATIN-ENGLISH DICTIONARY. By Rev. G. H. NALL.
[In preparation.
A SHORT GREEK-ENGLISH DICTIONARY. By the same. [In preparation.

PEILE.—See under Latin.

RUTHERFORD.—THE NEW PHRYNICHUS; being a Revised Text of the Ecloga of the Grammarian Phrynichus. With Introduction and Commentary. By the Rev. W. G. RUTHERFORD, M.A., LL.D., Headmaster of Westminster. 8vo. 18s.

STRACHAN—WILKINS.—See under Latin.

WHITE.—FIRST LESSONS IN GREEK. Adapted to GOODWIN'S GREEK GRAMMAR, and designed as an introduction to the ANABASIS OF XENOPHON. By JOHN WILLIAMS WHITE, Assistant Professor of Greek in Harvard University, U.S.A. Cr. 8vo. 3s. 6d.

WRIGHT.—ATTIC PRIMER. Arranged for the Use of Beginners. By J. WRIGHT, M.A. Ex. fcap. 8vo. 2s. 6d.

ANTIQUITIES, ANCIENT HISTORY, AND PHILOSOPHY.

ARNOLD.—A HISTORY OF THE EARLY ROMAN EMPIRE. By W. T. Arnold, M.A. Cr. 8vo. [*In preparation.*

ARNOLD.—THE SECOND PUNIC WAR. Being Chapters from THE HISTORY OF ROME by the late Thomas Arnold, D.D., Headmaster of Rugby. Edited, with Notes, by W. T. Arnold, M.A. With 8 Maps. Cr. 8vo. 5s.

*BEESLY.—STORIES FROM THE HISTORY OF ROME. By Mrs. Beesly. Fcap. 8vo. 2s. 6d.

BLACKIE.—HORÆ HELLENICÆ. By John Stuart Blackie, Emeritus Professor of Greek in the University of Edinburgh. 8vo. 12s.

BURN.—ROMAN LITERATURE IN RELATION TO ROMAN ART. By Rev. Robert Burn, M.A., late Fellow of Trinity College, Cambridge. Illustrated. Ex. cr. 8vo. 14s.

BURY.—A HISTORY OF THE LATER ROMAN EMPIRE FROM ARCADIUS TO IRENE, A.D. 395-800. By J. B. Bury, M.A., Fellow of Trinity College, Dublin. 2 vols. 8vo. 32s.
A SCHOOL HISTORY OF GREECE. By the same. Cr. 8vo. [*In preparation.*

BUTCHER.—SOME ASPECTS OF THE GREEK GENIUS. By S. H. Butcher, M.A., Professor of Greek, Edinburgh. Cr. 8vo. 7s. 6d. net.

*CLASSICAL WRITERS.—Edited by John Richard Green, M.A., LL.D. Fcap. 8vo. 1s. 6d. each.
SOPHOCLES. By Prof. L. Campbell, M.A.
EURIPIDES. By Prof. Mahaffy, D.D.
DEMOSTHENES. By Prof. S. H. Butcher, M.A.
VIRGIL. By Prof. Nettleship, M.A.
LIVY. By Rev. W. W. Capes, M.A.
TACITUS. By A. J. Church, M.A., and W. J. Brodribb, M.A.
MILTON. By Rev. Stopford A. Brooke, M.A.

DYER.—STUDIES OF THE GODS IN GREECE AT CERTAIN SANCTUARIES RECENTLY EXCAVATED. By Louis Dyer, B.A. Ex. Cr. 8vo. 8s. 6d. net.

FOWLER.—THE CITY-STATE OF THE GREEKS AND ROMANS. By W. Warde Fowler, M.A. Cr. 8vo. 5s.

FREEMAN.—HISTORICAL ESSAYS. By the late Edward A. Freeman, D.C.L., LL.D. Second Series. [Greek and Roman History.] 8vo. 10s. 6d.

GARDNER.—SAMOS AND SAMIAN COINS. An Essay. By Percy Gardner, Litt.D., Professor of Archæology in the University of Oxford. 8vo. 7s. 6d.

GEDDES.—THE PROBLEM OF THE HOMERIC POEMS. By Sir W. D. Geddes, Principal of the University of Aberdeen. 8vo. 14s.

GLADSTONE.—Works by the Rt. Hon. W. E. Gladstone, M.P.
THE TIME AND PLACE OF HOMER. Cr. 8vo. 6s. 6d.
LANDMARKS OF HOMERIC STUDY. Cr. 8vo. 2s. 6d.
*A PRIMER OF HOMER. 18mo. 1s.

GOW.—A COMPANION TO SCHOOL CLASSICS. By James Gow, Litt.D., Head Master of the High School, Nottingham. Illustrated. Cr. 8vo. 6s.

HARRISON—VERRALL.—MYTHOLOGY AND MONUMENTS OF ANCIENT ATHENS. Translation of a portion of the "Attica" of Pausanias. By Margaret de G. Verrall. With Introductory Essay and Archæological Commentary by Jane E. Harrison. With Illustrations and Plans. Cr. 8vo. 16s.

HOLM.—HISTORY OF GREECE. By Professor A. Holm. Translated. 4 vols. [*In preparation.*

JEBB.—Works by R. C. Jebb, Litt.D., Professor of Greek in the University of Cambridge.
THE ATTIC ORATORS FROM ANTIPHON TO ISAEOS. 2 vols. 8vo. 25s.
*A PRIMER OF GREEK LITERATURE. 18mo. 1s.
LECTURES ON GREEK POETRY. Cr. 8vo. [*In the Press.*

KIEPERT.—MANUAL OF ANCIENT GEOGRAPHY. By Dr. H. Kiepert. Cr. 8vo. 5s.

LANCIANI.—ANCIENT ROME IN THE LIGHT OF RECENT DISCOVERIES. By RODOLFO LANCIANI, Professor of Archæology in the University of Rome. Illustrated. 4to. 24s.

PAGAN AND CHRISTIAN ROME. By the same. Illustrated. 4to. 24s.

LEAF.—COMPANION TO THE ILIAD FOR ENGLISH READERS. By WALTER LEAF, Litt.D. Cr. 8vo. 7s. 6d.

MAHAFFY.—Works by J. P. MAHAFFY, D.D., Fellow of Trinity College, Dublin, and Professor of Ancient History in the University of Dublin.

SOCIAL LIFE IN GREECE; from Homer to Menander. Cr. 8vo. 9s.

GREEK LIFE AND THOUGHT; from the Age of Alexander to the Roman Conquest. Cr. 8vo. 12s. 6d.

THE GREEK WORLD UNDER ROMAN SWAY. From Plutarch to Polybius. Cr. 8vo. 10s. 6d.

PROBLEMS IN GREEK HISTORY. Cr. 8vo. 7s. 6d.

RAMBLES AND STUDIES IN GREECE. 4th Ed. Illust. Cr. 8vo. 10s. 6d.

A HISTORY OF CLASSICAL GREEK LITERATURE. Cr. 8vo. Vol. I. The Poets. Part I. Epic and Lyric. Part II. Dramatic. Vol. II. Prose Writers. Part I. Herodotus to Plato. Part II. Isocrates to Aristotle. 4s. 6d. each Part.

*A PRIMER OF GREEK ANTIQUITIES. With Illustrations. 18mo. 1s.

MAYOR.—BIBLIOGRAPHICAL CLUE TO LATIN LITERATURE. Edited after HÜBNER. By Prof. JOHN E. B. MAYOR. Cr. 8vo. 10s. 6d.

NEWTON.—ESSAYS ON ART AND ARCHÆOLOGY. By Sir CHARLES NEWTON, K.C.B., D.C.L. 8vo. 12s. 6d.

PATER.—PLATO AND PLATONISM. By W. PATER, Fellow of Brasenose College, Oxford. Ex. Cr. 8vo. 8s. 6d.

PHILOLOGY.—THE JOURNAL OF PHILOLOGY. Edited by W. A. WRIGHT, M.A., I. BYWATER, M.A., and H. JACKSON, Litt.D. 4s. 6d. each (half-yearly).

SAYCE.—THE ANCIENT EMPIRES OF THE EAST. By A. H. SAYCE, M.A., Deputy-Professor of Comparative Philology, Oxford. Cr. 8vo. 6s.

SCHMIDT—WHITE. AN INTRODUCTION TO THE RHYTHMIC AND METRIC OF THE CLASSICAL LANGUAGES. By Dr. J. H. H. SCHMIDT. Translated by JOHN WILLIAMS WHITE, Ph.D. 8vo. 10s. 6d.

SCHREIBER—ANDERSON.—ATLAS OF CLASSICAL ARCHAEOLOGY. By TH. SCHREIBER, with English Text by Prof. W. C. F. ANDERSON. [In the Press.

SCHUCHHARDT.—DR. SCHLIEMANN'S EXCAVATIONS AT TROY, TIRYNS, MYCENÆ, ORCHOMENOS, ITHACA, presented in the light of recent knowledge. By Dr. CARL SCHUCHHARDT. Translated by EUGENIE SELLERS. Introduction by WALTER LEAF, Litt.D. Illustrated. 8vo. 18s. net.

SHUCKBURGH.—A SCHOOL HISTORY OF ROME. By E. S. SHUCKBURGH, M.A. Cr. 8vo. [In the Press.

SMITH.—A HANDBOOK ON GREEK PAINTING. By CECIL SMITH. [In prep.

*STEWART.**—THE TALE OF TROY. Done into English by AUBREY STEWART. Gl. 8vo. 3s. 6d. [18mo. 1s.

*TOZER.**—A PRIMER OF CLASSICAL GEOGRAPHY. By H. F. TOZER, M.A.

WILKINS.—Works by Prof. WILKINS, Litt.D., LL.D.

*A PRIMER OF ROMAN ANTIQUITIES. Illustrated. 18mo. 1s.

*A PRIMER OF ROMAN LITERATURE. 18mo. 1s.

WILKINS—ARNOLD.—A MANUAL OF ROMAN ANTIQUITIES. By Prof. A. S. WILKINS, Litt.D., and W. T. ARNOLD, M.A. Cr. 8vo. [In prep.

MODERN LANGUAGES AND LITERATURE.

English; French; German; Modern Greek; Italian; Spanish.

ENGLISH.

*ABBOTT.**—A SHAKESPEARIAN GRAMMAR. An Attempt to Illustrate some of the Differences between Elizabethan and Modern English. By the Rev. E. A. ABBOTT, D.D., formerly Headmaster of the City of London School. Ex. fcap. 8vo. 6s.

*ADDISON.**—SELECTIONS FROM "THE SPECTATOR." With Introduction and Notes, by K. DEIGHTON. Gl. 8vo. 2s. 6d.

*BACON.—ESSAYS. With Introduction and Notes, by F. G. SELBY, M.A., Principal and Professor of Logic and Moral Philosophy, Deccan College, Poona. Gl. 8vo. 3s. ; sewed, 2s. 6d.
*THE ADVANCEMENT OF LEARNING. Book I. By the same. Gl. 8vo. 2s.
BROOKE.—EARLY ENGLISH LITERATURE. By Rev. STOPFORD A. BROOKE, M.A. 2 vols. 8vo. 20s. net.
BROWNING.—A PRIMER ON BROWNING. By F. M. WILSON. Gl 8vo. 2s. 6d.
*BURKE.—REFLECTIONS ON THE FRENCH REVOLUTION. By F. G. SELBY, M.A. Gl. 8vo. 5s.
BUTLER.—HUDIBRAS. With Introduction and Notes, by ALFRED MILNES, M.A. Ex. fcap. 8vo. Part I. 3s. 6d. Parts II. and III. 4s. 6d.
CAMPBELL.—SELECTIONS. With Introduction and Notes, by CECIL M. BARROW, M.A., Principal of Victoria College, Palghât. Gl. 8vo. [In preparation.
CHAUCER.—A PRIMER OF CHAUCER. By A. W. POLLARD, M.A. 18mo. 1s.
COLLINS.—THE STUDY OF ENGLISH LITERATURE: A Plea for its Recognition at the Universities. By J. CHURTON COLLINS, M.A. Cr. 8vo. 4s. 6d.
COWPER.—*THE TASK : an Epistle to Joseph Hill, Esq. ; TIROCINIUM, or a Review of the Schools ; and THE HISTORY OF JOHN GILPIN. Edited, with Notes, by W. BENHAM B.D. Gl. 8vo. 1s.
THE TASK. With Introduction and Notes, by F. J. ROWE, M.A., and W. T. WEBB, M.A. [In preparation.
CRAIK.—ENGLISH PROSE SELECTIONS. With Critical Introductions by various writers, and General Introductions to each Period. Edited by HENRY CRAIK, C.B., LL.D. In 5 vols. Vol. I. 14th to 16th Century. Cr. 8vo. 7s. 6d.
DRYDEN.—SELECT PROSE WORKS. Edited, with Introduction and Notes, by Prof. C. D. YONGE. Fcap. 8vo. 2s. 6d.
SELECT SATIRES. With Introduction and Notes. By J. CHURTON COLLINS, M.A. Gl. 8vo. [In preparation.
*GLOBE READERS. Edited by A. F. MURISON. Illustrated. Gl. 8vo.
Primer I. (48 pp.) 3d. Primer II. (48 pp.) 3d. Book I. (132 pp.) 8d. Book II. (136 pp.) 10d. Book III. (232 pp.) 1s. 3d. Book IV. (328 pp.) 1s. 9d. Book V. (408 pp.) 2s. Book VI. (436 pp.) 2s. 6d.
*THE SHORTER GLOBE READERS.—Illustrated. Gl. 8vo.
Primer I. (48 pp.) 3d. Primer II. (48 pp.) 8d. Book I. (132 pp.) 8d. Book II. (136 pp.) 10d. Book III. (178 pp.) 1s. Book IV. (182 pp.) 1s. Book V. (216 pp.) 1s. 3d. Book VI. (228 pp.) 1s. 6d.
*GOLDSMITH.—THE TRAVELLER, or a Prospect of Society ; and THE DESERTED VILLAGE. With Notes, Philological and Explanatory, by J. W. HALES, M.A. Cr. 8vo. 6d.
*THE TRAVELLER AND THE DESERTED VILLAGE. With Introduction and Notes, by A. BARRETT, B.A., Professor of English Literature, Elphinstone College, Bombay. Gl 8vo. 1s. 9d. ; sewed, 1s. 6d. The Traveller (separately), 1s., sewed.
*THE VICAR OF WAKEFIELD. With a Memoir of Goldsmith, by Prof. MASSON. Gl. 8vo. 1s.
SELECT ESSAYS. With Introduction and Notes, by Prof. C. D. YONGE. Fcap. 8vo. 2s. 6d.
GOW.—A METHOD OF ENGLISH, for Secondary Schools. Part I. By JAMES Gow, Litt.D. Gl. 8vo. 2s.
*GRAY.—POEMS. With Introduction and Notes, by JOHN BRADSHAW, LL.D. Gl. 8vo. 1s. 9d. ; sewed, 1s. 6d.
*HALES.—Works by J. W. HALES, M.A., Professor of English Literature at King's College, London.
LONGER ENGLISH POEMS. With Notes, Philological and Explanatory, and an Introduction on the Teaching of English. Ex. fcap. 8vo. 4s. 6d.
SHORTER ENGLISH POEMS. Ex. fcap. 8vo. [In preparation.
*HELPS.—ESSAYS WRITTEN IN THE INTERVALS OF BUSINESS. With Introduction and Notes, by F. J. ROWE, M.A., and W. T. WEBB, M.A. Gl. 8vo. 1s. 9d. ; sewed, 1s. 6d.
*JOHNSON.—LIVES OF THE POETS. The Six Chief Lives (Milton, Dryden, Swift, Addison, Pope, Gray), with Macaulay's "Life of Johnson." With Preface and Notes by MATTHEW ARNOLD. Cr. 8vo. 4s. 6d.

*LIFE OF MILTON. With Introduction and Notes, by K. DEIGHTON. Globe 8vo. 1s. 9d.

KELLNER.—HISTORICAL OUTLINES OF ENGLISH SYNTAX. By L. KELLNER, Ph.D. Globe 8vo. 6s.

LAMB.—TALES FROM SHAKESPEARE. With Introduction and Notes by Rev. A. AINGER, LL.D., Canon of Bristol. 18mo. 2s. 6d. net.

*LITERATURE PRIMERS.—Edited by J. R. GREEN, LL.D. 18mo. 1s. each.
ENGLISH GRAMMAR. By Rev. R. MORRIS, LL.D.
ENGLISH GRAMMAR EXERCISES. By R. MORRIS, LL.D., and H. C. BOWEN, M.A.
EXERCISES ON MORRIS'S PRIMER OF ENGLISH GRAMMAR. By J. WETHERELL, M.A.
ENGLISH COMPOSITION. By Professor NICHOL.
QUESTIONS AND EXERCISES ON ENGLISH COMPOSITION. By Prof. NICHOL and W. S. M'CORMICK.
ENGLISH LITERATURE. By STOPFORD BROOKE, M.A.
SHAKSPERE. By Professor DOWDEN.
CHAUCER. By A. W. POLLARD, M.A.
THE CHILDREN'S TREASURY OF LYRICAL POETRY. Selected and arranged with Notes by FRANCIS TURNER PALGRAVE. In Two Parts. 1s. each.
PHILOLOGY. By J. PEILE, Litt.D.
ROMAN LITERATURE. By Prof. A. S. WILKINS, Litt.D.
GREEK LITERATURE. By Prof. JEBB, Litt.D.
HOMER. By the Rt. Hon. W. E. GLADSTONE, M.P.

A HISTORY OF ENGLISH LITERATURE IN FOUR VOLUMES. Cr. 8vo.
EARLY ENGLISH LITERATURE. By STOPFORD BROOKE, M.A. [In preparation.
ELIZABETHAN LITERATURE. (1560-1665.) By GEORGE SAINTSBURY. 7s. 6d.
EIGHTEENTH CENTURY LITERATURE. (1660-1780.) By EDMUND GOSSE, M.A. 7s. 6d.
THE MODERN PERIOD. By Prof. DOWDEN. [In preparation.

LITTLEDALE.—ESSAYS ON TENNYSON'S IDYLLS OF THE KING. By H. LITTLEDALE, M.A., Vice-Principal and Professor of English Literature, Baroda College. Cr. 8vo. 4s. 6d.

MACLEAN.—ZUPITZA'S OLD AND MIDDLE ENGLISH READER. With Notes and Vocabulary by Prof. G. E. MACLEAN. [In the Press.

*MACMILLAN'S HISTORY READERS. (See History, p. 43.)

*MACMILLAN'S READING BOOKS.
PRIMER. 18mo. (48 pp.) 2d. BOOK I. (96 pp.) 4d. BOOK II. (144 pp.) 5d. BOOK III. (160 pp.) 6d. BOOK IV. (176 pp.) 8d. BOOK V. (380 pp.) 1s. BOOK VI. Cr. 8vo. (430 pp.) 2s.
Book VI. is fitted for Higher Classes, and as an Introduction to English Literature.

MACMILLAN'S RECITATION CARDS. Selections from TENNYSON, KINGSLEY, MATTHEW ARNOLD, CHRISTINA ROSSETTI, DOYLE. Annotated. Cr. 8vo. Nos. 1 to 18, 1d. each; Nos. 19 to 36, 2d. each.

*MACMILLAN'S COPY BOOKS.—1. Large Post 4to. Price 4d. each. 2. Post Oblong. Price 2d. each.
Nos. 3, 4, 5, 6, 7, 8, 9 may be had with Goodman's Patent Sliding Copies. Large Post 4to. Price 6d. each.

MACAULAY'S ESSAYS.—LORD CLIVE. With Introduction and Notes by K. DEIGHTON. Gl. 8vo.
WARREN HASTINGS. By the same. Gl. 8vo.
ADDISON. With Introduction and Notes by Prof. J. W. HALES, M.A. Gl. 8vo. [In preparation.

MARTIN.—*THE POET'S HOUR: Poetry selected for Children. By FRANCES MARTIN. 18mo. 2s. 6d.
*SPRING-TIME WITH THE POETS. By the same. 18mo. 3s. 6d.

*MILTON.—PARADISE LOST. Books I. and II. With Introduction and Notes, by MICHAEL MACMILLAN, B.A., Professor of English Literature. Elphinstone College, Bombay. Gl. 8vo. 1s. 9d. Or separately, 1s. 3d.; sewed 1s. each.
*L'ALLEGRO, IL PENSEROSO, LYCIDAS, ARCADES, SONNETS, &c. With Introduction and Notes, by W. BELL, M.A., Professor of Philosophy and Logic, Government College, Lahore. Gl. 8vo. 1s. 9d.

*COMUS. By the same. Gl. 8vo. 1s. 3d.
*SAMSON AGONISTES. By H. M. PERCIVAL, M.A., Professor of English Litera-
ture, Presidency College, Calcutta. Gl. 8vo. 2s.
*INTRODUCTION TO THE STUDY OF MILTON. By STOPFORD BROOKE,
M.A. Fcap. 8vo. 1s. 6d. (*Classical Writers.*)
MORRIS.—Works by the Rev. R. MORRIS, LL.D.
*A PRIMER OF ENGLISH GRAMMAR. 18mo. 1s.
*ELEMENTARY LESSONS IN HISTORICAL ENGLISH GRAMMAR, con-
taining Accidence and Word-Formation. 18mo. 2s. 6d.
*HISTORICAL OUTLINES OF ENGLISH ACCIDENCE, with Chapters on the
Development of the Language, and on Word-Formation. Ex. fcap. 8vo. 6s.
NICHOL—M'CORMICK.—A SHORT HISTORY OF ENGLISH LITERATURE.
By Prof. JOHN NICHOL and Prof. W. S. M'CORMICK. [*In preparation.*
OLIPHANT.—THE LITERARY HISTORY OF ENGLAND, 1790-1825. By
Mrs. OLIPHANT. 3 vols. 8vo. 21s.
OLIPHANT.—THE OLD AND MIDDLE ENGLISH. By T. L. KINGTON
OLIPHANT. 2nd Ed. Gl. 8vo. 9s.
THE NEW ENGLISH. By the same. 2 vols. Cr. 8vo. 21s.
PALGRAVE.—THE GOLDEN TREASURY OF SONGS AND LYRICS. Selected
by F. T. PALGRAVE. 18mo. 2s. 6d. net.
*THE CHILDREN'S TREASURY OF LYRICAL POETRY. Selected by the
same. 18mo. 2s. 6d. net. Also in Two Parts. 1s. each.
PATMORE.—THE CHILDREN'S GARLAND FROM THE BEST POETS.
Selected by COVENTRY PATMORE. 18mo. 2s. 6d. net.
*RANSOME.—SHORT STUDIES OF SHAKESPEARE'S PLOTS. By CYRIL
RANSOME, M.A., Professor of Modern History and Literature, Yorkshire College,
Leeds. Cr. 8vo. 3s. 6d. Also HAMLET, MACBETH, THE TEMPEST, 9d.
each, sewed.
*RYLAND.—CHRONOLOGICAL OUTLINES OF ENGLISH LITERATURE.
By F. RYLAND, M.A. Cr. 8vo. 6s.
SCOTT.—*LAY OF THE LAST MINSTREL, and THE LADY OF THE LAKE.
Edited by FRANCIS TURNER PALGRAVE. Gl. 8vo. 1s.
*THE LAY OF THE LAST MINSTREL. With Introduction and Notes, by G. H.
STUART, M.A., Principal of Kumbakonam College, and E. H. ELLIOT, B.A.
Gl. 8vo. 2s. Canto I. 9d. Cantos I. to III. and IV. to VI. Sewed, 1s. each.
*MARMION, and THE LORD OF THE ISLES. By F. T. PALGRAVE. Gl. 8vo. 1s.
*MARMION. With Introduction and Notes, by MICHAEL MACMILLAN, B.A.
Gl. 8vo. 3s. ; sewed, 2s. 6d.
*THE LADY OF THE LAKE. By G. H. STUART, M.A. Gl. 8vo. 2s. 6d. ;
sewed, 2s.
*ROKEBY. With Introduction and Notes, by MICHAEL MACMILLAN, B.A.
Gl. 8vo. 3s. ; sewed, 2s. 6d.
SHAKESPEARE.—*A SHAKESPEARIAN GRAMMAR. (*See* ABBOTT.)
*A PRIMER OF SHAKESPERE. By Prof. DOWDEN. 18mo. 1s.
*SHORT STUDIES OF SHAKESPEARE'S PLOTS. (*See* RANSOME.)
*THE TEMPEST. With Introduction and Notes, by K. DEIGHTON. Gl. 8vo. 1s. 9d.
*MUCH ADO ABOUT NOTHING. By the same. 2s.
*A MIDSUMMER NIGHT'S DREAM. By the same. 1s. 9d.
*THE MERCHANT OF VENICE. By the same. 1s. 9d.
*AS YOU LIKE IT. By the same. 1s. 9d.
*TWELFTH NIGHT. By the same. 1s. 9d.
*THE WINTER'S TALE. By the same. 2s.
*KING JOHN. By the same. 1s. 9d.
*RICHARD II. By the same. 1s. 9d.
*HENRY IV.—PART I. By the same. [*In preparation.*
*HENRY IV.—PART II. By the same. [*In preparation.*
*HENRY V. By the same. 1s. 9d.
*RICHARD III. By C. H. TAWNEY, M.A. 2s. 6d. ; sewed, 2s.
*CORIOLANUS. By K. DEIGHTON. 2s. 6d. ; sewed, 2s.
*ROMEO AND JULIET. By the same. [*In preparation.*
*JULIUS CÆSAR. By the same. 1s. 9d.
*MACBETH. By the same. 1s. 9d.
*HAMLET. By the same. 2s. 6d. ; sewed, 2s.

*KING LEAR. By the same. 1s. 9d.
*OTHELLO. By the same. 2s.
*ANTONY AND CLEOPATRA. By the same. 2s. 6d. ; sewed, 2s.
*CYMBELINE. By the same. 2s. 6d. ; sewed, 2s.
*SONNENSCHEIN—MEIKLEJOHN.—THE ENGLISH METHOD OF TEACHING TO READ. By A. Sonnenschein and J. M. D. Meiklejohn, M.A. Fcap. 8vo.
THE NURSERY BOOK, containing all the Two-Letter Words in the Language. 1d. (Also in Large Type on Sheets for School Walls. 5s.)
THE FIRST COURSE, consisting of Short Vowels with Single Consonants. 7d.
THE SECOND COURSE, with Combinations and Bridges, consisting of Short Vowels with Double Consonants. 7d.
THE THIRD AND FOURTH COURSES, consisting of Long Vowels, and all the Double Vowels in the Language. 7d.
*SOUTHEY.—LIFE OF NELSON. With Introduction and Notes, by Michael Macmillan, B.A. Gl. 8vo. 3s. ; sewed, 2s. 6d.
*SPENSER.—THE FAIRIE QUEENE. Book I. With Introduction and Notes, by H. M. Percival, M.A. Gl. 8vo. 3s. ; sewed, 2s. 6d.
TAYLOR.—WORDS AND PLACES; or, Etymological Illustrations of History, Ethnology, and Geography. By Rev. Isaac Taylor, Litt.D. Gl. 8vo. 6s.
TENNYSON.—THE COLLECTED WORKS. In 4 Parts. Cr. 8vo. 2s. 6d. each.
*TENNYSON FOR THE YOUNG. Edited by the Rev. Alfred Ainger, LL.D., Canon of Bristol. 18mo. 1s. net.
*SELECTIONS FROM TENNYSON. With Introduction and Notes, by F. J. Rowe, M.A., and W. T. Webb, M.A. New Ed. enlarged. Gl. 8vo. 3s. 6d. or in two parts. Part I. 2s. 6d. Part II. 2s. 6d.
*ENOCH ARDEN. By W. T. Webb, M.A. Gl. 8vo. 2s. 6d.
*AYLMER'S FIELD. By W. T. Webb, M.A. 2s. 6d.
*THE PRINCESS; A MEDLEY. By P. M. Wallace, M.A. 3s. 6d.
*THE COMING OF ARTHUR, and THE PASSING OF ARTHUR. By F. J. Rowe, M.A. Gl. 8vo. 2s. 6d.
*GARETH AND LYNETTE. By G. C. Macaulay, M.A. Globe 8vo. 2s. 6d.
*GERAINT AND ENID, and THE MARRIAGE OF GERAINT. By G. C. Macaulay, M.A. Gl. 8vo. 2s. 6d.
*THE HOLY GRAIL. By G. C. Macaulay, M.A. 2s. 6d.
THRING.—THE ELEMENTS OF GRAMMAR TAUGHT IN ENGLISH. By Edward Thring, M.A. With Questions. 4th Ed. 18mo. 2s.
*VAUGHAN.—WORDS FROM THE POETS. By C. M. Vaughan. 18mo. 1s.
WARD.—THE ENGLISH POETS. Selections, with Critical Introductions by various Writers. Edited by T. H. Ward, M.A. 4 Vols. Vol. I. Chaucer to Donne.—Vol. II. Ben Jonson to Dryden.—Vol. III. Addison to Blake.—Vol. IV. Wordsworth to Rossetti. 2nd Ed. Cr. 8vo. 7s. 6d. each.
WARD.—A HISTORY OF ENGLISH DRAMATIC LITERATURE, TO THE DEATH OF QUEEN ANNE. By A. W. Ward, Litt.D., Principal of Owens College, Manchester. 2 vols. 8vo. [New Ed. in preparation.
WOODS.—*A FIRST POETRY BOOK. By M. A. Woods. Fcap. 8vo. 2s. 6d.
*A SECOND POETRY BOOK. By the same. 4s. 6d.; or, Two Parts. 2s. 6d. each.
*A THIRD POETRY BOOK. By the same. 4s. 6d.
HYMNS FOR SCHOOL WORSHIP. By the same. 18mo. 1s. 6d.
WORDSWORTH.—SELECTIONS. With Introduction and Notes, by F. J. Rowe, M.A., and W. T. Webb, M.A. Gl. 8vo. [In preparation.
YONGE.—*A BOOK OF GOLDEN DEEDS. By Charlotte M. Yonge. 18mo. 2s. 6d. net.

FRENCH.

BEAUMARCHAIS.—LE BARBIER DE SEVILLE. With Introduction and Notes, by L. P. Blouet. Fcap. 8vo. 3s. 6d.
*BOWEN.—FIRST LESSONS IN FRENCH. By H. Courthope Bowen, M.A. Ex. fcap. 8vo. 1s.
BREYMANN.—FIRST FRENCH EXERCISE BOOK. By Hermann Breymann, Ph.D., Professor of Philology in the University of Munich. Ex. fcap. 8vo. 4s. 6d.
SECOND FRENCH EXERCISE BOOK. By the same. Ex. fcap. 8vo. 2s. 6d.

FASNACHT.—Works by G. E. FASNACHT, late Assistant Master at Westminster.
THE ORGANIC METHOD OF STUDYING LANGUAGES. Ex. fcap. 8vo. L. French. 3s. 6d.
A FRENCH GRAMMAR FOR SCHOOLS. Cr. 8vo. 3s. 6d.
GRAMMAR AND GLOSSARY OF THE FRENCH LANGUAGE OF THE SEVENTEENTH CENTURY. Cr. 8vo.   [In preparation.
STUDENT'S HANDBOOK OF FRENCH LITERATURE. Cr. 8vo. [In the Press.
MACMILLAN'S PRIMARY SERIES OF FRENCH READING BOOKS.—Edited by G. E. FASNACHT. Illustrations, Notes, Vocabularies, and Exercises. Gl. 8vo.
*FRENCH READINGS FOR CHILDREN. By G. E. FASNACHT. 1s. 6d.
*CORNAZ—NOS ENFANTS ET LEURS AMIS. By EDITH HARVEY. 1s. 6d.
*DE MAISTRE—LA JEUNE SIBERIENNE ET LE LÉPREUX DE LA CITÉ D'AOSTE. By STEPHANE BARLET, B.Sc. 1s. 6d.
*FLORIAN—FABLES. By Rev. CHARLES YELD, M.A., Headmaster of University School, Nottingham. 1s. 6d.
*LA FONTAINE—A SELECTION OF FABLES. By L. M. MORIARTY, B.A., Assistant Master at Harrow. 2s. 6d.
*MOLESWORTH—FRENCH LIFE IN LETTERS. By Mrs. MOLESWORTH. 1s. 6d.
*PERRAULT—CONTES DE FÉES. By G. E. FASNACHT. 1s. 6d.
*SOUVESTRE—UN PHILOSOPHE SOUS LES TOITS. By L. M. MORIARTY, B.A.   [In the Press.
MACMILLAN'S PROGRESSIVE FRENCH COURSE.—By G. E. FASNACHT. Ex. fcap. 8vo.
*FIRST YEAR, Easy Lessons on the Regular Accidence. 1s.
*SECOND YEAR, an Elementary Grammar with Exercises, Notes, and Vocabularies. 2s.
*THIRD YEAR, a Systematic Syntax, and Lessons in Composition. 2s. 6d.
THE TEACHER'S COMPANION TO THE ABOVE. With Copious Notes, Hints for Different Renderings, Synonyms, Philological Remarks, etc. By G. E. FASNACHT. Ex. fcap. 8vo. Each Year, 4s. 6d.
*MACMILLAN'S FRENCH COMPOSITION.—By G. E. FASNACHT. Part I. Elementary. Ex. fcap. 8vo. 2s. 6d. Part II. Advanced. Cr. 8vo. 5s.
THE TEACHER'S COMPANION TO THE ABOVE. By G. E. FASNACHT. Ex. fcap. 8vo. Part I. 4s. 6d. Part II. 5s. net.
A SPECIAL VOCABULARY TO MACMILLAN'S SECOND COURSE OF FRENCH COMPOSITION. By the Same.   [In the Press.
MACMILLAN'S PROGRESSIVE FRENCH READERS. By G. E. FASNACHT. Ex. fcap. 8vo.
*FIRST YEAR, containing Tales, Historical Extracts, Letters, Dialogues, Ballads, Nursery Songs, etc., with Two Vocabularies: (1) in the order of subjects; (2) in alphabetical order. With Imitative Exercises. 2s. 6d.
*SECOND YEAR, containing Fiction in Prose and Verse, Historical and Descriptive Extracts, Essays, Letters, Dialogues, etc. With Imitative Exercises. 2s. 6d.
MACMILLAN'S FOREIGN SCHOOL CLASSICS. Ed. by G. E. FASNACHT. 18mo.
*CORNEILLE—LE CID. By G. E. FASNACHT. 1s.
*DUMAS—LES DEMOISELLES DE ST. CYR. By VICTOR OGER, Lecturer at University College, Liverpool. 1s. 6d.
LA FONTAINE'S FABLES. By L. M. MORIARTY, B.A.   [In preparation.
*MOLIÈRE—L'AVARE. By the same. 1s.
*MOLIÈRE—LE BOURGEOIS GENTILHOMME. By the same. 1s. 6d.
*MOLIÈRE—LES FEMMES SAVANTES. By G. E. FASNACHT. 1s.
*MOLIÈRE—LE MISANTHROPE. By the same. 1s.
*MOLIÈRE—LE MÉDECIN MALGRÉ LUI. By the same. 1s.
*MOLIÈRE—LES PRÉCIEUSES RIDICULES. By the same. 1s.
*RACINE—BRITANNICUS. By E. PELLISSIER, M.A. 2s.
*FRENCH READINGS FROM ROMAN HISTORY. Selected from various Authors, by O. COLBECK, M.A., Assistant Master at Harrow. 4s. 6d.
*SAND, GEORGE—LA MARE AU DIABLE. By W. E. RUSSELL, M.A. Assistant Master at Haileybury. 1s.
*SANDEAU, JULES—MADEMOISELLE DE LA SEIGLIÈRE. By H. C. STEEL, Assistant Master at Winchester. 1s. 6d.
*VOLTAIRE—CHARLES XII. By G. E. FASNACHT. 3s. 6d.

*MASSON.—A COMPENDIOUS DICTIONARY OF THE FRENCH LANGUAGE. Adapted from the Dictionaries of Prof. A. ELWALL. By G. MASSON. Cr. 8vo. 3s. 6d.

LA LYRE FRANQAISE. Selected and arranged with Notes. 18mo. 2s. 6d. net.

MOLIÈRE.—LE MALADE IMAGINAIRE. With Introduction and Notes, by F. TARVER, M.A., Assistant Master at Eton. Fcap. 8vo. 2s. 6d.

PAYNE.—COMMERCIAL FRENCH. By J. B. PAYNE, King's College School, London. Gl. 8vo. [In preparation.

*PELLISSIER.—FRENCH ROOTS AND THEIR FAMILIES. A Synthetic Vocabulary, based upon Derivations. By E. PELLISSIER, M.A., Assistant Master at Clifton College. Gl. 8vo. 6s.

*STORM.—FRENCH DIALOGUES. A Systematic Introduction to the Grammar and Idiom of spoken French. By JOH. STORM, LL.D. Intermediate Course Translated by G. MACDONALD, M.A. Cr. 8vo. 4s. 6d.

GERMAN.

*BEHAGHEL.—A SHORT HISTORICAL GRAMMAR OF THE GERMAN LANGUAGE. By Dr. OTTO BEHAGHEL. Translated by EMIL TRECHMANN, M.A., Ph.D., University of Sydney. Gl. 8vo. 3s. 6d.

BUCHHEIM.—DEUTSCHE LYRIK. The Golden Treasury of the best German Lyrical Poems. Selected by Dr. BUCHHEIM. 18mo. 2s. 6d. net.

BALLADEN UND ROMANZEN. Selection of the best German Ballads and Romances. By the same. 18mo. 2s. 6d. net.

HUSS.—A SYSTEM OF ORAL INSTRUCTION IN GERMAN, by means of Progressive Illustrations and Applications of the leading Rules of Grammar. By H. C. O. HUSS, Ph.D. Cr. 8vo. 5s.

MACMILLAN'S PRIMARY SERIES OF GERMAN READING BOOKS. Edited by G. E. FASNACHT. With Notes, Vocabularies, and Exercises. Gl. 8vo.

*GRIMM—KINDER UND HAUSMÄRCHEN. By G. E. FASNACHT. 2s. 6d.

*HAUFF—DIE KARAVANE. By HERMAN HAGER, Ph.D. 3s.

*HAUFF—DAS WIRTHSHAUS IM SPESSART. By G. E. FASNACHT. [In the Press.

*SCHMID, CHR. VON—H. VON EICHENFELS. By G. E. FASNACHT. 2s. 6d.

MACMILLAN'S PROGRESSIVE GERMAN COURSE. By G. E. FASNACHT. Ex. fcap. 8vo.

*FIRST YEAR. Easy Lessons and Rules on the Regular Accidence. 1s. 6d.

*SECOND YEAR. Conversational Lessons in Systematic Accidence and Elementary Syntax. With Philological Illustrations and Vocabulary. 3s. 6d. [THIRD YEAR, in the Press.

THE TEACHER'S COMPANION TO THE ABOVE. With copious Notes, Hints for Different Renderings, Synonyms, Philological Remarks, etc. By G. E. FASNACHT. Ex. fcap. 8vo. Each Year. 4s. 6d.

MACMILLAN'S GERMAN COMPOSITION. By G. E. FASNACHT. Ex. fcap. 8vo.

*I. FIRST COURSE. Parallel German-English Extracts and Parallel English-German Syntax. 2s. 6d.

THE TEACHER'S COMPANION TO THE ABOVE. By G. E. FASNACHT. FIRST COURSE. Gl. 8vo. 4s. 6d.

MACMILLAN'S PROGRESSIVE GERMAN READERS. By G. E. FASNACHT. Ex. fcap. 8vo.

*FIRST YEAR, containing an Introduction to the German order of Words, with Copious Examples, extracts from German Authors in Prose and Poetry; Notes, and Vocabularies. 2s. 6d.

MACMILLAN'S FOREIGN SCHOOL CLASSICS.—Edited by G. E. FASNACHT. 18mo.

*GOETHE—GÖTZ VON BERLICHINGEN. By H. A. BULL, M.A. 2s.

*GOETHE—FAUST. PART I., followed by an Appendix on PART II. By JANE LEE, Lecturer in German Literature at Newnham College, Cambridge. 4s. 6d.

*HEINE—SELECTIONS FROM THE REISEBILDER AND OTHER PROSE WORKS. By C. COLBECK, M.A., Assistant Master at Harrow. 2s. 6d.

*SCHILLER—SELECTIONS FROM SCHILLER'S LYRICAL POEMS. With a Memoir. By E. J. TURNER, B.A., and E. D. A. MORSHEAD, M.A. 2s. 6d.

*SCHILLER—DIE JUNGFRAU VON ORLEANS. By JOSEPH GOSTWICK. 2s. 6d

*SCHILLER—MARIA STUART. By C. SHELDON, D.Litt. 2s. 6d.
*SCHILLER—WILHELM TELL. By G. E. FASNACHT. 2s. 6d.
*SCHILLER—WALLENSTEIN, DAS LAGER. By H. B. COTTERILL, M.A. 2s.
*UHLAND—SELECT BALLADS. Adapted for Beginners. With Vocabulary.
    By G. E. FASNACHT. 1s.
*PYLODET.—NEW GUIDE TO GERMAN CONVERSATION ; containing an Alpha-
    betical List of nearly 800 Familiar Words ; followed by Exercises, Vocabulary,
    Familiar Phrases and Dialogues. By L. PYLODET. 18mo. 2s. 6d.
*SMITH.—COMMERCIAL GERMAN. By F. C. SMITH, M.A. Gl. 8vo. 3s. 6d.
WHITNEY.—A COMPENDIOUS GERMAN GRAMMAR. By W. D. WHITNEY,
    Professor of Sanskrit and Instructor in Modern Languages in Yale College.
    Cr. 8vo. 4s. 6d.
  A GERMAN READER IN PROSE AND VERSE. By the same. With Notes
    and Vocabulary. Cr. 8vo. 5s.
*WHITNEY—EDGREN.—A COMPENDIOUS GERMAN AND ENGLISH DIC-
    TIONARY. By Prof. W. D. WHITNEY and A. H. EDGREN. Cr. 8vo. 5s.
  THE GERMAN-ENGLISH PART, separately, 3s. 6d.

MODERN GREEK.

CONSTANTINIDES.—NEO-HELLENICA. Dialogues illustrative of the develop-
    ment of the Greek Language. By Prof. M. CONSTANTINIDES. Cr. 8vo. 6s. net.
VINCENT—DICKSON.—HANDBOOK TO MODERN GREEK. By Sir EDGAR
    VINCENT, K.C.M.G., and T. G. DICKSON, M.A. With Appendix on the relation
    of Modern and Classical Greek by Prof. JEBB. Cr. 8vo. 6s.

ITALIAN.

DANTE.—With Translation and Notes, by A. J. BUTLER, M.A.
    THE HELL. Cr. 8vo. 12s. 6d.
    THE PURGATORY. 2nd Ed. Cr. 8vo. 12s. 6d.
    THE PARADISE. 2nd Ed. Cr. 8vo. 12s. 6d.
  READINGS ON THE PURGATORIO OF DANTE. Chiefly based on the Com-
    mentary of Benvenuto Da Imola. By Hon. W. WARREN VERNON, M.A. With
    Introduction by DEAN CHURCH. 2 vols. Cr. 8vo. 24s.
  THE DIVINE COMEDY. Transl. by C. E. NORTON. I. HELL. II. PURGA-
    TORY. III. PARADISE. Cr. 8vo. 6s. each. THE NEW LIFE. Cr. 8vo. 5s.
  THE PURGATORY. Translated by C. L. SHADWELL, M.A. Ex. Cr. 8vo. 10s. net.
  COMPANION TO DANTE. By Professor SCARTAZZINI. Translated by A. J.
    BUTLER, M.A. Cr. 8vo.   [In the Press.

SPANISH.

CALDERON.—FOUR PLAYS OF CALDERON. El Principe Constante, La Vida
    es Sueno, El Alcalde de Zalamea, and El Escondido y La Tapada. With Intro-
    duction and Notes. By NORMAN MACCOLL, M.A. Cr. 8vo. 14s.
DELBOS.—COMMERCIAL SPANISH. By Prof. DELBOS. Gl. 8vo. [In preparation.

MATHEMATICS.

Arithmetic, Book-keeping, Algebra, Euclid and Pure Geometry, Geometrical
    Drawing, Mensuration, Trigonometry, Analytical Geometry (Plane and
    Solid), Problems and Questions in Mathematics, Higher Pure Mathe-
    matics, Mechanics (Statics, Dynamics, Hydrostatics, Hydrodynamics: see
    also Physics), Physics (Sound, Light, Heat, Electricity, Elasticity, Attrac-
    tions, &c.), Astronomy, Historical.

ARITHMETIC.

*ALDIS.—THE GREAT GIANT ARITHMOS. A most Elementary Arithmetic
    for Children. By MARY STEADMAN ALDIS. Illustrated. Gl. 8vo. 2s. 6d.
*BRADSHAW.—A COURSE OF EASY ARITHMETICAL EXAMPLES FOR
    BEGINNERS. By J. G. BRADSHAW, B.A., Assistant Master at Clifton College.
    Gl. 8vo. 2s. With Answers, 2s. 6d.

*BROOKSMITH.—ARITHMETIC IN THEORY AND PRACTICE. By J. BROOK-SMITH, M.A. Cr. 8vo. 4s. 6d. KEY, for Teachers only. Crown 8vo. 10s. 6d.

*BROOKSMITH.—ARITHMETIC FOR BEGINNERS. By J. and E. J. BROOK-SMITH. Gl. 8vo. 1s. 6d. KEY, for Teachers only. Cr. 8vo. 6s. 6d.

CANDLER.—HELP TO ARITHMETIC. For the use of Schools. By H. CANDLER, Mathematical Master of Uppingham School. 2nd Ed. Ex. fcap. 8vo. 2s. 6d.

*COLLAR.—NOTES ON THE METRIC SYSTEM. By GEO. COLLAR, B.A., B.Sc. Gl. 8vo. 3d.

*DALTON.—RULES AND EXAMPLES IN ARITHMETIC. By Rev. T. DALTON, M.A., Senior Mathematical Master at Eton. With Answers. 18mo. 2s. 6d.

*GOYEN.—HIGHER ARITHMETIC AND ELEMENTARY MENSURATION. By P. GOYEN. Cr. 8vo. 5s.   [KEY, *June* 1893.

*HALL—KNIGHT.—ARITHMETICAL EXERCISES AND EXAMINATION PAPERS. With an Appendix containing Questions in LOGARITHMS and MENSURATION. By H. S. HALL, M.A., Master of the Military Side, Clifton College, and S. R. KNIGHT, B.A., M.B., Ch.B. Gl. 8vo. 2s. 6d.

HUNTER.—DECIMAL APPROXIMATIONS. By H. St. J. HUNTER, M.A., Fellow of Jesus College, Cambridge. 18mo. 1s. 6d.

JACKSON.—COMMERCIAL ARITHMETIC. By S. JACKSON, M.A. Gl. 8vo. 3s. 6d.

LOCK.—Works by Rev. J. B. LOCK, M.A., Senior Fellow and Bursar of Gonville and Caius College, Cambridge.

  *ARITHMETIC FOR SCHOOLS. With Answers and 1000 additional Examples for Exercise. 4th Ed., revised. Gl. 8vo. 4s. 6d. Or, Part I. 2s. Part II. 3s. KEY, for Teachers only. Cr. 8vo. 10s. 6d.

  *ARITHMETIC FOR BEGINNERS. A School Class-Book of Commercial Arithmetic. Gl. 8vo. 2s. 6d. KEY, for Teachers only. Cr. 8vo. 8s. 6d.

  *A SHILLING BOOK OF ARITHMETIC, FOR ELEMENTARY SCHOOLS. 18mo. 1s. With Answers. 1s. 6d.   [KEY *in the Press.*

LOCK—COLLAR.—ARITHMETIC FOR THE STANDARDS. By Rev. J. B. LOCK, M.A., and GEO. COLLAR, B.A., B.Sc. Standards I. II. III. and IV., 2d. each ; Standards V. VI. and VII., 3d. each. Answers to I. II. III. IV., 3d. each ; to V. VI. and VII., 4d. each.

MACMILLAN'S MENTAL ARITHMETIC. For the Standards. Containing 6000 Questions and Answers. Standards I. II., 6d. ; III. IV., 6d. ; V. VI., 6d.

*PEDLEY.—EXERCISES IN ARITHMETIC, containing 7000 Examples. By S. PEDLEY. Cr. 8vo. 5s. Also in Two Parts, 2s. 6d. each.

SMITH.—Works by Rev. BARNARD SMITH, M.A.

  *ARITHMETIC FOR SCHOOLS. Cr. 8vo. 4s. 6d. KEY, for Teachers. 8s. 6d.

  EXERCISES IN ARITHMETIC. Cr. 8vo. 2s. With Answers, 2s. 6d. Answers separately, 6d.

  SCHOOL CLASS-BOOK OF ARITHMETIC. 18mo. 3s. Or separately, in Three Parts, 1s. each. KEYS. Parts I. II. and III., 2s. 6d. each.

  SHILLING BOOK OF ARITHMETIC. 18mo. Or separately, Part I., 2d. ; Part II., 3d. ; Part III., 7d. Answers, 6d. KEY, for Teachers only. 18mo. 4s. 6d.

  *THE SAME, with Answers. 18mo, cloth. 1s. 6d.

  EXAMINATION PAPERS IN ARITHMETIC. 18mo. 1s. 6d. The Same, with Answers. 18mo. 2s. Answers, 6d. KEY. 18mo. 4s. 6d.

  THE METRIC SYSTEM OF ARITHMETIC, ITS PRINCIPLES AND APPLICATIONS, with Numerous Examples. 18mo. 3d.

  A CHART OF THE METRIC SYSTEM, on a Sheet, size 42 in. by 34 in. on Roller. New Ed. Revised by GEO. COLLAR, B.A., B.Sc. 4s. 6d.

  EASY LESSONS IN ARITHMETIC, combining Exercises in Reading, Writing, Spelling, and Dictation. Part I. Cr. 8vo. 9d.

  EXAMINATION CARDS IN ARITHMETIC. With Answers and Hints. Standards I. and II., in box, 1s. Standards III. IV. and V., in boxes, 1s. each. Standard VI. in Two Parts, in boxes, 1s. each.

SMITH (BARNARD)—HUDSON.—ARITHMETIC FOR SCHOOLS. By Rev. BARNARD SMITH, M.A., revised by W. H. H. HUDSON, M.A., Prof. of Mathematics, King's College, London. Cr. 8vo. 4s. 6d.

BOOK-KEEPING.

*THORNTON.—FIRST LESSONS IN BOOK-KEEPING. By J. THORNTON. Cr.
8vo. 2s. 6d. KEY. Oblong 4to. 10s. 6d.
*PRIMER OF BOOK-KEEPING. 18mo. 1s. KEY. Demy 8vo. 2s. 6d.
*EASY EXERCISES IN BOOK-KEEPING. 18mo. 1s.
*ADVANCED BOOK-KEEPING.   [*In preparation.*

ALGEBRA.

*DALTON.—RULES AND EXAMPLES IN ALGEBRA. By Rev. T. DALTON,
Senior Mathematical Master at Eton. Part I. 18mo. 2s. KEY. Cr. 8vo.
7s. 6d. Part II. 18mo. 2s. 6d.
DUPUIS.—PRINCIPLES OF ELEMENTARY ALGEBRA. By N. F. DUPUIS,
M.A., Professor of Mathematics, University of Queen's College, Kingston,
Canada. Cr. 8vo. 6s.
HALL—KNIGHT.—Works by H. S. HALL, M.A., Master of the Military Side,
Clifton College, and S. R. KNIGHT, B.A., M.B., Ch.B.
*ALGEBRA FOR BEGINNERS. Gl. 8vo. 2s. With Answers. 2s. 6d.
*ELEMENTARY ALGEBRA FOR SCHOOLS. 6th Ed. Gl. 8vo. 3s. 6d. With
Answers, 4s. 6d. Answers, 1s. KEY, for Teachers only. 8s. 6d.
*ALGEBRAICAL EXERCISES AND EXAMINATION PAPERS. To accom-
pany ELEMENTARY ALGEBRA. 2nd Ed., revised. Gl. 8vo. 2s. 6d.
*HIGHER ALGEBRA. 4th Ed. Cr. 8vo. 7s. 6d. KEY. Cr. 8vo. 10s. 6d.
*JARMAN.—ALGEBRAIC FACTORS. By J. ABBOT JARMAN. Gl. 8vo. 2s.
With Answers, 2s. 6d.
*JONES—CHEYNE.—ALGEBRAICAL EXERCISES. Progressively Arranged.
By Rev. C. A. JONES and C. H. CHEYNE, M.A., late Mathematical Masters
at Westminster School. 18mo. 2s. 6d.
KEY, for Teachers. By Rev. W. FAILES, M.A. Cr. 8vo. 7s. 6d.
SMITH.—Works by CHARLES SMITH, M.A., Master of Sidney Sussex College,
Cambridge.
*ELEMENTARY ALGEBRA. 2nd Ed., revised. Gl. 8vo. 4s. 6d. KEY, for
Teachers only. Cr. 8vo. 10s. 6d.
*A TREATISE ON ALGEBRA. 4th Ed. Cr. 8vo. 7s. 6d. KEY. Cr. 8vo. 10s. 6d.
TODHUNTER.—Works by ISAAC TODHUNTER, F.R.S.
*ALGEBRA FOR BEGINNERS. 18mo. 2s. 6d. KEY. Cr. 8vo. 6s. 6d.
*ALGEBRA FOR COLLEGES AND SCHOOLS. By ISAAC TODHUNTER, F.R.S.
Cr. 8vo. 7s. 6d. KEY, for Teachers. Cr. 8vo. 10s. 6d.

EUCLID AND PURE GEOMETRY.

COCKSHOTT—WALTERS.—A TREATISE ON GEOMETRICAL CONICS. By
A. COCKSHOTT, M.A., Assistant Master at Eton, and Rev. F. B. WALTERS,
M.A., Principal of King William's College, Isle of Man. Cr. 8vo. 5s.
CONSTABLE.—GEOMETRICAL EXERCISES FOR BEGINNERS. By SAMUEL
CONSTABLE. Cr. 8vo. 3s. 6d.
CUTHBERTSON.—EUCLIDIAN GEOMETRY. By FRANCIS CUTHBERTSON, M.A.,
LL.D. Ex. fcap. 8vo. 4s. 6d.
DAY.—PROPERTIES OF CONIC SECTIONS PROVED GEOMETRICALLY.
By Rev. H. G. DAY, M.A. Part I. The Ellipse, with an ample collection of
Problems. Cr. 8vo. 3s. 6d.
*DEAKIN.—RIDER PAPERS ON EUCLID. BOOKS I. AND II. By RUPERT
DEAKIN, M.A. 18mo. 1s.
DODGSON.—Works by CHARLES L. DODGSON, M.A., Student and late Mathematical
Lecturer, Christ Church, Oxford.
EUCLID, BOOKS I. AND II. 6th Ed., with words substituted for the Alge-
braical Symbols used in the 1st Ed. Cr. 8vo. 2s.
EUCLID AND HIS MODERN RIVALS. 2nd Ed. Cr. 8vo. 6s.
CURIOSA MATHEMATICA. Part I. A New Theory of Parallels. 3rd Ed.
Cr. 8vo. 2s. Part II. Pillow Problems. Cr. 8vo.   [*Immediately.*
DREW.—GEOMETRICAL TREATISE ON CONIC SECTIONS. By W. H.
DREW, M.A. New Ed., enlarged. Cr. 8vo. 5s.

DUPUIS.—ELEMENTARY SYNTHETIC GEOMETRY OF THE POINT, LINE AND CIRCLE IN THE PLANE. By N. F. Dupuis, M.A., Professor of Mathematics, University of Queen's College, Kingston, Canada. Gl. 8vo. 4s. 6d.

*****HALL—STEVENS.**—A TEXT-BOOK OF EUCLID'S ELEMENTS. Including Alternative Proofs, with additional Theorems and Exercises, classified and arranged. By H. S. Hall, M.A., and F. H. Stevens, M.A., Masters of the Military Side, Clifton College. Gl. 8vo. Book I., 1s.; Books I. and II., 1s. 6d.; Books I.-IV., 3s.; Books III.-IV., 2s.; Books III.-VI., 3s.; Books V.-VI. and XI., 2s. 6d.; Books I.-VI. and XI., 4s. 6d.; Book XI., 1s. KEY to Books I.-IV., 6s. 6d. KEY to VI. and XI., 3s. 6d. KEY to I.-VI. and XI., 8s. 6d.

HALSTED.—THE ELEMENTS OF GEOMETRY. By G. B. Halsted, Professor of Pure and Applied Mathematics in the University of Texas. 8vo. 12s. 6d.

HAYWARD.—THE ELEMENTS OF SOLID GEOMETRY. By R. B. Hayward, M.A., F.R.S. Gl. 8vo. 3s.

LACHLAN.—AN ELEMENTARY TREATISE ON MODERN PURE GEOMETRY. By R. Lachlan, M.A. 8vo. 9s.

*****LOCK.**—THE FIRST BOOK OF EUCLID'S ELEMENTS ARRANGED FOR BEGINNERS. By Rev. J. B. Lock, M.A. Gl. 8vo. 1s. 6d.

MILNE—DAVIS.—GEOMETRICAL CONICS. Part I. The Parabola. By Rev. J. J. Milne, M.A., and R. F. Davis, M.A. Cr. 8vo. 2s.

MUKHOPADHÁYA.—GEOMETRICAL CONIC SECTIONS. By Asutosh Mukhopadhaya, M.A. *[Ready shortly.*

*****RICHARDSON.**—THE PROGRESSIVE EUCLID. Books I. and II. With Notes, Exercises, and Deductions. Edited by A. T. Richardson, M.A.

SMITH.—GEOMETRICAL CONIC SECTIONS. By Charles Smith, M.A., Master of Sidney Sussex College, Cambridge. *[In the Press.*

SMITH.—INTRODUCTORY MODERN GEOMETRY OF POINT, RAY, AND CIRCLE. By W. B. Smith, A.M., Ph.D., Professor of Mathematics, Missouri University. Cr. 8vo. 5s.

SYLLABUS OF PLANE GEOMETRY (corresponding to Euclid, Books I.-VI.)—Prepared by the Association for the Improvement of Geometrical Teaching. Cr. 8vo. Sewed. 1s.

SYLLABUS OF MODERN PLANE GEOMETRY.—Prepared by the Association for the Improvement of Geometrical Teaching. Cr. 8vo. Sewed. 1s.

*****TODHUNTER.**—THE ELEMENTS OF EUCLID. By I. Todhunter, F.R.S. 18mo. 3s. 6d. *Books I. and II. 1s. KEY. Cr. 8vo. 6s. 6d.

WEEKS.—EXERCISES IN EUCLID, GRADUATED AND SYSTEMATIZED. By W. Weeks, Lecturer in Geometry, Training College, Exeter. 18mo. 2s.

WILSON.—Works by Archdeacon Wilson, M.A., late Headmaster of Clifton College.
ELEMENTARY GEOMETRY. BOOKS I.-V. (Corresponding to Euclid, Books I.-VI.) Following the Syllabus of the Geometrical Association. Ex. fcap. 8vo. 4s. 6d.
SOLID GEOMETRY AND CONIC SECTIONS. With Appendices on Transversals and Harmonic Division. Ex. fcap. 8vo. 3s. 6d.

GEOMETRICAL DRAWING.

EAGLES.—CONSTRUCTIVE GEOMETRY OF PLANE CURVES. By T. H. Eagles, M.A., Instructor, Roy. Indian Engineering Coll. Cr. 8vo. 12s.

EDGAR — PRITCHARD. — NOTE-BOOK ON PRACTICAL SOLID OR DESCRIPTIVE GEOMETRY. Containing Problems with help for Solutions. By J. H. Edgar and G. S. Pritchard. 4th Ed. Gl. 8vo. 4s. 6d.

·KITCHENER.—A GEOMETRICAL NOTE-BOOK. Containing Easy Problems in Geometrical Drawing. By F. E. Kitchener, M.A. 4to. 2s.

MILLAR.—ELEMENTS OF DESCRIPTIVE GEOMETRY. By J. B. Millar, Lecturer on Engineering in the Owens College, Manchester. Cr. 8vo. 6s.

PLANT.—PRACTICAL PLANE AND DESCRIPTIVE GEOMETRY. By E. C. Plant. Globe 8vo. *[In preparation.*

MENSURATION.

STEVENS.—ELEMENTARY MENSURATION. With Exercises on the Mensuration of Plane and Solid Figures. By F. H. Stevens, M.A. Gl. 8vo. *[In prep.*

TEBAY.—ELEMENTARY MENSURATION FOR SCHOOLS. By S. Tebay. Ex. fcap. 8vo. 3s. 6d.
*TODHUNTER.—MENSURATION FOR BEGINNERS. By Isaac Todhunter, F.R.S. 18mo. 2s. 6d. KEY. By Rev. Fr. L. McCarthy. Cr. 8vo. 7s. 6d.

TRIGONOMETRY.

BOTTOMLEY.—FOUR-FIGURE MATHEMATICAL TABLES. Comprising Logarithmic and Trigonometrical Tables, and Tables of Squares, Square Roots, and Reciprocals. By J. T. Bottomley, M.A., Lecturer in Natural Philosophy in the University of Glasgow. 8vo. 2s. 6d.
HAYWARD.—THE ALGEBRA OF CO-PLANAR VECTORS AND TRIGONO-METRY. By R. B. Hayward, M.A., F.R.S. Cr. 8vo. 8s. 6d.
JOHNSON.—A TREATISE ON TRIGONOMETRY. By W. E. Johnson, M.A., late Mathematical Lecturer at King's College, Cambridge. Cr. 8vo. 8s. 6d.
JONES.—LOGARITHMIC TABLES. By Prof. G. W. Jones, Cornell University. 8vo. 4s. 6d. net.
*LEVETT—DAVISON.—THE ELEMENTS OF PLANE TRIGONOMETRY. By Rawdon Levett, M.A., and C. Davison, M.A., Assistant Masters at King Edward's School, Birmingham. Gl. 8vo. 6s. 6d.; or, in 2 parts, 3s. 6d. each.
LOCK.—Works by Rev. J. B. Lock, M.A., Senior Fellow and Bursar of Gonville and Caius College, Cambridge.
*THE TRIGONOMETRY OF ONE ANGLE. Gl. 8vo. 2s. 6d.
*TRIGONOMETRY FOR BEGINNERS, as far as the Solution of Triangles. 3rd Ed. Gl. 8vo. 2s. 6d. KEY, for Teachers. Cr. 8vo. 6s. 6d.
*ELEMENTARY TRIGONOMETRY. 6th Ed. Gl. 8vo. 4s. 6d. KEY, for Teachers. Cr. 8vo. 8s. 6d.
HIGHER TRIGONOMETRY. 5th Ed. 4s. 6d. Both Parts complete in One Volume. 7s. 6d. [KEY *in preparation.*
M'CLELLAND — PRESTON. — A TREATISE ON SPHERICAL TRIGONO-METRY. By W. J. M'Clelland, M.A., Principal of the Incorporated Society's School, Santry, Dublin, and T. Preston, M.A. Cr. 8vo. 8s. 6d., or: Part I. To the End of Solution of Triangles, 4s. 6d. Part II., 5s.
MATTHEWS.—MANUAL OF LOGARITHMS. By G. F. Matthews, B.A. 8vo. 5s. net.
PALMER.—PRACTICAL LOGARITHMS AND TRIGONOMETRY. By J. H. Palmer, Headmaster, R.N., H.M.S. *Cambridge,* Devonport. Gl. 8vo. 4s. 6d.
SNOWBALL.—THE ELEMENTS OF PLANE AND SPHERICAL TRIGONO-METRY. By J. C. Snowball. 14th Ed. Cr. 8vo. 7s. 6d.
TODHUNTER.—Works by Isaac Todhunter, F.R.S.
*TRIGONOMETRY FOR BEGINNERS. 18mo. 2s. 6d. KEY. Cr. 8vo. 8s. 6d.
PLANE TRIGONOMETRY. Cr. 8vo. 5s. KEY. Cr. 8vo. 10s. 6d.
A TREATISE ON SPHERICAL TRIGONOMETRY. Cr. 8vo. 4s. 6d.
TODHUNTER—HOGG.—PLANE TRIGONOMETRY. By Isaac Todhunter. Revised by R. W. Hogg, M.A. Cr. 8vo. 5s. [KEY *in preparation.*
WOLSTENHOLME.—EXAMPLES FOR PRACTICE IN THE USE OF SEVEN-FIGURE LOGARITHMS. By Joseph Wolstenholme, D.Sc., late Professor of Mathematics, Royal Indian Engineering Coll., Cooper's Hill. 8vo. 5s.

ANALYTICAL GEOMETRY (Plane and Solid).

DYER.—EXERCISES IN ANALYTICAL GEOMETRY. By J. M. Dyer, M.A., Assistant Master at Eton. Illustrated. Cr. 8vo. 4s. 6d.
FERRERS.—AN ELEMENTARY TREATISE ON TRILINEAR CO-ORDIN-ATES, the Method of Reciprocal Polars, and the Theory of Projectors. By the Rev. N. M. Ferrers, D.D., F.R.S., Master of Gonville and Caius College, Cambridge. 4th Ed., revised. Cr. 8vo. 6s. 6d.
FROST.—Works by Percival Frost, D.Sc., F.R.S., Fellow and Mathematical Lecturer at King's College, Cambridge.
AN ELEMENTARY TREATISE ON CURVE TRACING. 8vo. 12s.
SOLID GEOMETRY. 3rd Ed. Demy 8vo. 16s.
HINTS FOR THE SOLUTION OF PROBLEMS in the above. 8vo. 8s. 6d.

JOHNSON.—CURVE TRACING IN CARTESIAN CO-ORDINATES. By W. WOOLSEY JOHNSON, Professor of Mathematics at the U.S. Naval Academy, Annapolis, Maryland. Cr. 8vo. 4s. 6d.

M'CLELLAND.—A TREATISE ON THE GEOMETRY OF THE CIRCLE, and some extensions to Conic Sections by the Method of Reciprocation. By W. J. M'CLELLAND, M.A. Cr. 8vo. 6s.

PUCKLE.—AN ELEMENTARY TREATISE ON CONIC SECTIONS AND ALGEBRAIC GEOMETRY. By G. H. PUCKLE, M.A. 5th Ed. Cr. 8vo. 7s. 6d.

SMITH.—Works by CHAS. SMITH, M.A., Master of Sidney Sussex Coll., Cambridge. CONIC SECTIONS. 7th Ed. Cr. 8vo. 7s. 6d. KEY. Cr. 8vo. 10s. 6d. AN ELEMENTARY TREATISE ON SOLID GEOMETRY. Cr. 8vo. 9s. 6d.

TODHUNTER.—Works by ISAAC TODHUNTER, F.R.S. PLANE CO-ORDINATE GEOMETRY, as applied to the Straight Line and the Conic Sections. Cr. 8vo. 7s. 6d. KEY. Cr. 8vo. 10s. 6d. EXAMPLES OF ANALYTICAL GEOMETRY OF THREE DIMENSIONS. New Ed., revised. Cr. 8vo. 4s.

PROBLEMS & QUESTIONS IN MATHEMATICS.

ARMY PRELIMINARY EXAMINATION, PAPERS 1882-Sept. 1891. With Answers to the Mathematical Questions. Cr. 8vo. 3s. 6d.

BALL.—MATHEMATICAL RECREATIONS AND PROBLEMS OF PAST AND PRESENT TIMES. By W. W. ROUSE BALL, M.A., Fellow and Lecturer of Trinity College; Cambridge, 2nd Ed. Cr. 8vo. 7s. net.

CAMBRIDGE SENATE-HOUSE PROBLEMS AND RIDERS, WITH SOLUTIONS:—
1875—PROBLEMS AND RIDERS. By A. G. GREENHILL, F.R.S. Cr. 8vo. 8s. 6d.
1878—SOLUTIONS OF SENATE-HOUSE PROBLEMS. Edited by J. W. L. GLAISHER, F.R.S., Fellow of Trinity College, Cambridge. Cr. 8vo. 12s.

CHRISTIE.—A COLLECTION OF ELEMENTARY TEST-QUESTIONS IN PURE AND MIXED MATHEMATICS. By J. R. CHRISTIE, F.R.S. Cr. 8vo. 8s. 6d.

CLIFFORD.—MATHEMATICAL PAPERS. By W. K. CLIFFORD. 8vo. 30s.

MACMILLAN'S MENTAL ARITHMETIC. (See page 21.)

MILNE.—WEEKLY PROBLEM PAPERS. By Rev. JOHN J. MILNE, M.A. Pott 8vo. 4s. 6d.
SOLUTIONS TO THE ABOVE. By the same. Cr. 8vo. 10s. 6d.
COMPANION TO WEEKLY PROBLEM PAPERS. Cr. 8vo. 10s. 6d.

*RICHARDSON.—PROGRESSIVE MATHEMATICAL EXERCISES FOR HOME WORK. By A. T. RICHARDSON, M.A. Gl. 8vo. First Series. 2s. With Answers, 2s. 6d. Second Series. 3s. With Answers, 3s. 6d.

SANDHURST MATHEMATICAL PAPERS, for Admission into the Royal Military College, 1881-1889. Edited by E. J. BROOKSMITH, B.A. Cr. 8vo. 3s. 6d.

THOMAS.—ENUNCIATIONS IN ARITHMETIC, ALGEBRA, EUCLID, AND TRIGONOMETRY, with Examples and Notes. By P. A. THOMAS, B.A.
[In the Press.

WOOLWICH MATHEMATICAL PAPERS, for Admission into the Royal Military Academy, Woolwich, 1880-1890 inclusive. By the same. Cr. 8vo. 6s.

WOLSTENHOLME.—MATHEMATICAL PROBLEMS, on Subjects included in the First and Second Divisions of Cambridge Mathematical Tripos. By JOSEPH WOLSTENHOLME, D.Sc. 3rd Ed., greatly enlarged. 8vo. 18s.
EXAMPLES FOR PRACTICE IN THE USE OF SEVEN-FIGURE LOGARITHMS. By the same. 8vo. 5s.

HIGHER PURE MATHEMATICS.

AIRY.—Works by Sir G. B. AIRY, K.C.B., formerly Astronomer-Royal.
ELEMENTARY TREATISE ON PARTIAL DIFFERENTIAL EQUATIONS. With Diagrams. 2nd Ed. Cr. 8vo. 5s. 6d.
ON THE ALGEBRAICAL AND NUMERICAL THEORY OF ERRORS OF OBSERVATIONS AND THE COMBINATION OF OBSERVATIONS. 2nd Ed., revised. Cr. 8vo. 6s. 6d.

BOOLE.—THE CALCULUS OF FINITE DIFFERENCES. By G. BOOLE. 3rd Ed., revised by J. F. MOULTON, Q.C. Cr. 8vo. 10s. 6d.

EDWARDS.—THE DIFFERENTIAL CALCULUS. By Joseph Edwards, M.A. With Applications and numerous Examples. New Ed. 8vo. 14s.
THE DIFFERENTIAL CALCULUS FOR SCHOOLS. By the Same. Gl. 8vo. 4s. 6d.
THE INTEGRAL CALCULUS. By the same. [In preparation.
THE INTEGRAL CALCULUS FOR SCHOOLS. By the same. [In preparation.

FORSYTH.—A TREATISE ON DIFFERENTIAL EQUATIONS. By Andrew Russell Forsyth, F.R.S., Fellow and Assistant Tutor of Trinity College, Cambridge. 2nd Ed. 8vo. 14s.

FROST.—AN ELEMENTARY TREATISE ON CURVE TRACING. By Percival Frost, M.A., D.Sc. 8vo. 12s.

GRAHAM.—GEOMETRY OF POSITION. By R. H. Graham. Cr. 8vo. 7s. 6d.

GREENHILL.—DIFFERENTIAL AND INTEGRAL CALCULUS. By A. G Greenhill, Professor of Mathematics to the Senior Class of Artillery Officers, Woolwich. New Ed. Cr. 8vo. 10s. 6d.
APPLICATIONS OF ELLIPTIC FUNCTIONS. By the same. 8vo. 12s.

HEMMING.—AN ELEMENTARY TREATISE ON THE DIFFERENTIAL AND INTEGRAL CALCULUS. By G. W. Hemming, M.A. 2nd Ed. 8vo. 9s.

JOHNSON.—Works by W. W. Johnson, Professor of Mathematics at the U.S. Naval Academy.
INTEGRAL CALCULUS, an Elementary Treatise. Founded on the Method of Rates or Fluxions. 8vo. 9s.
CURVE TRACING IN CARTESIAN CO-ORDINATES. Cr. 8vo. 4s. 6d.
A TREATISE ON ORDINARY AND DIFFERENTIAL EQUATIONS. Ex. cr. 8vo. 15s.

KELLAND—TAIT.—INTRODUCTION TO QUATERNIONS, with numerous examples. By P. Kelland and P. G. Tait, Professors in the Department of Mathematics in the University of Edinburgh. 2nd Ed. Cr. 8vo. 7s. 6d.

KEMPE.—HOW TO DRAW A STRAIGHT LINE: a Lecture on Linkages. By A. B. Kempe. Illustrated. Cr. 8vo. 1s. 6d.

KNOX.—DIFFERENTIAL CALCULUS FOR BEGINNERS. By Alexander Knox, M.A. Fcap. 8vo. 3s. 6d.

RICE—JOHNSON.—AN ELEMENTARY TREATISE ON THE DIFFERENTIAL CALCULUS. Founded on the Method of Rates or Fluxions. By J. M. Rice and W. W. Johnson. 3rd Ed. 8vo. 18s. Abridged Ed. 9s.

TODHUNTER.—Works by Isaac Todhunter, F.R.S.
AN ELEMENTARY TREATISE ON THE THEORY OF EQUATIONS. Cr. 8vo. 7s. 6d.
A TREATISE ON THE DIFFERENTIAL CALCULUS. Cr. 8vo. 10s. 6d. KEY. Cr. 8vo. 10s. 6d.
A TREATISE ON THE INTEGRAL CALCULUS AND ITS APPLICATIONS. Cr. 8vo. 10s. 6d. KEY. Cr. 8vo. 10s. 6d.
A HISTORY OF THE MATHEMATICAL THEORY OF PROBABILITY, from the time of Pascal to that of Laplace. 8vo. 18s.

WELD.—SHORT COURSE IN THE THEORY OF DETERMINANTS. By L. G. Weld, M.A. [In the Press.

MECHANICS: Statics, Dynamics, Hydrostatics, Hydrodynamics. (See also Physics.)

ALEXANDER—THOMSON.—ELEMENTARY APPLIED MECHANICS. By Prof. T. Alexander and A. W. Thomson. Part II. Transverse Stress. Cr. 8vo. 10s. 6d.

BALL.—EXPERIMENTAL MECHANICS. A Course of Lectures delivered at the Royal College of Science, Dublin. By Sir R. S. Ball, F.R.S. 2nd Ed. Illustrated. Cr. 8vo. 6s.

CLIFFORD.—THE ELEMENTS OF DYNAMIC. An Introduction to the Study of Motion and Rest in Solid and Fluid Bodies. By W. K. Clifford. Part I.—Kinematic. Cr. 8vo Books I.-III. 7s. 6d.; Book IV. and Appendix, 6s.

COTTERILL.—APPLIED MECHANICS: An Elementary General Introduction to the Theory of Structures and Machines. By J. H. COTTERILL, F.R.S., Professor of Applied Mechanics in the Royal Naval College, Greenwich. 8rd Ed. Revised. 8vo. 18s.

COTTERILL—SLADE.—LESSONS IN APPLIED MECHANICS. By Prof. J. H. COTTERILL and J. H. SLADE. Fcap. 8vo. 5s. 6d.

GANGUILLET—KUTTER.—A GENERAL FORMULA FOR THE UNIFORM FLOW OF WATER IN RIVERS AND OTHER CHANNELS. By E. GANGUILLET and W. R. KUTTER. Translated by R. HERING and J. C. TRAUTWINE. 8vo. 17s.

GRAHAM.—GEOMETRY OF POSITION. By R. H. GRAHAM. Cr. 8vo. 7s. 6d.

*GREAVES.—STATICS FOR BEGINNERS. By JOHN GREAVES, M.A., Fellow and Mathematical Lecturer at Christ's College, Cambridge. Gl. 8vo. 3s. 6d. A TREATISE ON ELEMENTARY STATICS. By the same. Cr. 8vo. 6s. 6d.

GREENHILL.—ELEMENTARY HYDROSTATICS. By A. G. GREENHILL, Professor of Mathematics to the Senior Class of Artillery Officers, Woolwich. Cr. 8vo. [In the Press.

*HICKS.—ELEMENTARY DYNAMICS OF PARTICLES AND SOLIDS. By W. M. HICKS, D.Sc., Principal and Professor of Mathematics and Physics, Firth College, Sheffield. Cr. 8vo. 6s. 6d.

HOSKINS.—ELEMENTS OF GRAPHIC STATICS. By L. M. HOSKINS. 8vo. 10s. net.

KENNEDY.—THE MECHANICS OF MACHINERY. By A. B. W. KENNEDY, F.R.S. Illustrated. Cr. 8vo. 8s. 6d.

LANGMAID—GAISFORD.—(See Engineering, p. 89.)

LOCK.—Works by Rev. J. B. LOCK, M.A.
*MECHANICS FOR BEGINNERS. Gl. 8vo. Part I. MECHANICS OF SOLIDS. 2s. 6d. [Part II. MECHANICS OF FLUIDS, in preparation.
*ELEMENTARY STATICS. 2nd Ed. Gl. 8vo. 3s. 6d. KEY. Cr. 8vo. 8s. 6d.
*ELEMENTARY DYNAMICS. 3rd Ed. Gl. 8vo. 8s. 6d. KEY. Cr. 8vo. 8s. 6d.
*ELEMENTARY DYNAMICS AND STATICS. Gl. 8vo. 6s. 6d.
ELEMENTARY HYDROSTATICS. Gl. 8vo. [In preparation.

MACGREGOR.—KINEMATICS AND DYNAMICS. An Elementary Treatise. By J. G. MACGREGOR, D.Sc., Munro Professor of Physics in Dalhousie College, Halifax, Nova Scotia. Illustrated. Cr. 8vo. 10s. 6d.

PARKINSON.—AN ELEMENTARY TREATISE ON MECHANICS. By S. PARKINSON, D.D., F.R.S., late Tutor and Prælector of St. John's College, Cambridge. 6th Ed., revised. Cr. 8vo. 9s. 6d.

PIRIE.—LESSONS ON RIGID DYNAMICS. By Rev. G. PIRIE, M.A., Professor of Mathematics in the University of Aberdeen. Cr. 8vo. 6s.

ROUTH.—Works by EDWARD JOHN ROUTH, D.Sc., LL.D., F.R.S., Hon. Fellow of St. Peter's College, Cambridge.
A TREATISE ON THE DYNAMICS OF THE SYSTEM OF RIGID BODIES. With numerous Examples. Two vols. 8vo. 5th Ed. Vol. I.—Elementary Parts. 14s. Vol. II.—The Advanced Parts. 14s.
STABILITY OF A GIVEN STATE OF MOTION, PARTICULARLY STEADY MOTION. Adams Prize Essay for 1877. 8vo. 8s. 6d.

*SANDERSON.—HYDROSTATICS FOR BEGINNERS. By F. W. SANDERSON, M.A., Assistant Master at Dulwich College. Gl. 8vo. 4s. 6d.

SYLLABUS OF ELEMENTARY DYNAMICS. Part I. Linear Dynamics. With an Appendix on the Meanings of the Symbols in Physical Equations. Prepared by the Association for the Improvement of Geometrical Teaching. 4to. 1s.

TAIT—STEELE.—A TREATISE ON DYNAMICS OF A PARTICLE. By Professor TAIT, M.A., and W. J. STEELE, B.A. 6th Ed., revised. Cr. 8vo. 12s.

TODHUNTER.—Works by ISAAC TODHUNTER, F.R.S.
*MECHANICS FOR BEGINNERS. 18mo. 4s. 6d. KEY. Cr. 8vo. 6s. 6d.
A TREATISE ON ANALYTICAL STATICS. 5th Ed. Edited by Prof. J. D. EVERETT, F.R.S. Cr. 8vo. 10s. 6d.

WEISBACH—HERMANN.—MECHANICS OF HOISTING MACHINERY. By Dr. J. WEISBACH and Prof. G. HERMANN. Translated by K. P. DAHLSTROM, M.E. [In the Press.

PHYSICS: Sound, Light, Heat, Electricity, Elasticity, Attractions, etc. (See also Mechanics.)

AIRY.—ON SOUND AND ATMOSPHERIC VIBRATIONS. By Sir G. B. AIRY, K.C.B., formerly Astronomer-Royal. With the Mathematical Elements of Music. Cr. 8vo. 9s.

BARKER.—PHYSICS. Advanced Course. By Prof. G. F. BARKER 8vo. 21s.

CUMMING.—AN INTRODUCTION TO THE THEORY OF ELECTRICITY. By LINNÆUS CUMMING, M.A., Assistant Master at Rugby. Illustrated. Cr. 8vo. 8s. 6d.

DANIELL.—A TEXT-BOOK OF THE PRINCIPLES OF PHYSICS. By ALFRED DANIELL, D.Sc. Illustrated. 2nd Ed., revised and enlarged. 8vo. 21s.

DAY.—ELECTRIC LIGHT ARITHMETIC. By R. E. DAY. Pott 8vo. 2s.

EVERETT.—ILLUSTRATIONS OF THE C. G. S. SYSTEM OF UNITS WITH TABLES OF PHYSICAL CONSTANTS. By J. D. EVERETT, F.R.S., Professor of Natural Philosophy, Queen's College, Belfast. New Ed. Ex. fcap. 8vo. 5s.

FESSENDEN.—PHYSICS FOR PUBLIC SCHOOLS. By C. FESSENDEN, Principal, Collegiate Institute, Peterboro, Ontario. Illustrated. Fcap. 8vo. 3s.

GRAY.—THE THEORY AND PRACTICE OF ABSOLUTE MEASUREMENTS IN ELECTRICITY AND MAGNETISM. By A. GRAY, F.R.S.E., Professor of Physics, University College, Bangor. Two vols. Cr. 8vo. Vol. I. 12s. 6d. Vol. II. In 2 Parts. 25s.

ABSOLUTE MEASUREMENTS IN ELECTRICITY AND MAGNETISM. 2nd Ed., revised and greatly enlarged. Fcap. 8vo. 5s. 6d.

ELECTRIC LIGHTING AND POWER DISTRIBUTION. [In preparation.

HANDBOOK OF ELECTRIC LIGHT ENGINEERING. [In preparation.

HEAVISIDE.—ELECTRICAL PAPERS. By O. HEAVISIDE. 2 vols. 8vo. 30s. net.

IBBETSON.—THE MATHEMATICAL THEORY OF PERFECTLY ELASTIC SOLIDS, with a Short Account of Viscous Fluids. By W. J. IBBETSON, late Senior Scholar of Clare College, Cambridge. 8vo. 21s.

JACKSON.—TEXT-BOOK ON ELECTRO-MAGNETISM AND THE CONSTRUCTION OF DYNAMOS. By Prof. D. C. JACKSON. [In the Press.

JOHNSON.—NATURE'S STORY BOOKS. SUNSHINE. By AMY JOHNSON, LL.A. Illustrated. Cr. 8vo. 6s.

*****JONES.**—EXAMPLES IN PHYSICS. With Answers and Solutions. By D. E. JONES, B.Sc., late Professor of Physics, University College of Wales, Aberystwith. 2nd Ed., revised and enlarged. Fcap. 8vo. 3s. 6d.

*****ELEMENTARY LESSONS IN HEAT, LIGHT, AND SOUND. By the same. Gl. 8vo. 2s. 6d.

LESSONS IN HEAT AND LIGHT. By the same. Globe 8vo. 3s. 6d.

KELVIN.—Works by Lord KELVIN, P.R.S., Professor of Natural Philosophy in the University of Glasgow.

ELECTROSTATICS AND MAGNETISM, REPRINTS OF PAPERS ON. 2nd Ed. 8vo. 18s.

POPULAR LECTURES AND ADDRESSES. 3 vols. Illustrated. Cr. 8vo. Vol. I. CONSTITUTION OF MATTER. 7s. 6d. Vol. III. NAVIGATION. 7s. 6d.

LODGE.—MODERN VIEWS OF ELECTRICITY. By OLIVER J. LODGE, F.R.S., Professor of Physics, University College, Liverpool. Illus. Cr. 8vo. 6d.

LOEWY.—*QUESTIONS AND EXAMPLES ON EXPERIMENTAL PHYSICS: Sound, Light, Heat, Electricity, and Magnetism. By B. LOEWY, Examiner in Experimental Physics to the College of Preceptors. Fcap. 8vo. 2s.

*****A GRADUATED COURSE OF NATURAL SCIENCE FOR ELEMENTARY AND TECHNICAL SCHOOLS AND COLLEGES. By the same. Part I. FIRST YEAR'S COURSE. Gl. 8vo. 2s. Part II. 2s. 6d.

LUPTON.—NUMERICAL TABLES AND CONSTANTS IN ELEMENTARY SCIENCE. By S. LUPTON, M.A. Ex. fcap. 8vo. 2s. 6d.

M'AULAY.—UTILITY OF QUATERNIONS IN PHYSICS. By ALEX. M'AULAY. 8vo. [In the Press.

MACFARLANE.—PHYSICAL ARITHMETIC. By A. MACFARLANE, D.Sc., late Examiner in Mathematics at the University of Edinburgh. Cr. 8vo. 7s. 6d.

*MAYER.—SOUND: A Series of Simple Experiments. By A. M. MAYER, Prof. of Physics in the Stevens Institute of Technology. Illustrated. Cr. 8vo. 3s. 6d.

*MAYER—BARNARD.—LIGHT: A Series of Simple Experiments. By A. M. MAYER and C. BARNARD. Illustrated. Cr. 8vo. 2s. 6d.

MOLLOY.—GLEANINGS IN SCIENCE: Popular Lectures. By Rev. GERALD MOLLOY, D.Sc., Rector of the Catholic University of Ireland. 8vo. 7s. 6d.

NEWTON.—PRINCIPIA. Edited by Prof. Sir W. THOMSON, P.R.S., and Prof. BLACKBURNE. 4to. 31s. 6d.

THE FIRST THREE SECTIONS OF NEWTON'S PRINCIPIA. With Notes, Illustrations, and Problems. By P. FROST, M.A., D.Sc. 3rd Ed. 8vo. 12s.

PARKINSON.—A TREATISE ON OPTICS. By S. PARKINSON, D.D., F.R.S., late Tutor of St. John's College, Cambridge. 4th Ed. Cr. 8vo. 10s. 6d.

PEABODY.—THERMODYNAMICS OF THE STEAM-ENGINE AND OTHER HEAT-ENGINES. By CECIL H. PEABODY. 8vo. 21s.

PERRY.—STEAM: An Elementary Treatise. By JOHN PERRY, Prof. of Applied Mechanics, Technical College, Finsbury. 18mo. 4s. 6d.

PICKERING.—ELEMENTS OF PHYSICAL MANIPULATION. By Prof. EDWARD C. PICKERING. Medium 8vo. Part I., 12s. 6d. Part II., 14s.

PRESTON.—THE THEORY OF LIGHT. By THOMAS PRESTON, M.A. Illustrated. 8vo. 15s. net.

THE THEORY OF HEAT. By the same. 8vo. [In the Press.

RAYLEIGH.—THE THEORY OF SOUND. By Lord RAYLEIGH, F.R.S. 8vo. Vol. I., 12s. 6d. Vol. II., 12s. 6d.

SANDERSON.—ELECTRICITY AND MAGNETISM FOR BEGINNERS. By F. W. SANDERSON. [In preparation.

SHANN.—AN ELEMENTARY TREATISE ON HEAT, IN RELATION TO STEAM AND THE STEAM-ENGINE. By G. SHANN, M.A. Cr. 8vo. 4s. 6d.

SPOTTISWOODE.—POLARISATION OF LIGHT. By the late W. SPOTTISWOODE, F.R.S. Illustrated. Cr. 8vo. 3s. 6d.

STEWART.—Works by BALFOUR STEWART, F.R.S., late Langworthy Professor of Physics, Owens College, Manchester.

*A PRIMER OF PHYSICS. Illustrated. With Questions. 18mo. 1s.

*LESSONS IN ELEMENTARY PHYSICS. Illustrated. Fcap. 8vo. 4s. 6d.

*QUESTIONS. By Prof. T. H. CORE. Fcap. 8vo. 2s.

STEWART—GEE.—LESSONS IN ELEMENTARY PRACTICAL PHYSICS. By BALFOUR STEWART, F.R.S., and W. W. HALDANE GEE, B.Sc. Cr. 8vo. Vol. I. GENERAL PHYSICAL PROCESSES, 6s. Vol. II. ELECTRICITY AND MAGNETISM. 7s. 6d. [Vol. III. OPTICS, HEAT, AND SOUND. In the Press.

*PRACTICAL PHYSICS FOR SCHOOLS AND THE JUNIOR STUDENTS OF COLLEGES. Gl. 8vo. Vol. I. ELECTRICITY AND MAGNETISM. 2s. 6d. [Vol. II. OPTICS, HEAT, AND SOUND. In the Press.

STOKES.—ON LIGHT. Burnett Lectures. By Sir G. G. STOKES, F.R.S., Lucasian Professor of Mathematics in the University of Cambridge. I. ON THE NATURE OF LIGHT. II. ON LIGHT AS A MEANS OF INVESTIGATION. III. ON THE BENEFICIAL EFFECTS OF LIGHT. 2nd Ed. Cr. 8vo. 7s. 6d.

STONE.—AN ELEMENTARY TREATISE ON SOUND. By W. H. STONE. Illustrated. Fcap. 8vo. 3s. 6d.

TAIT.—HEAT. By P. G. TAIT, Professor of Natural Philosophy in the University of Edinburgh. Cr. 8vo. 6s.

LECTURES ON SOME RECENT ADVANCES IN PHYSICAL SCIENCE. By the same. 3rd Edition. Crown 8vo. 9s.

TAYLOR.—SOUND AND MUSIC. An Elementary Treatise on the Physical Constitution of Musical Sounds and Harmony, including the Chief Acoustical Discoveries of Prof. Helmholtz. By S. TAYLOR, M.A. Ex. cr. 8vo. 8s. 6d.

*THOMPSON. — ELEMENTARY LESSONS IN ELECTRICITY AND MAGNETISM. By SILVANUS P. THOMPSON, Principal and Professor of Physics in the Technical College, Finsbury. Illustrated. Fcap. 8vo. 4s. 6d.

THOMSON.—Works by J. J. THOMSON, Professor of Experimental Physics in the University of Cambridge.

A TREATISE ON THE MOTION OF VORTEX RINGS. 8vo. 6s.

APPLICATIONS OF DYNAMICS TO PHYSICS AND CHEMISTRY. Cr. 8vo 7s. 6d.

TURNER.—A COLLECTION OF EXAMPLES ON HEAT AND ELECTRICITY. By H. H. TURNER, Fellow of Trinity College, Cambridge. Cr. 8vo. 2s. 6d.

WRIGHT.—LIGHT: A Course of Experimental Optics, chiefly with the Lantern. By LEWIS WRIGHT. Illustrated. New Ed. Cr. 8vo. 7s. 6d.

ASTRONOMY.

AIRY.—Works by Sir G. B. AIRY, K.C.B., formerly Astronomer-Royal.
*POPULAR ASTRONOMY. Revised by H. H. TURNER, M.A. 18mo. 4s. 6d.
GRAVITATION: An Elementary Explanation of the Principal Perturbations in the Solar System. 2nd Ed. Cr. 8vo. 7s. 6d.

CHEYNE.—AN ELEMENTARY TREATISE ON THE PLANETARY THEORY. By C. H. H. CHEYNE. With Problems. 3rd Ed., revised. Cr. 8vo. 7s. 6d.

CLARK—SADLER.—THE STAR GUIDE. By L. CLARK and H. SADLER. Roy. 8vo. 5s.

CROSSLEY—GLEDHILL—WILSON.—A HANDBOOK OF DOUBLE STARS. By E. CROSSLEY, J. GLEDHILL, and J. M. WILSON. 8vo. 21s.
CORRECTIONS TO THE HANDBOOK OF DOUBLE STARS. 8vo. 1s.

FORBES.—TRANSIT OF VENUS. By G. FORBES, Professor of Natural Philosophy in the Andersonian University, Glasgow. Illustrated. Cr. 8vo. 3s. 6d.

GODFRAY.—Works by HUGH GODFRAY, M.A., Mathematical Lecturer at Pembroke College, Cambridge.
A TREATISE ON ASTRONOMY. 4th Ed. 8vo. 12s. 6d.
AN ELEMENTARY TREATISE ON THE LUNAR THEORY. Cr. 8vo. 5s. 6d.

LOCKYER.—Works by J. NORMAN LOCKYER, F.R.S.
*A PRIMER OF ASTRONOMY. Illustrated. 18mo. 1s.
*ELEMENTARY LESSONS IN ASTRONOMY. With Spectra of the Sun, Stars, and Nebulæ, and Illus. 36th Thousand. Revised throughout. Fcap. 8vo. 5s. 6d.
*QUESTIONS ON THE ABOVE. By J. FORBES ROBERTSON. 18mo. 1s. 6d.
THE CHEMISTRY OF THE SUN. Illustrated. 8vo. 14s.
THE METEORITIC HYPOTHESIS OF THE ORIGIN OF COSMICAL SYSTEMS. Illustrated. 8vo. 17s. net.
STAR-GAZING PAST AND PRESENT. Expanded from Notes with the assistance of G. M. SEABROKE, F.R.A.S. Roy. 8vo. 21s.

LODGE.—PIONEERS OF SCIENCE. By OLIVER J. LODGE. Ex. Cr. 8vo. 7s. 6d.

NEWCOMB.—POPULAR ASTRONOMY. By S. NEWCOMB, LL.D., Professor U.S. Naval Observatory. Illustrated. 2nd Ed., revised. 8vo. 18s.

HISTORICAL.

BALL.—A SHORT ACCOUNT OF THE HISTORY OF MATHEMATICS. By W. W. ROUSE BALL, M.A. 2nd ed. Cr. 8vo. 10s. 6d.
MATHEMATICAL RECREATIONS, AND PROBLEMS OF PAST AND PRESENT TIMES. By the same. Cr. 8vo. 7s. net.

NATURAL SCIENCES.

Chemistry; Physical Geography, Geology, and Mineralogy; Biology (*Botany, Zoology, General Biology, Physiology*); Medicine.

CHEMISTRY.

ARMSTRONG.—A MANUAL OF INORGANIC CHEMISTRY. By H. E. ARMSTRONG, F.R.S., Professor of Chemistry, City and Guilds Central Institute [*In preparation.*]

BEHRENS. — MICRO - CHEMICAL METHODS OF ANALYSIS. By Prof. BEHRENS. With Preface by Prof. J. W. JUDD. Cr. 8vo. [*In preparation.*]

*COHEN.—THE OWENS COLLEGE COURSE OF PRACTICAL ORGANIC CHEMISTRY. By JULIUS B. COHEN, Ph.D., Assistant Lecturer on Chemistry, Owens College, Manchester. Fcap. 8vo. 2s. 6d.

*DOBBIN—WALKER.—CHEMICAL THEORY FOR BEGINNERS. By L. DOBBIN, Ph.D., and JAS. WALKER, Ph.D., Assistants in the Chemistry Department, University of Edinburgh. 18mo. 2s. 6d.

FLEISCHER.—A SYSTEM OF VOLUMETRIC ANALYSIS. By EMIL FLEISCHER. Translated, with Additions, by M. M. P. MUIR, F.R.S.E. Cr. 8vo. 7s. 6d.

FRANKLAND.—AGRICULTURAL CHEMICAL ANALYSIS. (*See* Agriculture.)

HARTLEY.—A COURSE OF QUANTITATIVE ANALYSIS FOR STUDENTS. By W. N. HARTLEY, F.R.S., Professor of Chemistry, Royal College of Science, Dublin. Gl. 8vo. 5s.

HEMPEL.—METHODS OF GAS ANALYSIS. By Dr. WALTHER HEMPEL. Translated by Dr. L. M. DENNIS. Cr. 8vo. 7s. 6d.

HIORNS.—Works by A. H. HIORNS, Principal of the School of Metallurgy, Birmingham and Midland Institute. Gl. 8vo.
A TEXT-BOOK OF ELEMENTARY METALLURGY. 4s.
PRACTICAL METALLURGY AND ASSAYING. 6s.
IRON AND STEEL MANUFACTURE. For Beginners. 3s. 6d.
MIXED METALS OR METALLIC ALLOYS. 6s.
METAL COLOURING AND BRONZING. By the same.

JONES.—*THE OWENS COLLEGE JUNIOR COURSE OF PRACTICAL CHEMISTRY. By FRANCIS JONES, F.R.S.E., Chemical Master at the Grammar School, Manchester. Illustrated. Fcap. 8vo. 2s. 6d.
*QUESTIONS ON CHEMISTRY. Inorganic and Organic. By the same. Fcap. 8vo. 3s.

LANDAUER.—BLOWPIPE ANALYSIS. By J. LANDAUER. Translated by J. TAYLOR, B.Sc. Revised Edition. Gl. 8vo. 4s. 6d.

LAURIE.—(*See* Agriculture, p. 40.)

LOCKYER.—THE CHEMISTRY OF THE SUN. By J. NORMAN LOCKYER, F.R.S. Illustrated. 8vo. 14s.

LUPTON.—CHEMICAL ARITHMETIC. With 1200 Problems. By S. LUPTON, M.A. 2nd Ed., revised. Fcap. 8vo. 4s. 6d.

MELDOLA.—THE CHEMISTRY OF PHOTOGRAPHY. By RAPHAEL MELDOLA, F.R.S., Professor of Chemistry, Technical College, Finsbury. Cr. 8vo. 6s.

MEYER.—HISTORY OF CHEMISTRY FROM THE EARLIEST TIMES TO THE PRESENT DAY. By ERNST VON MEYER, Ph.D. Translated by GEORGE McGOWAN, Ph.D. 8vo. 14s. net.

MIXTER.—AN ELEMENTARY TEXT-BOOK OF CHEMISTRY. By W.G. MIXTER, Professor of Chemistry, Yale College. 2nd Ed. Cr. 8vo. 7s. 6d.

MUIR.—PRACTICAL CHEMISTRY FOR MEDICAL STUDENTS: First M.B. Course. By M. M. P. MUIR, F.R.S.E., Fellow and Prælector in Chemistry at Gonville and Caius College, Cambridge. Fcap. 8vo. 1s. 6d.

MUIR.—WILSON.—THE ELEMENTS OF THERMAL CHEMISTRY. By M. M. P. MUIR, F.R.S.E.; assisted by D. M. WILSON. 8vo. 12s. 6d.

OSTWALD.—OUTLINES OF GENERAL CHEMISTRY: Physical and Theoretical. By Prof. W. OSTWALD. Trans. by JAS. WALKER, D.Sc. 8vo. 10s. net.

RAMSAY.—EXPERIMENTAL PROOFS OF CHEMICAL THEORY FOR BEGINNERS. By WILLIAM RAMSAY, F.R.S., Professor of Chemistry, University College, London. 18mo. 2s. 6d.

REMSEN.—Works by IRA REMSEN, Prof. of Chemistry, Johns Hopkins University.
*THE ELEMENTS OF CHEMISTRY. For Beginners. Fcap. 8vo. 2s. 6d.
AN INTRODUCTION TO THE STUDY OF CHEMISTRY (INORGANIC CHEMISTRY). Cr. 8vo. 6s. 6d.
COMPOUNDS OF CARBON: an Introduction to the Study of Organic Chemistry. Cr. 8vo. 6s. 6d.
A TEXT-BOOK OF INORGANIC CHEMISTRY. 8vo. 16s.

ROSCOE.—Works by Sir HENRY E. ROSCOE, F.R.S., formerly Professor of Chemistry, Owens College, Manchester.
*A PRIMER OF CHEMISTRY. Illustrated. With Questions. 18mo. 1s.
*CHEMISTRY FOR BEGINNERS. Gl. 8vo. [*Sept.* 1893.
*LESSONS IN ELEMENTARY CHEMISTRY, INORGANIC AND ORGANIC. With Illustrations and Chromolitho of the Solar Spectrum, and of the Alkalies and Alkaline Earths. New Ed., 1892. Fcap. 8vo. 4s. 6d.

ROSCOE—SCHORLEMMER.—A TREATISE ON INORGANIC AND ORGANIC CHEMISTRY. By Sir HENRY ROSCOE, F.R.S., and Prof. C. SCHORLEMMER, F.R.S. 8vo.

Vols. L and II.—INORGANIC CHEMISTRY. Vol. I.—The Non-Metallic Elements. 2nd Ed. 21s. Vol. II. Two Parts, 18s. each.

Vol. III.—ORGANIC CHEMISTRY. THE CHEMISTRY OF THE HYDRO-CARBONS and their Derivatives. Parts I. II. IV. and VI. 21s. each. Parts III. and V. 18s. each.

ROSCOE — SCHUSTER.—SPECTRUM ANALYSIS. By Sir HENRY ROSCOE, F.R.S. 4th Ed., revised by the Author and A. SCHUSTER, F.R.S., Professor of Applied Mathematics in the Owens College, Manchester. 8vo. 21s.

SCHORLEMMER.—RISE AND DEVELOPMENT OF ORGANIC CHEMISTRY. By Prof. SCHORLEMMER. N. E. Edited by Prof. A. H. SMITHELLS. [In the Press.

SCHULTZ—JULIUS.—SYSTEMATIC SURVEY OF THE ORGANIC COLOUR-ING MATTERS. By Dr. G. SCHULTZ and P. JULIUS. Translated and Edited, with extensive additions, by ARTHUR G. GREEN, F.I.C., F.C.S., Examiner in Coal Tar Products to the City and Guilds of London Institute. Royal 8vo. [In the Press.

*THORPE.—A SERIES OF CHEMICAL PROBLEMS. With Key. By T. E. THORPE, F.R.S., Professor of Chemistry, Royal College of Science. New Ed. Fcap. 8vo. 2s.

THORPE—RÜCKER.—A TREATISE ON CHEMICAL PHYSICS. By Prof. T. E. THORPE and Prof. A. W. RÜCKER. 8vo. [In preparation.

*TURPIN.—ORGANIC CHEMISTRY. By G. S. TURPIN, M.A. Part I. Elementary. Gl. 8vo. [In the Press.

WURTZ.—A HISTORY OF CHEMICAL THEORY. By AD. WURTZ. Translated by HENRY WATTS, F.R.S. Crown 8vo. 6s.

WYNNE.—COAL TAR PRODUCTS. By W. P. WYNNE, Royal College of Science. [In preparation.

PHYSICAL GEOGRAPHY, GEOLOGY, AND MINERALOGY.

BLANFORD.—THE RUDIMENTS OF PHYSICAL GEOGRAPHY FOR INDIAN SCHOOLS; with Glossary. By H. F. BLANFORD, F.G.S. Cr. 8vo. 2s. 6d.

FERREL.—A POPULAR TREATISE ON THE WINDS. By W. FERREL, M.A., Member of the American National Academy of Sciences. 8vo. 17s. net.

FISHER.—PHYSICS OF THE EARTH'S CRUST. By Rev. OSMOND FISHER, M.A., F.G.S., Hon. Fellow of King's College, London. 2nd Ed., enlarged. 8vo. 12s.

GEE.—SHORT STUDIES IN EARTH KNOWLEDGE. By WILLIAM GEE. Gl. 8vo. Illustrated. [In the Press.

GEIKIE.—Works by Sir ARCHIBALD GEIKIE, F.R.S., Director-General of the Geological Survey of the United Kingdom.

*A PRIMER OF PHYSICAL GEOGRAPHY. Illus. With Questions. 18mo. 1s.

*ELEMENTARY LESSONS IN PHYSICAL GEOGRAPHY. Illustrated. Fcap. 8vo. 4s. 6d. *QUESTIONS ON THE SAME. 1s. 6d.

*A PRIMER OF GEOLOGY. Illustrated. 18mo. 1s.

*CLASS-BOOK OF GEOLOGY. Illustrated. Cheaper Ed. Cr. 8vo. 4s. 6d.

TEXT-BOOK OF GEOLOGY. Illustrated. 3rd Ed. 8vo. 28s.

OUTLINES OF FIELD GEOLOGY. Illustrated. New Ed. Gl. 8vo. 3s. 6d.

THE SCENERY AND GEOLOGY OF SCOTLAND, VIEWED IN CONNEXION WITH ITS PHYSICAL GEOLOGY. Illustrated. Cr. 8vo. 12s. 6d.

HUXLEY.—PHYSIOGRAPHY. An Introduction to the Study of Nature. By T. H. HUXLEY, F.R.S. Illustrated. Cr. 8vo. 6s.

LESSING.—TABLES FOR THE DETERMINATION OF THE ROCK-FORMING MINERALS. Compiled by F. L. LOEWINSON-LESSING, Professor of Geology at the University of Dorpat. Translated from the Russian by J. W. GREGORY, B.Sc., F.G.S., of the British Museum. With a Glossary added by Prof. G. A. J. COLE, F.G.S. 8vo.

LOCKYER.—OUTLINES OF PHYSIOGRAPHY—THE MOVEMENTS OF THE EARTH. By J. NORMAN LOCKYER, F.R.S., Examiner in Physiography for the Science and Art Department. Illustrated. Cr. 8vo. Sewed, 1s. 6d.

LOUIS.—HANDBOOK OF GOLD MILLING. By HENRY LOUIS. [In the Press.

*MARR—HARKER. PHYSIOGRAPHY FOR BEGINNERS. By J. E. MARR, M.A., and A. HARKER, M.A. Gl. 8vo. [In the Press.

MIERS.—A TREATISE ON MINERALOGY. By H. A. MIERS, of the British
  Museum. 8vo. *[In preparation.*
MIERS—CROSSKEY.—(*See* Hygiene, p. 40.)
PHILLIPS.—A TREATISE ON ORE DEPOSITS. By J.A. PHILLIPS, F.R.S. 8vo. 25s.
WILLIAMS.—ELEMENTS OF CRYSTALLOGRAPHY, for students of Chemistry,
  Physics, and Mineralogy. By G. H. WILLIAMS, Ph.D. Cr. 8vo. 6s.

BIOLOGY.

(*Botany, Zoology, General Biology, Physiology.*)

Botany.

ALLEN.—ON THE COLOURS OF FLOWERS, as Illustrated in the British Flora.
  By GRANT ALLEN. Illustrated. Cr. 8vo. 3s. 6d.
BALFOUR—WARD.—A GENERAL TEXT-BOOK OF BOTANY. By Prof. I. B.
  BALFOUR, F.R.S., University of Edinburgh, and Prof. H. MARSHALL WARD,
  F.R.S., Roy. Indian Engineering Coll. *[In preparation.*
*BETTANY.—FIRST LESSONS IN PRACTICAL BOTANY. By G. T. BETTANY.
  18mo. 1s.
*BOWER.—A COURSE OF PRACTICAL INSTRUCTION IN BOTANY. By F.
  O. BOWER, D.Sc., F.R.S., Regius Professor of Botany in the University of
  Glasgow. Cr. 8vo. 10s. 6d. *[Abridged Ed. in preparation.*
CHURCH—VINES.—MANUAL OF VEGETABLE PHYSIOLOGY. By Prof.
  A. H. CHURCH, F.R.S., and S. H. VINES. Illustrated. Cr. 8vo. *[In prep.*
GOODALE.—PHYSIOLOGICAL BOTANY. I. Outlines of the Histology of
  Phænogamous Plants. II. Vegetable Physiology. By G. L. GOODALE, M.A.,
  M.D., Professor of Botany in Harvard University. 8vo. 10s. 6d.
GRAY.—STRUCTURAL BOTANY, OR ORGANOGRAPHY ON THE BASIS
  OF MORPHOLOGY. By Prof. ASA GRAY, LL.D. 8vo. 10s. 6d.
HARTIG.—TEXT-BOOK OF THE DISEASES OF TREES. (*See* Agriculture, p. 39.)
HOOKER.—Works by Sir JOSEPH HOOKER, F.R.S., &c.
*PRIMER OF BOTANY. Illustrated. 18mo. 1s.
  THE STUDENT'S FLORA OF THE BRITISH ISLANDS. 3rd Ed., revised.
  Gl. 8vo. 10s. 6d.
LUBBOCK—FLOWERS, FRUITS, AND LEAVES. By the Right Hon. Sir J.
  LUBBOCK, F.R.S. Illustrated. 2nd Ed. Cr. 8vo. 4s. 6d.
MÜLLER.—THE FERTILISATION OF FLOWERS. By HERMANN MÜLLER.
  Translated by D'ARCY W. THOMPSON, B.A., Professor of Biology in University
  College, Dundee. Preface by CHARLES DARWIN. Illustrated. 8vo. 21s.
NISBET.—BRITISH FOREST TREES. (*See* Agriculture, p. 40.)
OLIVER.—*LESSONS IN ELEMENTARY BOTANY. By DANIEL OLIVER, F.R.S.,
  late Professor of Botany in University College, London. Fcap. 8vo. 4s. 6d.
  FIRST BOOK OF INDIAN BOTANY. By the same. Ex. fcap. 8vo. 6s. 6d.
SMITH.—DISEASES OF FIELD AND GARDEN CROPS. (*See* Agriculture, p. 40.)
WARD.—TIMBER AND SOME OF ITS DISEASES. (*See* Agriculture, p. 40.)

Zoology.

BALFOUR.—A TREATISE ON COMPARATIVE EMBRYOLOGY. By F. M.
  BALFOUR, F.R.S. Illustrated. 2 vols. 8vo. Vol. I. 18s. Vol. II. 21s.
BERNARD—THE APODIDAE. By H. M. BERNARD, M.A., LL.D. Cr. 8vo. 7s. 6d.
BUCKTON.—MONOGRAPH OF THE BRITISH CICADÆ, OR TETTIGIDÆ.
  By G. B. BUCKTON. 2 vols. 8vo. 33s. 6d. each, net.
COUES.—HANDBOOK OF FIELD AND GENERAL ORNITHOLOGY. By
  Prof. ELLIOTT COUES, M.A. Illustrated. 8vo. 10s. net.
FLOWER — GADOW.—AN INTRODUCTION TO THE OSTEOLOGY OF
  THE MAMMALIA. By Sir W. H. FLOWER, F.R.S., Director of the Natural
  History Museum. Illus. 3rd Ed., revised with the help of HANS GADOW, Ph.D.
  Cr. 8vo. 10s. 6d.
FOSTER — BALFOUR.—THE ELEMENTS OF EMBRYOLOGY. By Prof.
  MICHAEL FOSTER, M.D., F.R.S., and the late F. M. BALFOUR, F.R.S., 2nd Ed.
  revised, by A. SEDGWICK, M.A., Fellow and Assistant Lecturer of Trinity
  College, Cambridge, and W. HEAPE, M.A. Illustrated. Cr. 8vo. 10s. 6d.
GÜNTHER.—GUIDE TO BRITISH FISHES. By Dr. A. GÜNTHER. Cr. 8vo.
  [In the Press.

HERDMAN.—BRITISH MARINE FAUNA. By Prof. W. A. HERDMAN. Cr. 8vo.
[*In preparation.*

LANG.—TEXT-BOOK OF COMPARATIVE ANATOMY. By Dr. ARNOLD LANG, Professor of Zoology in the University of Zurich. Transl. by H. M. and M. BERNARD. Introduction by Prof. HAECKEL. 2 vols. Illustrated. 8vo. Part I. 17s. net. [*Part II. in the Press.*

LUBBOCK.—THE ORIGIN AND METAMORPHOSES OF INSECTS. By the Right Hon. Sir JOHN LUBBOCK, F.R.S., D.C.L. Illus. Cr. 8vo. 3s. 6d.

MARTIN—MOALE.—ON THE DISSECTION OF VERTEBRATE ANIMALS. By Prof. H. N. MARTIN and W. A. MOALE. Cr. 8vo. [*In preparation.*

MEYRICK.—BRITISH LEPIDOPTERA. By L. MEYRICK. [*In preparation.*

MIALL.—AQUATIC INSECTS. By Prof. L. C. MIALL. [*In preparation.*

MIVART.—LESSONS IN ELEMENTARY ANATOMY. By ST. G. MIVART, F.R.S., Lecturer on Comparative Anatomy at St. Mary's Hospital. Fcap. 8vo. 6s. 6d.

PARKER.—A COURSE OF INSTRUCTION IN ZOOTOMY (VERTEBRATA). By T. JEFFERY PARKER, F.R.S., Professor of Biology in the University of Otago, New Zealand. Illustrated. Cr. 8vo. 8s. 6d.

PARKER—HASWELL.—A TEXT-BOOK OF ZOOLOGY. By Prof. T. J. PARKER, F.R.S., and Prof. HASWELL. 8vo. [*In preparation.*

SEDGWICK.—TREATISE ON EMBRYOLOGY. By ADAM SEDGWICK, F.R.S., Fellow and Lecturer of Trinity College, Cambridge. 8vo. [*In preparation.*

SHUFELDT.—THE MYOLOGY OF THE RAVEN (*Corvus corax sinuatus*). A Guide to the Study of the Muscular System in Birds. By R. W. SHUFELDT. Illustrated. 8vo. 13s. net.

WIEDERSHEIM.—ELEMENTS OF THE COMPARATIVE ANATOMY OF VERTEBRATES. By Prof. R. WIEDERSHEIM. Adapted by W. NEWTON PARKER, Professor of Biology, University College, Cardiff. 8vo. 12s. 6d.

General Biology.

BALL.—ARE THE EFFECTS OF USE AND DISUSE INHERITED? By W. PLATT BALL. Cr. 8vo. 3s. 6d.

BATESON.—MATERIALS FOR THE STUDY OF VARIATION IN ANIMALS. Part I. Discontinuous Variation. By W. BATESON. 8vo. Illus. [*In the Press.*

CALDERWOOD.—EVOLUTION AND MAN'S PLACE IN NATURE. By Prof. H. CALDERWOOD, LL.D. Cr. 8vo. 7s. 6d.

EIMER.—ORGANIC EVOLUTION as the Result of the Inheritance of Acquired Characters according to the Laws of Organic Growth. By Dr. G. H. T. EIMER. Transl. by J. T. CUNNINGHAM, F.R.S.E. 8vo. 12s. 6d.

HOWES.—AN ATLAS OF PRACTICAL ELEMENTARY BIOLOGY. By G. B. HOWES, Assistant Professor of Zoology, Royal College of Science. 4to. 14s.

*HUXLEY.—INTRODUCTORY PRIMER OF SCIENCE. By Prof. T. H. HUXLEY, F.R.S. 18mo. 1s.

HUXLEY — MARTIN.—A COURSE OF PRACTICAL INSTRUCTION IN ELEMENTARY BIOLOGY. By Prof. T. H. HUXLEY, F.R.S., assisted by H. N. MARTIN, F.R.S., Professor of Biology in the Johns Hopkins University. New Ed., revised by G. B. HOWES, Assistant Professor, Royal College of Science, and D. H. SCOTT, D.Sc. Cr. 8vo. 10s. 6d.

LUBBOCK.—ON BRITISH WILD FLOWERS CONSIDERED IN RELATION TO INSECTS. By the Right Hon. Sir J. LUBBOCK, F.R.S. Illustrated. Cr. 8vo. 4s. 6d.

PARKER.—LESSONS IN ELEMENTARY BIOLOGY. By Prof. T. JEFFERY PARKER, F.R.S. Illustrated. 2nd Ed. Cr. 8vo. 10s. 6d.

VARIGNY.—EXPERIMENTAL EVOLUTION. By H. DE VARIGNY. Cr. 8vo. 5s.

WALLACE.—Works by ALFRED RUSSEL WALLACE, LL.D.
DARWINISM: An Exposition of the Theory of Natural Selection. Cr. 8vo. 9s.
NATURAL SELECTION: AND TROPICAL NATURE. New Ed. Cr. 8vo. 6s.
ISLAND LIFE. New Ed. Cr. 8vo. 6s.

Physiology.

FEARNLEY.—A MANUAL OF ELEMENTARY PRACTICAL HISTOLOGY. By WILLIAM FEARNLEY. Illustrated. Cr. 8vo. 7s. 6d.

FOSTER.—Works by MICHAEL FOSTER, M.D., F.R.S., Professor of Physiology in the University of Cambridge.

*A PRIMER OF PHYSIOLOGY. Illustrated. 18mo. 1s.

A TEXT-BOOK OF PHYSIOLOGY. Illustrated. 5th Ed., largely revised. 8vo. Part I. Blood—The Tissues of Movement, The Vascular Mechanism. 10s. 6d. Part II. The Tissues of Chemical Action, with their Respective Mechanisms —Nutrition. 10s. 6d. Part III. The Central Nervous System. 7s. 6d. Part IV. The Senses and some Special Muscular Mechanisms. The Tissues and Mechanisms of Reproduction. 10s. 6d. APPENDIX—THE CHEMICAL BASIS OF THE ANIMAL BODY. By A. S. LEA, M.A. 7s. 6d.

FOSTER—LANGLEY.—A COURSE OF ELEMENTARY PRACTICAL PHY-SIOLOGY AND HISTOLOGY. By Prof. MICHAEL FOSTER, and J. N. LANGLEY, F.R.S., Fellow of Trinity College, Cambridge. 6th Ed. Cr. 8vo. 7s. 6d.

FOSTER—SHORE.—PHYSIOLOGY FOR BEGINNERS. By MICHAEL FOSTER, M.A., and L. E. SHORE, M.A. Gl. 8vo. [In the Press.

GAMGEE.—A TEXT-BOOK OF THE PHYSIOLOGICAL CHEMISTRY OF THE ANIMAL BODY. By A. GAMGEE, M.D., F.R.S. 8vo. Vol. I. 18s.
[Vol. II. in the Press.

*HUXLEY.—LESSONS IN ELEMENTARY PHYSIOLOGY. By Prof. T. H. HUXLEY, F.R.S. Illust. Fcap. 8vo. 4s. 6d.

*QUESTIONS ON THE ABOVE. By T. ALCOCK, M.D. 18mo. 1s. 6d.

MEDICINE.

BLYTH.—(See Hygiene, p. 40).

BRUNTON.—Works by T. LAUDER BRUNTON, M.D., F.R.S., Examiner in Materia Medica in the University of London, in the Victoria University, and in the Royal College of Physicians, London.

A TEXT-BOOK OF PHARMACOLOGY, THERAPEUTICS, AND MATERIA MEDICA. Adapted to the United States Pharmacopœia by F. H. WILLIAMS, M.D., Boston, Mass. 3rd Ed. Adapted to the New British Pharmacopœia, 1885, and additions, 1891. 8vo. 21s. Or in 2 vols. 22s. 6d. Supplement. 1s.

TABLES OF MATERIA MEDICA: A Companion to the Materia Medica Museum. Illustrated. Cheaper Issue. 8vo. 5s.

AN INTRODUCTION TO MODERN THERAPEUTICS. 8vo. 3s. 6d. net.

GRIFFITHS.—LESSONS ON PRESCRIPTIONS AND THE ART OF PRESCRIB-ING. By W. H. GRIFFITHS. Adapted to the Pharmacopœia, 1885. 18mo. 3s. 6d.

HAMILTON.—A TEXT-BOOK OF PATHOLOGY, SYSTEMATIC AND PRAC-TICAL. By D. J. HAMILTON, F.R.S.E., Professor of Pathological Anatomy, University of Aberdeen. Illustrated. Vol. I. 8vo. 25s. [Vol. II. in the Press.

KLEIN.—Works by E. KLEIN, F.R.S., Lecturer on General Anatomy and Physio-logy in the Medical School of St. Bartholomew's Hospital, London.

MICRO-ORGANISMS AND DISEASE. An Introduction into the Study of Specific Micro-Organisms. Illustrated. 3rd Ed., revised. Cr. 8vo. 6s.

THE BACTERIA IN ASIATIC CHOLERA. Cr. 8vo. 5s.

VON KAHLDEN.—HANDBOOK OF HISTOLOGICAL METHODS. By Dr. VON KAHLDEN. Translated by H. MORLEY FLETCHER, M.D. 8vo. Being a Companion to Ziegler's "Pathological Anatomy." [In preparation.

WHITE.—A TEXT-BOOK OF GENERAL THERAPEUTICS. By W. HALE WHITE, M.D., Senior Assistant Physician to and Lecturer in Materia Medica at Guy's Hospital. Illustrated. Cr. 8vo. 8s. 6d.

WILLOUGHBY.—(See Hygiene, p. 40.)

ZIEGLER—MACALISTER.—TEXT-BOOK OF PATHOLOGICAL ANATOMY AND PATHOGENESIS. By Prof. E. ZIEGLER. Translated and Edited by DONALD MACALISTER, M.A., M.D., Fellow and Medical Lecturer of St. John's College, Cambridge. Illustrated. 8vo.

Part I.—GENERAL PATHOLOGICAL ANATOMY. 2nd Ed. 12s. 6d.

Part II.—SPECIAL PATHOLOGICAL ANATOMY. Sections I.-VIII. 2nd Ed. 12s. 6d. Sections IX.-XII. 12s. 6d.

HUMAN SCIENCES.

Mental and Moral Philosophy ; Political Economy ; Law and Politics ;
Anthropology ; Education.

MENTAL AND MORAL PHILOSOPHY.

BALDWIN.—HANDBOOK OF PSYCHOLOGY: SENSES AND INTELLECT.
By Prof. J. M. BALDWIN, M.A., LL.D. 2nd Ed., revised. 8vo. 12s. 6d.
FEELING AND WILL. By the same. 8vo. 12s. 6d.

BOOLE.—THE MATHEMATICAL ANALYSIS OF LOGIC. Being an Essay
towards a Calculus of Deductive Reasoning. By GEORGE BOOLE. 8vo. 5s.

CALDERWOOD.—HANDBOOK OF MORAL PHILOSOPHY. By Rev. HENRY
CALDERWOOD, LL.D., Professor of Moral Philosophy in the University of
Edinburgh. 14th Ed., largely rewritten. Cr. 8vo. 6s.

CLIFFORD.—SEEING AND THINKING. By the late Prof. W. K. CLIFFORD,
F.R.S. With Diagrams. Cr. 8vo. 3s. 6d.

HÖFFDING.—OUTLINES OF PSYCHOLOGY. By Prof. H. HÖFFDING. Translated by M. E. LOWNDES. Cr. 8vo. 6s.

JAMES.—THE PRINCIPLES OF PSYCHOLOGY. By WM. JAMES, Professor
of Psychology in Harvard University. 2 vols. 8vo. 25s. net.
A TEXT-BOOK OF PSYCHOLOGY. By the same. Cr. 8vo. 7s. net.

JARDINE.—THE ELEMENTS OF THE PSYCHOLOGY OF COGNITION. By
Rev. ROBERT JARDINE, D.Sc. 3rd Ed., revised. Cr. 8vo. 6s. 6d.

JEVONS.—Works by W. STANLEY JEVONS, F.R.S.
*A PRIMER OF LOGIC. 18mo. 1s.
*ELEMENTARY LESSONS IN LOGIC, Deductive and Inductive, with Copious
Questions and Examples, and a Vocabulary. Fcap. 8vo. 3s. 6d.
THE PRINCIPLES OF SCIENCE. Cr. 8vo. 12s. 6d.
STUDIES IN DEDUCTIVE LOGIC. 2nd Ed. Cr. 8vo. 6s.
PURE LOGIC: AND OTHER MINOR WORKS. Edited by R. ADAMSON,
M.A., LL.D., Professor of Logic at Owens College, Manchester, and HARRIET
A. JEVONS. With a Preface by Prof. ADAMSON. 8vo. 10s. 6d.

KANT—MAX MÜLLER.—CRITIQUE OF PURE REASON. By IMMANUEL KANT.
2 vols. 8vo. 16s. each. Vol. I. HISTORICAL INTRODUCTION, by LUD-
WIG NOIRÉ ; Vol. II. CRITIQUE OF PURE REASON, translated by F. MAX
MÜLLER.

**KANT—MAHAFFY—BERNARD. — KANT'S CRITICAL PHILOSOPHY FOR
ENGLISH READERS.** By J. P. MAHAFFY, D.D., Professor of Ancient History
in the University of Dublin, and JOHN H. BERNARD, B.D., Fellow of Trinity
College, Dublin. A new and complete Edition in 2 vols. Cr. 8vo.
Vol. I. THE KRITIK OF PURE REASON EXPLAINED AND DEFENDED. 7s. 6d.
Vol. II. THE PROLEGOMENA. Translated with Notes and Appendices. 6s.

KANT.—KRITIK OF JUDGMENT. Translated with Introduction and Notes by
J. H. BERNARD, D.D. 8vo. 10s. net.

KEYNES.—FORMAL LOGIC, Studies and Exercises in. By J. N. KEYNES, D.Sc.
2nd Ed., revised and enlarged. Cr. 8vo. 10s. 6d.

McCOSH.—Works by JAMES McCOSH, D.D., President of Princeton College.
PSYCHOLOGY. Cr. 8vo. I. THE COGNITIVE POWERS. 6s. 6d. II. THE
MOTIVE POWERS. 6s. 6d.
FIRST AND FUNDAMENTAL TRUTHS: a Treatise on Metaphysics. 8vo. 9s.
THE PREVAILING TYPES OF PHILOSOPHY. CAN THEY LOGICALLY
REACH REALITY ? 8vo. 3s. 6d.

MAURICE.—MORAL AND METAPHYSICAL PHILOSOPHY. By F. D.
MAURICE, M.A., late Professor of Moral Philosophy in the University of Cambridge. 4th Ed. 2 vols. 8vo. 16s.

***RAY.—A TEXT-BOOK OF DEDUCTIVE LOGIC FOR THE USE OF STUDENTS.**
By P. K. RAY, D.Sc., Professor of Logic and Philosophy, Presidency College,
Calcutta. 4th Ed. Globe 8vo. 4s. 6d.

**SIDGWICK.—Works by HENRY SIDGWICK, LL.D., D.C.L., Knightbridge Professor
of Moral Philosophy in the University of Cambridge.**
THE METHODS OF ETHICS. 4th Ed. 8vo. 14s.

OUTLINES OF THE HISTORY OF ETHICS. 3rd Ed. Cr. 8vo. 8s. 6d.
VENN.—Works by JOHN VENN, F.R.S., Examiner in Moral Philosophy in the
University of London.
THE LOGIC OF CHANCE. An Essay on the Foundations and Province of the
Theory of Probability. 3rd Ed., rewritten and enlarged. Cr. 8vo. 10s. 6d.
SYMBOLIC LOGIC. Cr. 8vo. 10s. 6d.
THE PRINCIPLES OF EMPIRICAL OR INDUCTIVE LOGIC. 8vo. 18s.
WILLIAMS.—REVIEW OF THE SYSTEM OF ETHICS FOUNDED ON THE
THEORY OF EVOLUTION. By C. M. WILLIAMS. Ex. Cr. 8vo. 12s. net.

POLITICAL ECONOMY.

BASTABLE.—PUBLIC FINANCE. By C. F. BASTABLE, Professor of Political
Economy in the University of Dublin. 8vo. 12s. 6d. net.
BÖHM-BAWERK.—CAPITAL AND INTEREST. Translated by WILLIAM SMART,
M.A. 8vo. 12s. net.
THE POSITIVE THEORY OF CAPITAL. By the same. 8vo. 12s. net.
CAIRNES.—THE CHARACTER AND LOGICAL METHOD OF POLITICAL
ECONOMY. By J. E. CAIRNES. Cr. 8vo. 6s.
SOME LEADING PRINCIPLES OF POLITICAL ECONOMY NEWLY EX-
POUNDED. By the same. 8vo. 14s.
CLARE.—ABC OF THE FOREIGN EXCHANGES. By GEORGE CLARE. Crown
8vo. 3s. net.
COSSA.—INTRODUCTION TO THE STUDY OF POLITICAL ECONOMY.
Being an entirely rewritten third edition of the Guide to the Study of Political
Economy by LUIGI COSSA, Professor in the Royal University of Pavia. Trans-
lated, with the author's sanction and assistance, from the original Italian by a
former Taylorian scholar in Italian of the University of Oxford. Crown 8vo.
[In the Press.
*FAWCETT.—POLITICAL ECONOMY FOR BEGINNERS, WITH QUESTIONS.
By Mrs. HENRY FAWCETT. 7th Ed. 18mo. 2s. 6d.
FAWCETT.—A MANUAL OF POLITICAL ECONOMY. By the Right Hon. HENRY
FAWCETT, F.R.S. 7th Ed., revised. Cr. 8vo. 12s.
AN EXPLANATORY DIGEST of above. By C. A. WATERS, B.A. Cr. 8vo. 2s.6d.
GILMAN.—PROFIT-SHARING BETWEEN EMPLOYER AND EMPLOYEE.
By N. P. GILMAN. Cr. 8vo. 7s. 6d.
SOCIALISM AND THE AMERICAN SPIRIT. By the Same. Cr. 8vo. 6s. 6d.
GUNTON.—WEALTH AND PROGRESS: An examination of the Wages Question
and its Economic Relation to Social Reform. By GEORGE GUNTON. Cr. 8vo. 6s.
HOWELL.—THE CONFLICTS OF CAPITAL AND LABOUR HISTORICALLY
AND ECONOMICALLY CONSIDERED. Being a History and Review of the
Trade Unions of Great Britain. By GEORGE HOWELL, M.P. 2nd Ed., revised.
Cr. 8vo. 7s. 6d.
JEVONS.—Works by W. STANLEY JEVONS, F.R.S.
*PRIMER OF POLITICAL ECONOMY. 18mo. 1s.
THE THEORY OF POLITICAL ECONOMY. 3rd Ed., revised. 8vo. 10s. 6d.
KEYNES.—THE SCOPE AND METHOD OF POLITICAL ECONOMY. By
J. N. KEYNES, D.Sc. 7s. net.
MARSHALL.—PRINCIPLES OF ECONOMICS. By ALFRED MARSHALL, M.A.,
Professor of Political Economy in the University of Cambridge. 2 vols. 8vo.
Vol. I. 2nd Ed. 12s. 6d. net.
ELEMENTS OF ECONOMICS OF INDUSTRY. By the same. New Ed.,
1892. Cr. 8vo. 3s. 6d.
PALGRAVE.—A DICTIONARY OF POLITICAL ECONOMY. By various Writers.
Edited by R. H. INGLIS PALGRAVE, F.R.S. 3s. 6d. each, net. No. I. July 1891.
PANTALEONI.—MANUAL OF POLITICAL ECONOMY. By Prof. M. PANTA-
LEONI. Translated by T. BOSTON BRUCE. [In preparation.
SIDGWICK.—THE PRINCIPLES OF POLITICAL ECONOMY. By HENRY
SIDGWICK, LL.D., D.C.L., Knightbridge Professor of Moral Philosophy in the
University of Cambridge. 2nd Ed., revised. 8vo. 16s.
SMART.—AN INTRODUCTION TO THE THEORY OF VALUE. By WILLIAM
SMART, M.A. Crown 8vo. 3s. net.
THOMPSON.—THE THEORY OF WAGES. By H. M. THOMPSON. Cr. 8vo. 3s. 6d.

WALKER.—Works by Francis A. Walker, M.A.
FIRST LESSONS IN POLITICAL ECONOMY. Cr. 8vo. 5s.
A BRIEF TEXT-BOOK OF POLITICAL ECONOMY. Cr. 8vo. 6s. 6d.
POLITICAL ECONOMY. 2nd Ed., revised and enlarged. 8vo. 12s. 6d.
THE WAGES QUESTION. Ex. Cr. 8vo. 8s. 6d. net.
MONEY. Ex. Cr. 8vo. 8s. 6d. net.
WICKSTEED.—ALPHABET OF ECONOMIC SCIENCE. By P. H. Wicksteed, M.A. Part I. Elements of the Theory of Value or Worth. Gl. 8vo. 2s. 6d.

LAW AND POLITICS.

BALL.—THE STUDENT'S GUIDE TO THE BAR. By W. W. Rouse Ball, M.A., Fellow of Trinity College, Cambridge. 4th Ed., revised. Cr. 8vo. 2s. 6d.
BOUTMY. — STUDIES IN CONSTITUTIONAL LAW. By Emile Boutmy. Translated by Mrs. Dicey, with Preface by Prof. A. V. Dicey. Cr. 8vo. 6s.
THE ENGLISH CONSTITUTION. By the same. Translated by Mrs. Eaden, with Introduction by Sir F. Pollock, Bart. Cr. 8vo. 6s.
*BUCKLAND.**—OUR NATIONAL INSTITUTIONS. By A. Buckland. 18mo. 1s.
CHERRY.—LECTURES ON THE GROWTH OF CRIMINAL LAW IN ANCIENT COMMUNITIES. By R. R. Cherry, LL.D., Reid Professor of Constitutional and Criminal Law in the University of Dublin. 8vo. 5s. net.
DICEY.—INTRODUCTION TO THE STUDY OF THE LAW OF THE CONSTITU-TION. By A. V. Dicey, B.C.L., Vinerian Professor of English Law in the University of Oxford. 3rd Ed. 8vo. 12s. 6d.
HOLMES.—THE COMMON LAW. By O. W. Holmes, Jun. Demy 8vo. 12s.
JENKS.—THE GOVERNMENT OF VICTORIA. By Edward Jenks, B.A., LL.B., late Professor of Law in the University of Melbourne. 14s.
MUNRO.—COMMERCIAL LAW. (See Commerce, p. 41.)
PHILLIMORE.—PRIVATE LAW AMONG THE ROMANS. From the Pandects. By J. G. Phillimore, Q.C. 8vo. 16s.
POLLOCK.—ESSAYS IN JURISPRUDENCE AND ETHICS. By Sir Frederick Pollock, Bart. 8vo. 10s. 6d.
INTRODUCTION TO THE HISTORY OF THE SCIENCE OF POLITICS. By the same. Cr. 8vo. 2s. 6d.
SIDGWICK.—THE ELEMENTS OF POLITICS. By Henry Sidgwick, LL.D. 8vo. 14s. net.
STEPHEN.—Works by Sir James Fitzjames Stephen, Bart.
A DIGEST OF THE LAW OF EVIDENCE. 5th Ed. Cr. 8vo. 6s.
A DIGEST OF THE CRIMINAL LAW: CRIMES AND PUNISHMENTS. 4th Ed., revised. 8vo. 16s.
A DIGEST OF THE LAW OF CRIMINAL PROCEDURE IN INDICTABLE OFFENCES. By Sir J. F. Stephen, Bart., and H. Stephen. 8vo. 12s. 6d.
A HISTORY OF THE CRIMINAL LAW OF ENGLAND. 3 vols. 8vo. 48s.
A GENERAL VIEW OF THE CRIMINAL LAW OF ENGLAND. 8vo. 14s.

ANTHROPOLOGY.

TYLOR.—ANTHROPOLOGY. By E. B. Tylor, F.R.S., Reader in Anthropology in the University of Oxford. Illustrated. Cr. 8vo. 7s. 6d.

EDUCATION.

ARNOLD.—REPORTS ON ELEMENTARY SCHOOLS. 1852-1882. By Matthew Arnold. Edited by Lord Sandford. Cr. 8vo. 3s. 6d.
HIGHER SCHOOLS AND UNIVERSITIES IN GERMANY. By the same. Crown 8vo. 6s.
A FRENCH ETON, AND HIGHER SCHOOLS AND UNIVERSITIES IN FRANCE. By the same. Cr. 8vo. 6s.
BALL.—THE STUDENT'S GUIDE TO THE BAR. (See Law, above.)
*BLAKISTON.**—THE TEACHER. Hints on School Management. By J. R. Blakiston, H.M.I.S. Cr. 8vo. 2s. 6d.
CALDERWOOD.—ON TEACHING. By Prof. Henry Calderwood. New Ed. Ex. fcap. 8vo. 2s. 6d.
FEARON.—SCHOOL INSPECTION. By D. R. Fearon. 6th Ed. Cr. 8vo. 2s. 6d.

FITCH.—NOTES ON AMERICAN SCHOOLS AND TRAINING COLLEGES. By J. G. FITCH, M.A., LL.D. Gl. 8vo. 2s. 6d.
GEIKIE.—THE TEACHING OF GEOGRAPHY. (See Geography, p. 41.)
GLADSTONE.—SPELLING REFORM FROM A NATIONAL POINT OF VIEW By J. H. GLADSTONE. Cr. 8vo. 1s. 6d.
HERTEL.—OVERPRESSURE IN HIGH SCHOOLS IN DENMARK. By Dr. HERTEL. Introd. by Sir J. CRICHTON-BROWNE, F.R.S. Cr. 8vo. 3s. 6d.
RECORD OF TECHNICAL AND SECONDARY EDUCATION. 8vo. Sewed, 2s., net. Part I. Nov. 1891.

TECHNICAL KNOWLEDGE.

Civil and Mechanical Engineering; Military and Naval Science; Agriculture; Domestic Economy; Hygiene; Commerce; Manual Training.

CIVIL AND MECHANICAL ENGINEERING.

ALEXANDER—THOMSON.—ELEMENTARY APPLIED MECHANICS. (See Mechanics, p. 26.)
CHALMERS.—GRAPHICAL DETERMINATION OF FORCES IN ENGINEERING STRUCTURES. By J. B. CHALMERS, C.E. Illustrated. 8vo. 24s.
COTTERILL.—APPLIED MECHANICS. (See Mechanics, p. 27.)
COTTERILL—SLADE.—LESSONS IN APPLIED MECHANICS. (See Mechanics, p. 27.)
GRAHAM.—GEOMETRY OF POSITION. (See Mechanics, 27.)
KENNEDY.—THE MECHANICS OF MACHINERY. (See Mechanics, 27.)
LANGMAID—GAISFORD.—ELEMENTARY LESSONS IN STEAM MACHINERY AND IN MARINE STEAM ENGINES. By T. LANGMAID, Chief Engineer R.N., and H. GAISFORD, R.N. [Shortly.
PEABODY.—THERMODYNAMICS OF THE STEAM-ENGINE AND OTHER HEAT-ENGINES. (See Physics, p. 29.)
SHANN.—AN ELEMENTARY TREATISE ON HEAT IN RELATION TO STEAM AND THE STEAM-ENGINE. (See Physics, p. 29.)
YOUNG.—SIMPLE PRACTICAL METHODS OF CALCULATING STRAINS ON GIRDERS, ARCHES, AND TRUSSES. By E. W. YOUNG, C.E. 8vo. 7s. 6d.

MILITARY AND NAVAL SCIENCE.

ARMY PRELIMINARY EXAMINATION PAPERS, 1882-1891. (See Mathematics.)
FLAGG.—A PRIMER OF NAVIGATION. By A. T. FLAGG. 18mo. [In preparation.
KELVIN.—POPULAR LECTURES AND ADDRESSES. By Lord KELVIN, P.R.S. 3 vols. Illustrated. Cr. 8vo. Vol. III. Navigation. 7s. 6d.
MATTHEWS.—MANUAL OF LOGARITHMS. (See Mathematics, p. 24.)
MAURICE.—WAR. By Col. G. F. MAURICE, C.B., R.A. 8vo. 5s. net.
MERCUR.—ELEMENTS OF THE ART OF WAR. Prepared for the use of Cadets of the United States Military Academy. By JAMES MERCUR. 8vo. 17s.
PALMER.—TEXT-BOOK OF PRACTICAL LOGARITHMS AND TRIGONOMETRY. (See Mathematics, p. 24.)
ROBINSON.—TREATISE ON MARINE SURVEYING. For younger Naval Officers. By Rev. J. L. ROBINSON. Cr. 8vo. 7s. 6d.
SANDHURST MATHEMATICAL PAPERS. (See Mathematics, p. 25.)
SHORTLAND.—NAUTICAL SURVEYING. By Vice-Adm. SHORTLAND. 8vo. 21s.
WOLSELEY.—Works by General Viscount WOLSELEY, G.C.M.G.
THE SOLDIER'S POCKET-BOOK FOR FIELD SERVICE. 16mo. Roan. 5s.
FIELD POCKET-BOOK FOR THE AUXILIARY FORCES. 16mo. 1s. 6d.
WOOLWICH MATHEMATICAL PAPERS. (See Mathematics, p. 25.)

AGRICULTURE AND FORESTRY.

FRANKLAND.—AGRICULTURAL CHEMICAL ANALYSIS. By P. F. FRANKLAND, F.R.S., Prof. of Chemistry, University College, Dundee. Cr. 8vo. 7s. 6d.
HARTIG.—TEXT-BOOK OF THE DISEASES OF TREES. By Dr. ROBERT HARTIG. Translated by WM. SOMERVILLE, B.S., D.Œ., Professor of Agriculture and Forestry, Durham College of Science. 8vo. [In the Press.

LASLETT.—TIMBER AND TIMBER TREES, NATIVE AND FOREIGN. By THOMAS LASLETT. Cr. 8vo. 8s. 6d.

LAURIE.—THE FOOD OF PLANTS. By A. P. LAURIE, M.A. 18mo. 1s.

MUIR.—MANUAL OF DAIRY-WORK. By Professor JAMES MUIR, Yorkshire College, Leeds. 18mo. 1s.

NICHOLLS.—A TEXT-BOOK OF TROPICAL AGRICULTURE. By H. A. ALFORD NICHOLLS, M.D. Illustrated. Crown 8vo. 6s.

NISBET.—BRITISH FOREST TREES AND THEIR AGRICULTURAL CHAR-ACTERISTICS AND TREATMENT. By JOHN NISBET, D.Œ., of the Indian Forest Service. Cr. 8vo. 6s.

SOMERVILLE.—INSECTS IN RELATION TO AGRICULTURE. By Dr. W. SOMERVILLE. 18mo. [In preparation.

SMITH.—DISEASES OF FIELD AND GARDEN CROPS, chiefly such as are caused by Fungi. By WORTHINGTON G. SMITH, F.L.S. Fcap. 8vo. 4s. 6d.

TANNER.—*ELEMENTARY LESSONS IN THE SCIENCE OF AGRICULTURAL PRACTICE. By HENRY TANNER, F.C.S., M.R.A.C., Examiner in Agriculture under the Science and Art Department. Fcap. 8vo. 3s. 6d.

*FIRST PRINCIPLES OF AGRICULTURE. By the same. 18mo. 1s.

*THE PRINCIPLES OF AGRICULTURE. For use in Elementary Schools. By the same. Ex. fcap. 8vo. I. The Alphabet. 6d. II. Further Steps. 1s. III. Elementary School Readings for the Third Stage. 1s.

WARD.—TIMBER AND SOME OF ITS DISEASES. By H. MARSHALL WARD, F.R.S., Prof. of Botany, Roy. Ind. Engin. Coll., Cooper's Hill. Cr. 8vo. 6s.

WRIGHT.—A PRIMER OF PRACTICAL HORTICULTURE. By J. WRIGHT, F.R.H.S. 18mo. 1s.

DOMESTIC ECONOMY.

*BARKER.—FIRST LESSONS IN THE PRINCIPLES OF COOKING. By LADY BARKER. 18mo. 1s.

*BARNETT—O'NEILL.—A PRIMER OF DOMESTIC ECONOMY. By E. A. BARNETT and H. C. O'NEILL. 18mo. 1s.

*COOKERY BOOK.—THE MIDDLE-CLASS COOKERY BOOK. Edited by the Manchester School of Domestic Cookery. Fcap. 8vo. 1s. 6d.

CRAVEN.—A GUIDE TO DISTRICT NURSES. By Mrs. CRAVEN. Cr. 8vo. 2s. 6d.

*GRAND'HOMME.—CUTTING-OUT AND DRESSMAKING. From the French of Mdlle. E. GRAND'HOMME. With Diagrams. 18mo. 1s.

*GRENFELL.—DRESSMAKING. A Technical Manual for Teachers. By Mrs. HENRY GRENFELL. With Diagrams. 18mo. 1s.

JEX-BLAKE.—THE CARE OF INFANTS. A Manual for Mothers and Nurses. By SOPHIA JEX-BLAKE, M.D. 18mo. 1s.

ROSEVEAR.—MANUAL OF NEEDLEWORK. By E. ROSEVEAR, Lecturer on Needlework, Training College, Stockwell. Cr. 8vo. 6s.

*TEGETMEIER.—HOUSEHOLD MANAGEMENT AND COOKERY. Compiled for the London School Board. By W. B. TEGETMEIER. 18mo. 1s.

*WRIGHT.—THE SCHOOL COOKERY-BOOK. Compiled and Edited by C. E. GUTHRIE WRIGHT, Hon. Sec. to the Edinburgh School of Cookery. 18mo. 1s.

HYGIENE.

*BERNERS.—FIRST LESSONS ON HEALTH. By J. BERNERS. 18mo. 1s.

BLYTH.—A MANUAL OF PUBLIC HEALTH. By A. WYNTER BLYTH, M.R.C.S. 8vo. 17s. net.

LECTURES ON SANITARY LAW. By the same Author. 8vo. [In the Press.

MIERS—CROSSKEY.—THE SOIL IN RELATION TO HEALTH. By H. A. MIERS, M.A., F.G.S., F.C.S., Assistant in the British Museum, and R. CROSS-KEY, M.A., D.P.H., Fellow of the British Institute of Public Health. Cr. 8vo. 3s. 6d.

REYNOLDS.—A PRIMER OF HYGIENE. By E. S. REYNOLDS, M.D., Victoria University Extension Lecturer in Hygiene. 18mo. [In preparation.

WILLOUGHBY.—HANDBOOK OF PUBLIC HEALTH AND DEMOGRAPHY. By Dr. E. F. WILLOUGHBY. Fcap. 8vo. [In the Press.

COMMERCE.

MACMILLAN'S ELEMENTARY COMMERCIAL CLASS BOOKS. Edited by JAMES GOW, Litt.D., Headmaster of the High School, Nottingham. Globe 8vo.
*THE HISTORY OF COMMERCE IN EUROPE. By H. DE B. GIBBINS, M.A. 3s. 6d.
*COMMERCIAL ARITHMETIC. By S. JACKSON, M.A. 3s. 6d.
ADVANCED BOOKKEEPING. By J. THORNTON. *[In the Press.*
COMMERCIAL GEOGRAPHY. By E. C. K. GONNER, M.A., Professor of Political Economy in University College, Liverpool. *[In preparation.*
*INTRODUCTION TO COMMERCIAL GERMAN. By F. C. SMITH, B.A., formerly Scholar of Magdalene College, Cambridge. 3s. 6d.
COMMERCIAL FRENCH. By JAMES B. PAYNE, King's College School, London. *[In preparation.*
COMMERCIAL SPANISH. By Prof. DELBOS, Instructor, H.M.S. *Britannia*, Dartmouth. *[In preparation.*
COMMERCIAL LAW. By J. E. C. MUNRO, LL.D., late Professor of Law and Political Economy in the Owens College, Manchester. *[In the Press.*

MANUAL TRAINING.

BENSON.—ELEMENTARY HANDICRAFT. By W. A. S. BENSON. *[In the Press.*
DEGERDON.—THE GRAMMAR OF WOODWORK. By W. E. DEGERDON, Head Instructor, Whitechapel Craft School. 4to. 2s.
LETHABY.—CAST IRON AND LEAD WORK. By W. R. LETHABY. Illustrated. Cr. 8vo. *[In preparation.*

GEOGRAPHY.

(See also PHYSICAL GEOGRAPHY, p. 32.)

BARTHOLOMEW.—*THE ELEMENTARY SCHOOL ATLAS. By JOHN BARTHOLOMEW, F.R.G.S. 4to. 1s.
*MACMILLAN'S SCHOOL ATLAS, PHYSICAL AND POLITICAL. 80 Maps and Index. By the same. Royal 4to. 8s. 6d. Half-morocco, 10s. 6d.
THE LIBRARY REFERENCE ATLAS OF THE WORLD. By the same. 84 Maps and Index to 100,000 places. Half-morocco. Gilt edges. Folio. £2:12:6 net. Also in parts, 5s. each, net. Index, 7s. 6d. net.
*CLARKE.—CLASS-BOOK OF GEOGRAPHY. By C. B. CLARKE, F.R.S. With 18 Maps. Fcap. 8vo. 3s. ; sewed, 2s. 6d.
*GREEN.—A SHORT GEOGRAPHY OF THE BRITISH ISLANDS. By JOHN RICHARD GREEN, LL.D., and A. S. GREEN. With Maps. Fcap. 8vo. 3s. 6d.
*GROVE.—A PRIMER OF GEOGRAPHY. By Sir GEORGE GROVE. 18mo. 1s.
KIEPERT.—A MANUAL OF ANCIENT GEOGRAPHY. By Dr. H. KIEPERT. Cr. 8vo. 5s.
MACMILLAN'S GEOGRAPHICAL SERIES.—Edited by Sir ARCHIBALD GEIKIE, F.R.S., Director-General of the Geological Survey of the United Kingdom.
*THE TEACHING OF GEOGRAPHY. A Practical Handbook for the Use of Teachers. By Sir ARCHIBALD GEIKIE, F.R.S. Cr. 8vo. 2s.
*MAPS AND MAP-DRAWING. By W. A. ELDERTON. 18mo. 1s.
*GEOGRAPHY OF THE BRITISH ISLES. By Sir A. GEIKIE, F.R.S. 18mo. 1s.
*AN ELEMENTARY CLASS-BOOK OF GENERAL GEOGRAPHY. By H. R. MILL, D.Sc. Illustrated. Cr. 8vo. 3s. 6d.
*GEOGRAPHY OF EUROPE. By J. SIME, M.A. Illustrated. Gl. 8vo. 3s.
*ELEMENTARY GEOGRAPHY OF INDIA, BURMA, AND CEYLON. By H. F. BLANFORD, F.G.S. Gl. 8vo. 2s. 6d.
GEOGRAPHY OF NORTH AMERICA. By Prof. N. S. SHALER. *[In preparation.*
*ELEMENTARY GEOGRAPHY OF THE BRITISH COLONIES. By G. M. DAWSON, LL.D., and A. SUTHERLAND. Globe 8vo. 3s.
STRACHEY.—LECTURES ON GEOGRAPHY. By General RICHARD STRACHEY, R.E. Cr. 8vo. 4s. 6d.
*TOZER.—A PRIMER OF CLASSICAL GEOGRAPHY. By H. F. TOZER, M.A. 18mo. 1s.

HISTORY.

ARNOLD.—THE SECOND PUNIC WAR. (*See* Antiquities, p. 12.)

ARNOLD.—A HISTORY OF THE EARLY ROMAN EMPIRE. (*See* p. 12.)

*BEESLY.—STORIES FROM THE HISTORY OF ROME. (*See* p. 12.)

BRYCE.—THE HOLY ROMAN EMPIRE. By JAMES BRYCE, M.P., D.C.L., Cr. 8vo. 7s. 6d. Library Edition. 8vo. 14s.

*BUCKLEY.—A HISTORY OF ENGLAND FOR BEGINNERS. By ARABELLA B. BUCKLEY. With Maps and Tables. Gl. 8vo. 3s.

BURY.—A HISTORY OF THE LATER ROMAN EMPIRE FROM ARCADIUS TO IRENE. (*See* Antiquities, p. 12.)

CASSEL.—MANUAL OF JEWISH HISTORY AND LITERATURE. By Dr. D. CASSEL. Translated by Mrs. HENRY LUCAS. Fcap. 8vo. 2s. 6d.

ENGLISH STATESMEN, TWELVE. Cr. 8vo. 2s. 6d. each.
WILLIAM THE CONQUEROR. By EDWARD A. FREEMAN, D.C.L., LL.D.
HENRY II. By Mrs. J. R. GREEN.
EDWARD I. By Prof. T. F. TOUT.
HENRY VII. By JAMES GAIRDNER.
CARDINAL WOLSEY. By Bishop CREIGHTON.
ELIZABETH. By E. S. BEESLY.
OLIVER CROMWELL. By FREDERIC HARRISON.
WILLIAM III. By H. D. TRAILL.
WALPOLE. By JOHN MORLEY.
CHATHAM. By JOHN MORLEY.   [*In preparation.*
PITT. By Lord ROSEBERY.
PEEL. By J. R. THURSFIELD.

FISKE.—Works by JOHN FISKE, formerly Lecturer on Philosophy at Harvard University.
THE CRITICAL PERIOD IN AMERICAN HISTORY, 1783–1789. 10s. 6d.
THE BEGINNINGS OF NEW ENGLAND. Cr. 8vo. 7s. 6d.
THE AMERICAN REVOLUTION. 2 vols. Cr. 8vo. 18s.
THE DISCOVERY OF AMERICA. 2 vols. Cr. 8vo. 18s.

FREEMAN.—Works by the late EDWARD A. FREEMAN, D.C.L.
*OLD ENGLISH HISTORY. With Maps. Ex. fcap. 8vo. 6s.
METHODS OF HISTORICAL STUDY. 8vo. 10s. 6d.
THE CHIEF PERIODS OF EUROPEAN HISTORY. 8vo. 10s. 6d.
HISTORICAL ESSAYS. 8vo. First Series. 10s. 6d. Second Series. 10s. 6d. Third Series. 12s. Fourth Series. 12s. 6d.
THE GROWTH OF THE ENGLISH CONSTITUTION FROM THE EARLIEST TIMES. 5th Ed. Cr. 8vo. 5s.

GREEN.—Works by JOHN RICHARD GREEN, LL.D.
*A SHORT HISTORY OF THE ENGLISH PEOPLE. Cr. 8vo. 8s. 6d.
*Also in Four Parts. With Analysis. Crown 8vo. 3s. each. Part I. 607–1265. Part II. 1204–1553. Part III. 1540–1689. Part IV. 1660–1873. Illustrated Edition. 8vo. Monthly parts, 1s. net. Part I. *Oct.* 1891. Vols. I. and II. 12s. each net.
HISTORY OF THE ENGLISH PEOPLE. In four vols. 8vo. 16s. each.
Vol. I.—Early England, 449–1071; Foreign Kings, 1071–1214; The Charter, 1214–1291; The Parliament, 1307–1461. 8 Maps.
Vol. II.—The Monarchy, 1461–1540; The Reformation, 1540–1603.
Vol. III.—Puritan England, 1603–1660; The Revolution, 1660–1688. 4 Maps.
Vol. IV.—The Revolution, 1688–1760; Modern England, 1760–1815.
THE MAKING OF ENGLAND (449–829). With Maps. 8vo. 16s.
THE CONQUEST OF ENGLAND (758–1071). With Maps and Portrait. 8vo. 18s.
*ANALYSIS OF ENGLISH HISTORY, based on Green's "Short History of the English People." By C. W. A. TAIT, M.A. Crown 8vo. 4s. 6d.
*READINGS IN ENGLISH HISTORY. Selected by J. R. GREEN. Three Parts. Gl. 8vo. 1s. 6d. each. I. Hengist to Cressy. II. Cressy to Cromwell. III. Cromwell to Balaklava.

GUEST.—LECTURES ON THE HISTORY OF ENGLAND. By M. J. GUEST. With Maps. Cr. 8vo. 6s.

HISTORICAL COURSE FOR SCHOOLS.—Edited by E. A. FREEMAN. 18mo.
GENERAL SKETCH OF EUROPEAN HISTORY. By E. A. FREEMAN. 3s. 6d.
HISTORY OF ENGLAND. By EDITH THOMPSON. 2s. 6d.
HISTORY OF SCOTLAND. By MARGARET MACARTHUR. 2s.
HISTORY OF FRANCE. By CHARLOTTE M. YONGE. 3s. 6d.
HISTORY OF GERMANY. By J. SIME, M.A. 3s.
HISTORY OF ITALY. By Rev. W. HUNT, M.A. 3s. 6d.
HISTORY OF AMERICA. By JOHN A. DOYLE. 4s. 6d.
HISTORY OF EUROPEAN COLONIES. By E. J. PAYNE, M.A. 4s. 6d.

*HISTORY PRIMERS.—Edited by JOHN RICHARD GREEN, LL.D. 18mo. 1s. each.
ROME. By Bishop CREIGHTON.
GREECE. By C. A. FYFFE, M.A., late Fellow of University College, Oxford.
EUROPE. By E. A. FREEMAN, D.C.L.
FRANCE. By CHARLOTTE M. YONGE.
ROMAN ANTIQUITIES. By Prof. WILKINS, Litt.D. Illustrated.
GREEK ANTIQUITIES. By Rev. J. P. MAHAFFY, D.D. Illustrated.
GEOGRAPHY. By Sir G. GROVE, D.C.L. Maps.
CLASSICAL GEOGRAPHY. By H. F. TOZER, M.A.
ENGLAND. By ARABELLA B. BUCKLEY.
ANALYSIS OF ENGLISH HISTORY. By Prof. T. F. TOUT, M.A.
INDIAN HISTORY: ASIATIC AND EUROPEAN. By J. TALBOYS WHEELER.

HOLE.—A GENEALOGICAL STEMMA OF THE KINGS OF ENGLAND AND FRANCE. By Rev. C. HOLE. On Sheet. 1s.

JENNINGS.—CHRONOLOGICAL TABLES OF ANCIENT HISTORY. By Rev. A. C. JENNINGS. 8vo. 5s.

LABBERTON.—NEW HISTORICAL ATLAS AND GENERAL HISTORY. By R. H. LABBERTON. 4to. 15s.

LETHBRIDGE.—A SHORT MANUAL OF THE HISTORY OF INDIA. With an Account of INDIA AS IT IS. By Sir ROPER LETHBRIDGE. Cr. 8vo. 5s.

*MACMILLAN'S HISTORY READERS. Adapted to the New Code, 1893. Gl. 8vo. Book I. 9d. Book II. 10d. Book III. 1s. Book IV. 1s. 3d. Book V. 1s. 6d. Book VI. 1s. 6d. Book VII. 1s. 6d.

MAHAFFY.—GREEK LIFE AND THOUGHT FROM THE AGE OF ALEXANDER TO THE ROMAN CONQUEST. (See Classics, p. 13.)
THE GREEK WORLD UNDER ROMAN SWAY. (See Classics, p. 13.)
PROBLEMS IN GREEK HISTORY. (See Classics, p. 13.)

MARRIOTT.—THE MAKERS OF MODERN ITALY: MAZZINI, CAVOUR, GARIBALDI. By J. A. R. MARRIOTT, M.A. Cr. 8vo. 1s. 6d.

MICHELET.—A SUMMARY OF MODERN HISTORY. By M. MICHELET. Translated by M. C. M. SIMPSON. Gl. 8vo. 4s. 6d.

NORGATE.—ENGLAND UNDER THE ANGEVIN KINGS. By KATE NORGATE. With Maps and Plans. 2 vols. 8vo. 32s.

OTTÉ.—SCANDINAVIAN HISTORY. By E. C. OTTÉ. With Maps. Gl. 8vo. 6s.

RHOADES. — HISTORY OF THE UNITED STATES. 1850-1880. By J. F. RHOADES. 2 vols. 8vo. 24s.

SHUCKBURGH.—A SCHOOL HISTORY OF ROME. (See p. 13.)

SEELEY.—THE EXPANSION OF ENGLAND. By J. R. SEELEY, M.A., Regius Professor of Modern History in the University of Cambridge. Cr. 8vo. 4s. 6d.
OUR COLONIAL EXPANSION. Extracts from the above. Cr. 8vo. Sewed. 1s.

SEWELL—YONGE.—EUROPEAN HISTORY. Selections from the Best Authorities. Edited by E. M. SEWELL and C. M. YONGE. Cr. 8vo. First Series, 1003-1154. 6s. Second Series, 1088-1228. 6s.

*TAIT.—ANALYSIS OF ENGLISH HISTORY. (See under Green, p. 42.)

WHEELER.—Works by J. TALBOYS WHEELER.
*A PRIMER OF INDIAN HISTORY. 18mo. 1s.
*COLLEGE HISTORY OF INDIA. With Maps. Cr. 8vo. 3s.; sewed, 2s. 6d.
A SHORT HISTORY OF INDIA AND OF THE FRONTIER STATES OF AFGHANISTAN, NEPAUL, AND BURMA. With Maps. Cr. 8vo. 12s.

YONGE.—Works by CHARLOTTE M. YONGE.
CAMEOS FROM ENGLISH HISTORY. Ex. fcap. 8vo. 5s. each. (1) From Rollo to Edward II. (2) The Wars in France. (3) The Wars of the Roses. (4) Reformation Times. (5) England and Spain. (6) Forty Years of Stewart Rule (1603–1643). (7) Rebellion and Restoration (1642–1678).
THE VICTORIAN HALF CENTURY. Cr. 8vo. 1s. 6d. ; sewed, 1s.

ART.

*ANDERSON.—LINEAR PERSPECTIVE AND MODEL DRAWING. With Questions and Exercises. By LAURENCE ANDERSON. Illustrated. 8vo. 2s.
COLLIER.—A PRIMER OF ART. By Hon. JOHN COLLIER. 18mo. 1s.
COOK.—THE NATIONAL GALLERY, A POPULAR HANDBOOK TO. By E. T. COOK, with preface by Mr. RUSKIN, and Selections from his Writings. 3rd Ed. Cr. 8vo. Half-mor., 14s. Large Paper Edition. 2 vols. 8vo.
DELAMOTTE.—A BEGINNER'S DRAWING BOOK. By P. H. DELAMOTTE, F.S.A. Progressively arranged. Cr. 8vo. 3s. 6d.
ELLIS.—SKETCHING FROM NATURE. A Handbook. By TRISTRAM J. ELLIS. Illustrated by H. STACY MARKS, R.A., and the Author. Cr. 8vo. 3s. 6d.
GROVE.—A DICTIONARY OF MUSIC AND MUSICIANS. 1450–1889. Edited by Sir GEORGE GROVE. 4 vols. 8vo. 21s. each. INDEX. 7s. 6d.
HUNT.—TALKS ABOUT ART. By WILLIAM HUNT. Cr. 8vo. 3s. 6d.
HUTCHINSON.—SOME HINTS ON LEARNING TO DRAW. Containing Examples from Leighton, Watts, Poynter, etc. By G. W. C. HUTCHINSON, Art Master at Clifton College. Sup. Roy. 8vo. 8s. 6d.
LETHABY.—(See under Manual Training, p. 41.)
MELDOLA.—THE CHEMISTRY OF PHOTOGRAPHY. By RAPHAEL MELDOLA, F.R.S., Professor of Chemistry in the Technical College, Finsbury. Cr. 8vo. 6s.
TAYLOR.—A PRIMER OF PIANOFORTE-PLAYING. By F. TAYLOR. 18mo. 1s.
TAYLOR.—A SYSTEM OF SIGHT-SINGING FROM THE ESTABLISHED MUSICAL NOTATION; based on the Principle of Tonic Relation. By SEDLEY TAYLOR, M.A. 8vo. 5s. net.
TYRWHITT.—OUR SKETCHING CLUB. Letters and Studies on Landscape Art. By Rev. R. ST. JOHN TYRWHITT. With reproductions of the Lessons and Woodcuts in Mr. Ruskin's "Elements of Drawing." Cr. 8vo. 7s. 6d.

DIVINITY.

The Bible ; History of the Christian Church ; The Church of England ; The Fathers ; Hymnology.

THE BIBLE.

History of the Bible.—THE ENGLISH BIBLE ; A Critical History of the various English Translations. By Prof. JOHN EADIE. 2 vols. 8vo. 28s.
THE BIBLE IN THE CHURCH. By Right Rev. B. F. WESTCOTT, Bishop of Durham. 10th Ed. 18mo. 4s. 6d.
Biblical History.—BIBLE LESSONS. By Rev. E. A. ABBOTT. Cr. 8vo. 4s. 6d.
SIDE-LIGHTS UPON BIBLE HISTORY. By Mrs. SYDNEY BUXTON. Cr. 8vo. 5s.
STORIES FROM THE BIBLE. By Rev. A. J. CHURCH. Illustrated. Cr. 8vo. 2 parts. 3s. 6d. each.
*BIBLE READINGS SELECTED FROM THE PENTATEUCH AND THE BOOK OF JOSHUA. By Rev. J. A. CROSS. Gl. 8vo. 2s. 6d.
*THE CHILDREN'S TREASURY OF BIBLE STORIES. By Mrs. H. GASKOIN. 18mo. 1s. each. Part I. OLD TESTAMENT. Part II. NEW TESTAMENT. Part III. THE APOSTLES.
*A CLASS-BOOK OF OLD TESTAMENT HISTORY. By Rev. G. F. MACLEAR, D.D. 18mo. 4s. 6d.
*A CLASS-BOOK OF NEW TESTAMENT HISTORY. 18mo. 5s. 6d.
*A SHILLING BOOK OF OLD TESTAMENT HISTORY. 18mo. 1s.
*A SHILLING BOOK OF NEW TESTAMENT HISTORY. 18mo. 1s.

*SCRIPTURE READINGS FOR SCHOOLS AND FAMILIES. By C. M.
YONGE. Globe 8vo. 1s. 6d. each; also with comments, 3s. 6d. each.
GENESIS TO DEUTERONOMY. JOSHUA TO SOLOMON. KINGS AND THE PROPHETS.
THE GOSPEL TIMES. APOSTOLIC TIMES.

The Old Testament.—THE PATRIARCHS AND LAWGIVERS OF THE OLD
TESTAMENT. By F. D. MAURICE. Cr. 8vo. 3s. 6d.
THE PROPHETS AND KINGS OF THE OLD TESTAMENT. By the same.
Cr. 8vo. 3s. 6d.
THE CANON OF THE OLD TESTAMENT. By Rev. H. E. RYLE, B.D.,
Hulsean Professor of Divinity in the University of Cambridge. Cr. 8vo. 6s.
THE EARLY NARRATIVES OF GENESIS. By the same. Cr. 8vo. 3s. net.
THE DIVINE LIBRARY OF THE OLD TESTAMENT. By A. F. KIRK-
PATRICK, M.A., Professor of Hebrew in the University of Cambridge. Cr. 8vo
3s. net.

The Pentateuch.—AN HISTORICO-CRITICAL INQUIRY INTO THE ORIGIN
AND COMPOSITION OF THE PENTATEUCH AND BOOK OF JOSHUA.
By Prof. A. KUENEN. Trans. by P. H. WICKSTEED, M.A. 8vo. 14s.

The Psalms.—THE PSALMS CHRONOLOGICALLY ARRANGED. By FOUR
FRIENDS. Cr. 8vo. 5s. net.
GOLDEN TREASURY PSALTER. Student's Edition of above. 18mo. 3s. 6d.
THE PSALMS, WITH INTRODUCTION AND NOTES. By A. C. JENNINGS,
M.A., and W. H. LOWE, M.A. 2 vols. Cr. 8vo. 10s. 6d. each.
INTRODUCTION TO THE STUDY AND USE OF THE PSALMS. By Rev.
J. F. THRUPP. 2nd Ed. 2 vols. 8vo. 21s.

Isaiah.—ISAIAH XL.-LXVI. With the Shorter Prophecies allied to it. Edited by
MATTHEW ARNOLD. Cr. 8vo. 5s.
ISAIAH OF JERUSALEM. In the Authorised English Version, with Intro-
duction and Notes. By the same. Cr. 8vo. 4s. 6d.
A BIBLE-READING FOR SCHOOLS,—THE GREAT PROPHECY OF
ISRAEL'S RESTORATION (Isaiah, Chapters xl.-lxvi.) Arranged and
Edited for Young Learners. By the same. 18mo. 1s.
COMMENTARY ON THE BOOK OF ISAIAH: CRITICAL, HISTORICAL,
AND PROPHETICAL; with Translation. By T. R. BIRKS. 8vo. 12s. 6d.
THE BOOK OF ISAIAH CHRONOLOGICALLY ARRANGED. By T. K.
CHEYNE. Cr. 8vo. 7s. 6d.

Zechariah.—THE HEBREW STUDENT'S COMMENTARY ON ZECHARIAH,
HEBREW AND LXX. By W. H. LOWE, M.A. 8vo. 10s. 6d.

The Minor Prophets.—DOCTRINE OF THE PROPHETS. By Prof. A. F. KIRK-
PATRICK. Cr. 8vo. 6s.

The New Testament.—THE NEW TESTAMENT. Essay on the Right Estimation
of MS. Evidence in the Text of the New Testament. By T. R. BIRKS. Cr.
8vo. 3s. 6d.
THE MESSAGES OF THE BOOKS. Discourses and Notes on the Books of
the New Testament. By Archd. FARRAR. 8vo. 14s.
THE CLASSICAL ELEMENT IN THE NEW TESTAMENT. Considered as a
proof of its Genuineness, with an Appendix on the Oldest Authorities used
in the Formation of the Canon. By C. H. HOOLE. 8vo. 10s. 6d.
ON A FRESH REVISION OF THE ENGLISH NEW TESTAMENT. With
an Appendix on the Last Petition of the Lord's Prayer. By Bishop LIGHT-
FOOT. Cr. 8vo. 7s. 6d.
THE UNITY OF THE NEW TESTAMENT. By F. D. MAURICE. 2 vols.
Cr. 8vo. 12s.
A GENERAL SURVEY OF THE HISTORY OF THE CANON OF THE NEW
TESTAMENT DURING THE FIRST FOUR CENTURIES. By Bishop
WESTCOTT. Cr. 8vo. 10s. 6d.
THE NEW TESTAMENT IN THE ORIGINAL GREEK. The Text revised
by Bishop WESTCOTT, D.D., and Prof. F. J. A. HORT, D.D. 2 vols. Cr. 8vo.
10s. 6d. each. Vol. I. Text. Vol. II. Introduction and Appendix.
SCHOOL EDITION OF THE ABOVE. 18mo, 4s. 6d.; 18mo, roan, 5s. 6d.;
morocco, gilt edges, 6s. 6d.

The Gospels.—THE COMMON TRADITION OF THE SYNOPTIC GOSPELS, in the Text of the Revised Version. By Rev. E. A. ABBOTT and W. G. RUSHBROOKE. Cr. 8vo. 3s. 6d.

SYNOPTICON: AN EXPOSITION OF THE COMMON MATTER OF THE SYNOPTIC GOSPELS. By W. G. RUSHBROOKE. Printed in Colours. In six Parts, and Appendix. 4to. Part I. 3s. 6d. Parts II. and III. 7s. Parts IV. V. and VI., with Indices, 10s. 6d. Appendices, 10s. 6d. Complete in 1 vol. 35s. "Indispensable to a Theological Student."—*The Cambridge Guide.*

ESSAYS ON THE WORK ENTITLED "SUPERNATURAL RELIGION." A discussion of the authenticity of the Gospels. By Bishop LIGHTFOOT. 8vo. 10s. 6d.

INTRODUCTION TO THE STUDY OF THE FOUR GOSPELS. By Bishop WESTCOTT. Cr. 8vo. 10s. 6d.

THE COMPOSITION OF THE FOUR GOSPELS. By Rev. A. WRIGHT. Cr. 8vo. 5s.

The Gospel according to St. Matthew.—*THE GREEK TEXT With Introduction and Notes by Rev. A. SLOMAN. Fcap. 8vo. 2s. 6d.

CHOICE NOTES ON ST. MATTHEW. Drawn from Old and New Sources. Cr. 8vo. 4s. 6d. (St. Matthew and St. Mark in 1 vol. 9s.)

The Gospel according to St. Mark.—*SCHOOL READINGS IN THE GREEK TESTAMENT. Being the Outlines of the Life of our Lord as given by St. Mark, with additions from the Text of the other Evangelists. Edited, with Notes and Vocabulary, by Rev. A. CALVERT, M.A. Fcap. 8vo. 2s. 6d.

THE GREEK TEXT, with Introduction and Notes. By Rev. J. O. F. MURRAY, M.A. [*In preparation.*

CHOICE NOTES ON ST. MARK. Drawn from Old and New Sources. Cr. 8vo. 4s. 6d. (St. Matthew and St. Mark in 1 vol. 9s.)

The Gospel according to St. Luke.—*THE GREEK TEXT, with Introduction and Notes. By Rev. J. BOND, M.A. Fcap. 8vo. 2s. 6d.

CHOICE NOTES ON ST. LUKE. Drawn from Old and New Sources. Cr. 8vo. 4s. 6d.

THE GOSPEL OF THE KINGDOM OF HEAVEN. A Course of Lectures on the Gospel of St. Luke. By F. D. MAURICE. Cr. 8vo. 3s. 6d.

The Gospel according to St. John.—THE GOSPEL OF ST. JOHN. By F. D. MAURICE. 8th Ed. Cr. 8vo. 6s.

CHOICE NOTES ON ST. JOHN. Drawn from Old and New Sources. Cr. 8vo. 4s. 6d.

The Acts of the Apostles.—*THE GREEK TEXT, with Notes by T. E. PAGE, M.A. Fcap. 8vo. 3s. 6d.

THE CHURCH OF THE FIRST DAYS: THE CHURCH OF JERUSALEM, THE CHURCH OF THE GENTILES, THE CHURCH OF THE WORLD. Lectures on the Acts of the Apostles. By Very Rev. C. J. VAUGHAN. Cr. 8vo. 10s. 6d.

THE CODEX BEZAE OF THE ACTS OF THE APOSTLES. By Rev. F. H. CHASE. [*In the Press.*

The Epistles of St. Paul.—THE EPISTLE TO THE ROMANS. The Greek Text, with English Notes. By the Very Rev. C. J. VAUGHAN. 7th Ed. Cr. 8vo. 7s. 6d.

THE EPISTLES TO THE CORINTHIANS. Greek Text, with Commentary. By Rev. W. KAY. 8vo. 9s.

THE EPISTLE TO THE GALATIANS. A Revised Text, with Introduction, Notes, and Dissertations. By Bishop LIGHTFOOT. 10th Ed. 8vo. 12s.

THE EPISTLE TO THE PHILIPPIANS. A Revised Text, with Introduction, Notes, and Dissertations. By the same. 8vo. 12s.

THE EPISTLE TO THE PHILIPPIANS. With Translation, Paraphrase, and Notes for English Readers. By Very Rev. C. J. VAUGHAN. Cr. 8vo. 5s.

THE EPISTLE TO THE COLOSSIANS AND TO PHILEMON. A Revised Text, with Introductions, etc. By Bishop LIGHTFOOT. 9th Ed. 8vo. 12s.

THE EPISTLES TO THE EPHESIANS, THE COLOSSIANS, AND PHILEMON. With Introduction and Notes. By Rev. J. LL. DAVIES. 8vo. 7s. 6d.

THE FIRST EPISTLE TO THE THESSALONIANS. By Very Rev. C. J. VAUGHAN. 8vo. Sewed, 1s. 6d.

THE EPISTLES TO THE THESSALONIANS. Commentary on the Greek Text. By Prof. JOHN EADIE. 8vo. 12s.
INTRODUCTORY LECTURES ON THE EPISTLES TO THE ROMANS AND TO THE EPHESIANS. By the late Prof. HORT. Cr. 8vo. [*In preparation.*
The Epistle of St. James.—THE GREEK TEXT, with Introduction and Notes. By Rev. JOSEPH B. MAYOR. 8vo. 14s.
The Epistles of St. John.—THE EPISTLES OF ST. JOHN. By F. D. MAURICE. Cr. 8vo. 3s. 6d.
THE GREEK TEXT, with Notes. By Bishop WESTCOTT. 2nd Ed. 8vo. 12s. 6d.
The Epistle to the Hebrews.—GREEK AND ENGLISH. Edited by Rev. F. RENDALL. Cr. 8vo. 6s.
ENGLISH TEXT, with Commentary. By the same. Cr. 8vo. 7s. 6d.
THE GREEK TEXT, with Notes. By Very Rev. C. J. VAUGHAN. Cr. 8vo. 7s. 6d.
THE GREEK TEXT, with Notes and Essays. By Bishop WESTCOTT. 8vo. 14s.
Revelation.—LECTURES ON THE APOCALYPSE. By F. D. MAURICE. Cr. 8vo. 3s. 6d.
THE REVELATION OF ST. JOHN. By Prof. W. MILLIGAN. Cr. 8vo. 7s. 6d.
LECTURES ON THE APOCALYPSE. By the same. Cr. 8vo. 5s.
DISCUSSIONS ON THE APOCALYPSE. By the same. Crown 8vo. 5s.
LECTURES ON THE REVELATION OF ST. JOHN. By Very Rev. C. J. VAUGHAN. 5th Ed. Cr. 8vo. 10s. 6d.

WRIGHT.—THE BIBLE WORD-BOOK. By W. ALDIS WRIGHT. Cr. 8vo. 7s. 6d.

HISTORY OF THE CHRISTIAN CHURCH.

CUNNINGHAM.—THE GROWTH OF THE CHURCH IN ITS ORGANISATION AND INSTITUTIONS. By Rev. JOHN CUNNINGHAM. 8vo. 9s.
CUNNINGHAM.—THE CHURCHES OF ASIA: A METHODICAL SKETCH OF THE SECOND CENTURY. By Rev. WILLIAM CUNNINGHAM. Cr. 8vo. 6s.
DALE.—THE SYNOD OF ELVIRA, AND CHRISTIAN LIFE IN THE FOURTH CENTURY. By A. W. W. DALE. Cr. 8vo. 10s. 6d.
HARDWICK.—Works by Archdeacon HARDWICK.
A HISTORY OF THE CHRISTIAN CHURCH: MIDDLE AGE. Edited by Bishop STUBBS. Cr. 8vo. 10s. 6d.
A HISTORY OF THE CHRISTIAN CHURCH DURING THE REFORMATION. 9th Ed., revised by Bishop STUBBS. Cr. 8vo. 10s. 6d.
HORT.—TWO DISSERTATIONS. 1. ON ΜΟΝΟΓΕΝΗΣ ΘΕΟΣ IN SCRIPTURE AND TRADITION. II. ON THE "CONSTANTINOPOLITAN" CREED AND OTHER CREEDS OF THE FOURTH CENTURY. By the late Prof. HORT. 8vo. 7s. 6d.
LECTURES ON JUDAISTIC CHRISTIANITY. By the same. Cr. 8vo. [*In the Press.*
LECTURES ON EARLY CHURCH HISTORY. By the same. Cr. 8vo. [*In the Press.*
KILLEN.—ECCLESIASTICAL HISTORY OF IRELAND, from the earliest date to the present time. By W. D. KILLEN. 2 vols. 8vo. 25s.
SIMPSON.—AN EPITOME OF THE HISTORY OF THE CHRISTIAN CHURCH. By Rev. W. SIMPSON. 7th Ed. Fcap. 8vo. 3s. 6d.
VAUGHAN.—THE CHURCH OF THE FIRST DAYS: THE CHURCH OF JERUSALEM, THE CHURCH OF THE GENTILES, THE CHURCH OF THE WORLD. By Very Rev. C. J. VAUGHAN. Cr. 8vo. 10s. 6d.

THE CHURCH OF ENGLAND.

BENHAM.—A COMPANION TO THE LECTIONARY. By Rev. W. BENHAM, B.D. Cr. 8vo. 4s. 6d.
COLENSO.—THE COMMUNION SERVICE FROM THE BOOK OF COMMON PRAYER. With Select Readings from the Writings of the Rev. F. D MAURICE. Edited by Bishop COLENSO. 6th Ed. 16mo. 2s. 6d.

MACLEAR.—Works by Rev. G. F. MACLEAR, D.D.

*A CLASS-BOOK OF THE CATECHISM OF THE CHURCH OF ENGLAND. 18mo. 1s. 6d.

*A FIRST CLASS-BOOK OF THE CATECHISM OF THE CHURCH OF ENGLAND. 18mo. 6d.

THE ORDER OF CONFIRMATION. With Prayers and Devotions. 32mo. 6d.

FIRST COMMUNION. With Prayers and Devotions for the newly Confirmed. 32mo. 6d.

*A MANUAL OF INSTRUCTION FOR CONFIRMATION AND FIRST COMMUNION. With Prayers and Devotions. 32mo. 2s.

*AN INTRODUCTION TO THE CREEDS. 18mo. 3s. 6d.

AN INTRODUCTION TO THE THIRTY-NINE ARTICLES.   [In the Press.

PROCTER.—A HISTORY OF THE BOOK OF COMMON PRAYER. By Rev. F. PROCTER. 18th Ed. Cr. 8vo. 10s. 6d.

*PROCTER—MACLEAR.— AN ELEMENTARY INTRODUCTION TO THE BOOK OF COMMON PRAYER. By Rev. F. PROCTER and Rev. G. F. MACLEAR, D.D. 18mo. 2s. 6d.

VAUGHAN.—TWELVE DISCOURSES ON SUBJECTS CONNECTED WITH THE LITURGY AND WORSHIP OF THE CHURCH OF ENGLAND. By Very Rev. C. J. VAUGHAN. Fcap. 8vo. 6s.

NOTES FOR LECTURES ON CONFIRMATION. With suitable Prayers. By the same. 18mo. 1s. 6d.

THE FATHERS.

CUNNINGHAM.—THE EPISTLE OF ST. BARNABAS. A Dissertation, including a Discussion of its Date and Authorship. Together with the Greek Text, the Latin Version, and a new English Translation and Commentary. By Rev. W. CUNNINGHAM. Cr. 8vo. 7s. 6d.

DONALDSON.—THE APOSTOLICAL FATHERS. A Critical Account of their Genuine Writings, and of their Doctrines. By Prof. JAMES DONALDSON. 2nd Ed. Cr. 8vo. 7s. 6d.

GWATKIN.—SELECTIONS FROM THE EARLY CHRISTIAN WRITERS. By Rev. Prof. GWATKIN. 8vo.   [In the Press.

EARLY HISTORY OF THE CHRISTIAN CHURCH. By the same. [In prep.

LIGHTFOOT.—THE APOSTOLIC FATHERS. Part I. ST. CLEMENT OF ROME. Revised Texts, with Introductions, Notes, Dissertations, and Translations. By Bishop LIGHTFOOT. 2 vols. 8vo. 32s.

THE APOSTOLIC FATHERS. Part II. ST. IGNATIUS to ST. POLYCARP. Revised Texts, with Introductions, Notes, Dissertations, and Translations. By the same. 3 vols. 2nd Ed. Demy 8vo. 48s.

THE APOSTOLIC FATHERS. Abridged Edition. With short Introductions, Greek Text, and English Translation. By the same. 8vo. 16s.

HYMNOLOGY.

PALGRAVE.—ORIGINAL HYMNS. By Prof. F. T. PALGRAVE. 18mo. 1s. 6d.

SELBORNE.—THE BOOK OF PRAISE. By EARL OF SELBORNE. 18mo. 2s. 6d. net.

A HYMNAL. A. 32mo. 6d. B. 18mo, larger type. 1s. C. Fine Paper. 1s. 6d. Edited, with Music, by JOHN HULLAH. 18mo. 3s. 6d.

WOODS.—HYMNS FOR SCHOOL WORSHIP. By M. A. WOODS. 18mo. 1s. 6d.

www.ingramcontent.com/pod-product-compliance
Lightning Source LLC
Chambersburg PA
CBHW030732280326
41926CB00086B/1205